The British Empire in the 1950s

Also by Martin Lynn

COMMERCE AND ECONOMIC CHANGE IN WEST AFRICA

(*ed.*) NIGERIA 1943–60

(*ed. with B. Wood*) TRAVEL, TRADE AND POWER IN THE ATLANTIC 1765–1884

The British Empire in the 1950s

Retreat or Revival?

Edited by

Martin Lynn
Professor of African History
Queen's University, Belfast

palgrave
macmillan

First published in 2006 by
PALGRAVE MACMILLAN
Houndmills, Basingstoke, Hampshire RG21 6XS and
175 Fifth Avenue, New York, N.Y. 10010
Companies and representatives throughout the world.

PALGRAVE MACMILLAN is the global academic imprint of the Palgrave Macmillan division of St. Martin's Press, LLC and of Palgrave Macmillan Ltd. Macmillan® is a registered trademark in the United States, United Kingdom and other countries. Palgrave is a registered trademark in the European Union and other countries.

ISBN-13: 978–1–4039–3226–6
ISBN-10: 1–4039–3226–3

This book is printed on paper suitable for recycling and made from fully managed and sustained forest sources.

A catalogue record for this book is available from the British Library.

Library of Congress Cataloging-in-Publication Data

The British Empire in the 1950s : retreat or revival? / edited by Martin Lynn.
        p. cm.
    Originally presented as papers at the Wiles Colloquium held at Queen's University, Belfast on 9–10 Sept. 2004.
    Includes bibliographical references and index.
    Contents : Was there a fourth British Empire? / John Darwin – Keeping change within bounds : a Whitehall reassessment / S.R. Ashton – "Government by blackmail" : the origins of the Central African Federation reconsidered / Philip Murphy – African prospects : mining the empire from Britain in the 1950s / Sarah Stockwell – Decolonisation in the 1950s : the version according to British business / Nicholas J. White – Things fall apart : the erosion of local government, local justice and civil rights in Ghana, 1955–60 / Richard Rathbone – "We cannot let the North down" : British policy and Nigeria in the 1950s / Martin Lynn – Anglo-Amercian revival and empire during the Macmillan years, 1957–63 / Nigel J. Ashton-Public enemy number one: the British Empire in the dock at the United Nations 1957–1971 / Wm. Roger Louis – When (if ever) did Empire end? : "internal decolonisation" in British culture since the 1950s / Stephen Howe.

        ISBN 1–4039–3226–3 (cloth)
        1. Great Britain – Colonies – History – 20th century – Congresses.
    2. Imperialism – Government policy – Great Britain – History – 20th century – Congresses. 3. Decolonization – Great Britain – Colonies – History – 20th century – Congresses. I. Lynn, Martin, 1951– II. Wiles Colloquium (2004 : Queen's University of Belfast).

DA16.B695 2005
325'. 341'09045—dc22   2005045405

10 9 8 7 6 5 4 3 2 1
15 14 13 12 11 10 09 08 07 06

Printed and bound in Great Britain by
Antony Rowe Ltd, Chippenham and Eastbourne

To Alice, Hannah and Megan

Contents

Martin Lynn (1951–2005)

Teacher and Colleague at Queen's: A Tribute

Peter Jupp

Martin Lynn joined the History Department at Queen's University, Belfast in 1980, as a lecturer in modern British and imperial history, in succession to Deborah Lavin. Throughout his time at Queen's he gave sterling service to the cause of British history, teaching on the staple survey courses on the nineteenth and twentieth centuries. But he also broadened the outlook of the department in developing more specialised courses in imperial and African history, including a very successful special subject on the end of empire in West Africa, and at the time of his death was preparing to offer an advanced option on Chinese history, building on his very successful first year course on modern China. He had been promoted to Senior Lecturer, Reader and finally, in 2004, to a personal chair in African History.

Martin was a colleague with an outstanding, and very distinctive, set of qualities. In the British history courses, on which we collaborated for over two decades, his impact was immediate and continuous. As the evidence of student feedback questionnaires confirmed, he was an outstandingly successful lecturer. Students were presented with a clear line of interpretation, supported by a manageable number of key points, underlined, it is said, by his walking up and down the aisles of the raked lecture hall, making sure that everyone understood them. There was commitment, enthusiasm, and an ability to cut through the literature on a topic and present an argument that was lucid and fully up-to-date. He brought similar qualities to his conduct of tutorials. Students would be presented at the start of a course with the sequence of topics to be covered and clear guidelines on what Martin expected of them. As the student questionnaires also confirmed, he had a gift for encouraging students of all levels of ability to feel that their contributions were valued and that they could achieve good marks in the examination. He then completed the process by sending personal notes of congratulation to those of his students who had done particularly well, often on picture postcards that had been carefully chosen to reflect some aspect of the subject they had been investigating together.

The qualities displayed in the British history courses were also evident in those specialist modules for which he was personally responsible. His lectures on the history of China to Year 1 students became legendary. Their clarity and cogency were such that students could not refrain from reproducing them in examinations, no matter what the particular slant of the question happened to be. However, it was typical of Martin that he disapproved strongly of such responses and was inclined to mark them down for ignoring his well-known rule that lectures were meant to be a guide to how students should prepare their own thoughts on a subject. As for his courses on imperial history, the student questionnaires spoke for themselves. Without being especially enamoured of the system of questionnaires, seeing them in fact as part of an increasing level of bureaucratic obligation that diminished time for serious teaching and research, he nevertheless kept meticulous digests of them. These demonstrated excellence (a word that Martin was not too keen on) in every aspect. Indeed, when they were reviewed, either at 'appraisal' time or collectively in a 'module review', many of us were left scratching our heads, wondering how Martin was able to achieve what he did.

One of the answers, I think, was the clarity of his thinking on what could be expected of students. Martin believed profoundly in the virtues of traditional methods – the lecture, the tutorial and the written examination. The goal for students was the ability to write three answers in three hours to clearly stated questions on subjects that had been covered in the course. This was the ultimate test of a conscientious application to the course as a whole; of the ability to construct an answer with an introduction, a discussion of the evidence and a conclusion; and of literacy. The tutor's task, therefore, was to enthuse and guide students to that end. In the case of team-taught courses, he sometimes encountered colleagues who did not share his views, but throughout discussions Martin always maintained his steadfast support for the traditional methods of university pedagogy.

Martin took his teaching very seriously. Every session that he undertook, be it lecture, seminar or tutorial, would be followed by a period of reflection, and the noting down in his teaching 'logs' of whatever had gone well, or badly, and what could be done to improve the delivery of the material. But it was not just a matter of pride in performance – exceptional professionalism, in other words – for he really cared, and cared passionately, that his students should be enabled to learn as much as possible from his classes. And he relished their successes. He always made a point of attending the graduation garden parties, to congratulate those he had taught, and his office was full of photographs he had taken of smiling graduates. He kept in touch with many of them, long after graduation, following their careers and offering encouragement and advice, by letter, postcard and, more recently, by e-mail. The affection in which he was held by his students was evident in the huge numbers that thronged the memorial meeting held for him by the Society of Friends, and in a deeply moving anonymous tribute posted by one of his last tutorial groups on the departmental noticeboard.

In personal terms, Martin was a delight to know and to work with. In his early days at Queen's, when there seemed to be much more time for socialising, he was a stalwart member of the staff cricket team and was even able to organise a 'History Eleven', comprising members of the then separate departments of Modern History and Economic and Social History (since merged into a single School), a surviving photograph of which demonstrates very different ideas on appropriate garb and equipment. He also went on several field trips to places of historic interest in Ireland and Britain, during which he alerted students to the fact that there was more to history than the big houses and landed estates to which the present writer, as organiser, seemed addicted. Further, although Martin never sought administrative duties, he carried out those that were asked of him with great efficiency and commitment. Of these, the ones connected with student welfare were (characteristically) what attracted him most. He was for many years a University liaison officer with overseas students, and a trustee for the Duke of Abercorn's Trust for Overseas Students in Northern Ireland, and within the department took special responsibility for disabled students. He even introduced his habitual good humour to the unenviable task of 'Safety Officer', managing to bring all staff and students onto the pavement outside the department with smiles on their faces at an unannounced ringing of the fire bells.

A conscientious temperament and wider interests beyond the walls of the university meant that Martin sometimes imposed limits – perhaps increasingly strict limits – on the time he could afford for departmental sociability. What mattered to him most were his family, his Quaker faith, his teaching and the causes that his faith led him to. These could leave little time for anything else. He did cherish close friendships among his colleagues – particularly with David Hempton, Martin Ingram, Alvin Jackson, Gillian McIntosh and Lucy Wooding – and was esteemed and liked by everyone. That said, an abiding impression of Martin in the context of the department in recent years, is of someone keeping a tight rein on his natural sociability as other demands – scholarly and bureaucratic – took their toll on his time. In one respect, however, he remained a sheet anchor of collegiality, acting as mentor – formally and informally – to the younger members of staff and to tutorial assistants. The time and care that he devoted to explaining the arcana of departmental lore to new appointees, and to counselling them on the development of their teaching – usually showing by example how the highest standards should be striven for and might be achieved – was typical of the man and of immense value to the department he served so well and so loyally for the great majority of his working life.

Martin's death was an immense loss to Queen's University and to his colleagues in the School of History. He represented a beacon of integrity in what he often lamented was an academic world in decline: bedevilled by the increased bureaucratisation of university life, and undermined by the unavoidable short-cuts in a curriculum modularised to suit twelve-week semesters ('History Lite', was his trenchant characterisation of modern cafeteria-style degree programmes). He was properly sceptical of modish innovations and committed to the enduring principles of his subject. He was also an example to us all in the care and enthusiasm which he continued to devote to research and teaching, and may be said to have inspired not only generations of Belfast students, but generations of academic colleagues. He died at the height of his powers, when his department was beginning to undertake major reconstructive changes and he was in a position to contribute significantly to those changes. This tragic event has robbed both his colleagues and his students of an outstanding teacher and a true friend.

A Note by the Contributors

For those who attended, at Martin Lynn's invitation, the colloquium at Queen's University, Belfast in September 2004 and whose names now appear in this volume as chapter authors, Martin was a rare figure in academic life. He had a deserved reputation as a dedicated and distinguished scholar but he was also universally liked and respected. He was one of the few historians of empire who managed successfully to bridge what is often a gulf between the exponents of regional or local history, in his case that of West Africa, and those of metropolitan history. And both from nineteenth- and twentieth-century perspectives he was firmly establishing himself as the authoritative historian of Nigeria, the country of his birth. On a personal level Martin was a private individual but he was also warm and welcoming, and generous to a fault. During our two-day stay in Belfast for the colloquium he took one of our number to one side and remarked how proud he was to have brought us as a group to Queen's. The feeling was mutual, and it was a pleasure to be there. His passing saddened us all and we still feel the loss. But he bequeathed a fine academic legacy, and this volume now forms part of it. We dedicate it to his wife Alice and to his daughters, Hannah and Megan.

Preface

The essays collected in this volume were originally presented as papers at the Wiles Colloquium held at Queen's University, Belfast on 9–10 September 2004. The Wiles Trust was established in 1953 by Mrs Janet Boyd in memory of her father, Mr Thomas Wiles of Albany, New York; the purpose of the Wiles Colloquium is to bring together a group of specialists on a particular topic to discuss their research in an informal setting. The participants in the 2004 Colloquium would like to thank the Wiles Trust for the opportunity for making this gathering of scholars possible.

The subject of the 2004 Colloquium was the decolonisation of the British Empire in the 1950s. It is accepted that choosing a decade like the 1950s and making its boundaries the limit of analysis is a somewhat arbitrary process. As all historians know, history does not work like that. The chapters in this volume reflect the fact that the issues they address in many cases both predate the 1950s and postdate it too. The choice of the 1950s as the focus for the Colloquium was made for a number of reasons. It was made partly from the desire to avoid covering the well-worked ground of British imperial policy in the 1940s, and partly to address the tendency in the historiography of British decolonisation to see the late 1940s and the years 1959–68 as the critical eras in the story of British retreat from overseas commitments, while ignoring the years between. As outlined in the Introduction to this volume, the 1950s sit oddly in the long-term ebb of British imperial power and for many historians the decade is seen as a period characterised by an attempt to stem the tide of retreat before the Suez crisis and its aftermath brought reality home to British policymakers. The ideas of retreat and revival were made the broad themes of the Colloquium and the scholars whose essays are collected in this volume have each attempted to address these issues in relation to their own field of research. No claim is made that these ten essays represent a definitive attempt to resolve these questions or even a comprehensive history of the Empire in these years; what is collected herein are simply the reflections of ten leading historians on this topic. The hope is that their work will provide a guide to the current state of debate and will generate an impetus to further research.

Thanks are due to the Wiles Trustees and to the School of History at Queen's University for providing the funding for the Colloquium.

Thanks are also due to Sean Connolly, Grainne Devlin, Shane Gavaghan, Siobhan Gunn and David Hayton for their assistance with the Colloquium. The editor would particularly like to thank Peter Jupp and Peter Marshall without whose advice and support the Colloquium would not have been possible.

Martin Lynn

Notes on Contributors

Nigel J. Ashton is Senior Lecturer in International History at the London School of Economics and Political Science. He is the author of *Eisenhower, Macmillan and the Problem of Nasser: Anglo-American Relations and Arab Nationalism, 1955–59* (Basingstoke, 1996), and *Kennedy, Macmillan and the Cold War: The Irony of Interdependence* (Basingstoke, 2002), which won the 2003 Cambridge Donner book prize.

Stephen Ashton was formerly Senior Research Fellow at the Institute of Commonwealth Studies, University of London, where he was General Editor of the British Documents on the End of Empire Project. In the BDEEP series he co-edited with Sarah Stockwell *Imperial Policy and Colonial Practice 1925–1945* (1996), with David Killingray *The West Indies* (1999), and with Roger Louis *East of Suez and the Commonwealth 1964–1971* (2004). In the Foreign and Commonwealth Office series of Documents on British Policy Overseas he edited *Britain and China 1945–1950* (2001). He is the author of a number of articles about British relations with Burma before and after Burma's independence in 1948.

John Darwin is Beit Lecturer in the History of the British Commonwealth, University of Oxford, and Fellow of Nuffield College. His books include *Britain, Egypt and the Middle East: Imperial Policy in the Aftermath of War 1918–22* (Cambridge, 1981) and *Britain and Decolonisation: The Retreat from Empire in the Post-War World* (Basingstoke, 1988).

Stephen Howe is Professor in the History and Cultures of Colonialism in the University of Bristol. Previously he taught contemporary History at Ruskin College, Oxford. He has been a Research Fellow at Corpus Christi College and a columnist for the *New Statesman*. He is editor of *Lines of Dissent: Writing from the New Statesman, 1913–1988* (London, 1988) and author of *Anticolonialism in British Politics: The Left and the End of Empire, 1918–1964* (Oxford, 1993); *Afrocentrism: Mythical Pasts and Imagined Homes* (London, 1998); *Ireland and Empire: Colonial Legacies in Irish History and Culture* (Oxford, 2000); and *Empire: A Very Short Introduction* (Oxford, 2002). *His Intellectual Consequences of Decolonisation* is forthcoming from Oxford.

Wm. Roger Louis is Kerr Professor of English History and Culture and Distinguished Teaching Professor at the University of Texas at Austin. He is an Honorary Fellow of St. Antony's College, Oxford. His books include *Imperialism at Bay* (1976) and *The British Empire in the Middle East* (1984). He is the Editor-in-Chief of the *Oxford History of the British Empire*. In 2001 he was President of the American Historical Association.

The late **Martin Lynn** was Professor of African History at Queens University, Belfast. His publications include *Commerce and Economic Change in West Africa* (Cambridge, 1997) and *Nigeria 1943–1960* (ed. 2 vols, London, 2001), in the British Documents on End of Empire series.

Philip Murphy is Reader in Imperial and Commonwealth History at the University of Reading. He is author of *Party Politics and Decolonization: The Conservative Party and British Colonial Policy in Tropical Africa 1951–1964* (Oxford, 1995) and *Alan Lennox Boyd: A Biography* (London, 1999). He is the editor of the *Central Africa* volume in the British Documents on the End of Empire series (London, 2005).

Richard Rathbone is Emeritus Professor of History in the University of London and Honorary Professor of History in the University of Wales, Aberystwyth. He is editor of the Ghana volume in the British Documents on the End of Empire series (London, 1992) and author of, amongst other publications, *Murder and Politics in Colonial Ghana* (New Haven, 1993) and *Nkrumah and the Chiefs* (Oxford, 2000).

Sarah Stockwell is Lecturer in Imperial and Commonwealth History at King's College London. Her publications include *The Business of Decolonization: British Business Strategies in the Gold Coast* (Oxford, 2000), and with S.R. Ashton, *Imperial Policy and Colonial Practice 1925–1945* in the British Documents on the End of Empire series (London, 1996).

Nicholas J. White is Senior Lecturer in Economic and Social History in the School of Social Science, Liverpool John Moores University where he specialises in the history of European imperialism and decolonisation, as well as the recent history of East and Southeast Asia. His major works include *Business, Government and the End of Empire: Malaya, 1942–57* (Kuala Lumpur, 1996), *Decolonisation: The British Experience since 1945* (Harlow, 1999) and *British Business in Post-Colonial Malaysia, 1957–70: 'Neo-colonialism' or 'disengagement'?* (London, 2004). Dr. White has also published articles in scholarly journals such as *Economic History Review, Journal of Imperial & Commonwealth History, Modern Asian Studies, Journal of Southeast Asian Studies, South East Asia Research, Asia Pacific Business Review, Twentieth Century British History*.

Introduction

Martin Lynn

As is often the case, the more that historians have published on the ending of the British Empire after the Second World War the more, not less, complex the phenomenon has come to appear. The relative importance to be given in explaining decolonisation to changes in international relations, to the growth of anti-colonial nationalism and to developments within Britain remains unclear.[1] Even whether the ending of imperial rule represents imperial retreat at all, but should rather be seen as the continuation of imperialism by other means, is debated. On one thing however, many historians agree. Decolonisation should not be seen in terms of a linear progress towards an inevitable conclusion, beginning in 1945 and ending, say, in 1968 with the decision to withdraw from 'east of Suez'.[2] The view that characterises decolonisation as an inexorable process that progressed predictably to an inevitable 'fullstop' in the late 1960s, ignores both the determination of policy-makers to maintain Britain as a world power after 1945 and the potentialities within Britain's imperial position in these years. Policy-makers in 1945 most certainly did not see the future in terms of inexorable imperial retreat – Harold Macmillan famously wrote in 1952 of the march to a 'third British Empire' while Winston Churchill a year earlier talked of imperial 'consolidation' – and there is no reason to suggest they were anachronistic in thinking this way.[3]

Moreover, the view that sees decolonisation in these linear terms ignores the differences in emphasis and approach between the various British governments of this period.[4] Far from being a simple phenomenon, resulting from a single set of decisions and reflecting a shared imperial consensus within Westminster, British imperial withdrawal after 1945 was a complex and intermittent process that ebbed and flowed over time. If decolonisation is seen as a symptom of the waning

1

of British power, then for many periods during this era, it is arguable that it is the waxing not the waning of that power, that was so remarkable. Decolonisation in fact occurred in a series of uneven phases over the years after 1945 as successive British governments adjusted to changes in Britain's external relationships. It is the desire to examine one of these phases, the 1950s, that underpins this volume.

In the story of Britain's withdrawal from empire after 1945, the 1950s have suffered by comparison with what might be seen as the more dramatic events of the 1940s and 1960s. Of course, decades do not fit neatly into phases of historical change and even 'the 1950s' as an era in the periodisation of decolonisation, has emerged by default; the 1950s, it is implied, is that period that is 'not the 1940s' when India was abandoned and critical decisions were taken to move towards decolonisation in other parts of the empire, and also 'not the 1960s' when those decisions were driven to their logical conclusion as the remnants of the empire were discarded, culminating in withdrawal from east of Suez. Nor can the overlap between these periods be ignored; developments that began in the 1950s were to be played out for many years afterwards. Yet it is the argument of this volume that the years between the end of the Labour government in 1951 and the quickening impulse to decolonisation that accompanied the arrival of Iain Macleod as Secretary of State for the Colonies (1959–61) represent a 'distinctive period' in the history of Britain's withdrawal from her empire.[5]

Indeed the years 1951–59 were far from being a period when imperial policy marked time, but were rather an era of significant initiatives. It was the time of the Suez crisis, intervention in British Guiana, independence for the Gold Coast, counter-insurgency campaigns in colonies as different as Cyprus, Malaya and Kenya, Macmillan's renowned 'cost-benefit analysis' of the empire and the 1956–57 defence review and all that flowed from it. This was a period when critical developments occurred with long-term consequences for Britain's overseas role.[6] Yet it is also true that the precise significance of these years remains uncertain. In McIntyre's description these were 'the Ambiguous Fifties' when policy swung between a determination to hold the line and an acceptance of the need for more rapid withdrawal from overseas commitments.[7] It is unclear which approach prevailed. Did this era see an attempt to revive the empire and re-assert an ambitious overseas role for Britain? If it did, how successful was it?

Clearly the Conservative government that came to power in 1951 under Churchill as Prime Minister (1951–55), shared much with its Labour predecessor as far as the empire was concerned. Like Labour it faced an enfeebled economy, whose attempts at sterling convertibility in 1947–49 had failed disastrously, a heavy dependence on US economic and military aid at a time of Soviet threats in Europe, and difficulties in Malaya, Egypt and elsewhere in the Middle East, and in territories as diverse as British Guiana, the Gold Coast and Sudan. However it is important not to exaggerate these problems, not least because nationalism remained attenuated across much of the empire in the early 1950s. Indeed the international climate facing the empire in 1951 was a good deal more favourable than had been the case in 1945. This was not just because of Britain's burgeoning economic recovery in the early 1950s. The Cold War, and Britain's commitment to the conflict against communism, for example in Korea (1950–53), meant that US policy was much more willing to tolerate, even underpin, a continuing British Empire than before.[8] Britain remained in 1951 one of the 'Big Three' great powers, ruler of an empire that still covered significant parts of Asia, Africa, the Pacific and the Americas.

Yet for all Churchill's talk of 'consolidation' and his obduracy and resistance to increasingly emboldened demands from nationalists, it was recognised that a die-hard, reactionary refusal to adapt was unlikely to take Britain very far after 1951.[9] Adjusting to demands for constitutional advance, or even self-government, from nationalists was necessary if Britain was to remain an imperial power. For some in the government, like the Secretary of State for the Colonies, Oliver Lyttelton (1951–54), and, but to a much lesser extent, his successor, Alan Lennox-Boyd (1954–59), a pragmatic willingness to co-operate with demands for self-government in some areas was seen as necessary for the empire to survive at all. Thus the moves to self-government in West Africa begun under Labour, though strongly criticised by both Churchill and the Foreign Secretary, Anthony Eden (1951–55), continued in this period with Kwame Nkrumah appointed Prime Minister of the Gold Coast in 1952.[10]

Yet Lyttelton was no radical and no one welcomed a policy of too rapid a withdrawal from the empire in these years. Churchill was determined to resist a continuation of what he saw as Labour's too hasty 'retreat' from overseas territories in the late 1940s; India was to be an exception rather than the start of a wider move in the dependent empire towards self-government. The empire – whether the 'third' or even 'fourth' British Empire – still had a critical role in the defence of Britain's overseas interests and this required, it was believed, a determined resistance to too hasty moves to self-government.[11] For the Conservatives, self-government for much of the empire, while an acknowledged goal of policy, was so many decades away – in some views even a century away – that it could effectively be ignored; for some colonies indeed, it might never occur. The Colonial Office Minister Henry Hopkinson in 1954 made clear his view that Cyprus would 'never' gain independence while similar sentiments were expressed with regard to Kenya as late as 1959.[12] The point has often been made that during the premierships of Churchill and his successor Eden (1955–57), no territory received its independence from Britain with the exceptions of Libya and Sudan, both of which had an unusual status.[13]

If a determined resistance to the moves to independence initiated in the 1940s by Labour was one feature of the Conservative governments' policy of these years, another was its ready willingness to use force in managing nationalism. The Conservatives were determined, as it were, to 'pick' their nationalists and to use military action to do this. It can be argued that this was not a new policy, but clearly the increased willingness in these years to use force against nationalists represented a break with the immediate past, or at the very least a change in emphasis. Force was used in these years to help restore the pro-western Shah of Iran in 1953, to intervene in British Guiana, also in 1953, to attempt to crush the Ethniki Orhanosis Kyrion Agoniston (EOKA) rising in Cyprus after 1955 and to continue the emergency in Malaya begun in 1948.[14] Consideration was even given to military intervention in Nigeria in 1955–56 in order to slow down what officials saw as the precipitate move to self-government begun under Labour.[15] Most notably however, force was used in Kenya following the commencement of the so-called Mau Mau emergency in 1952. Heavy military intervention over the next years involving the processing and 'rehabilitation' in camps of large numbers of Africans, and, as is now clear, serious brutality, was coupled with the jailing of the Kenyan leader, Jomo Kenyatta, and the banning of his party, the Kenyan African Union; this was accompanied by political and economic measures designed to undermine support for the Mau Mau insurgents.[16] What is striking about the intervention in Kenya, as about the Malayan equivalent, is the relative success of these military actions in these years.

Picking one's nationalists, also meant supporting settlers. The Conservative governments, at least in the early to mid-1950s, unquestionably pursued a policy of reinforcing settlers' interests. The rhetoric may have been about 'kith and kin' but the reality was the more pragmatic one that settlers' interests were seen as being congruent with Britain's interests. The moves towards self-government in the Gold Coast and Nigeria gave a renewed importance to settlers elsewhere in the continent. Africa, given its likely economic potential, was clearly to play a major role in the remodelled empire that was central to Conservative overseas ambitions and clearly settlers would be an important part of this.

In 1952 the Empire Settlement Act was renewed while the following year the Central African Federation was established.[17] The Federation, based on an overwhelmingly white franchise, was seen by the Conservatives as being on the road to self-government within a decade or so, but this was a self-government that, for all the safeguards London apparently pursued for the African majority, would be under white leadership.[18] The driving motor of British policy here was to maintain British interests in Central Africa through a bolstered white regime. Meanwhile in East Africa discussions about a Federation, initiated in the late 1940s, were followed by the moves during the 1950s to increase African political rights in Kenya and to encourage power-sharing. Yet there were strict limits to African rights in Kenya; in Darwin's words, these initiatives were 'an ambitious effort to outflank and outmanoeuvre any demand for universal suffrage'.[19] They were, in truth, designed to sustain white settler rule in Kenya, for 'multi-racialism' as it was termed, meant 50,000 Kenyan settlers having the same representation as five million Africans. Conservative policy in Kenya, as enunciated in the Commons as late as April 1959 by Lennox-Boyd, was to maintain, not dilute, a British presence in the territory.[20]

Concessions where essential, military resistance to nationalism where necessary, support for settlers where possible: these were the characteristics of Conservative imperial policy under Churchill and Eden. This was not however a reactionary, knee-jerk policy of blind intransigence and a refusal to accept that the world had changed. Conservative policy was to conserve the empire: to preserve a world role for Britain in the 1950s. This required, it was believed, a more assertive stance than what was seen as Labour's 'retreat' after 1945. The aim was to regroup and to reshape Britain's empire. There was a future for a remodelled empire, it was felt, based around a new emphasis on Britain's future in Africa, a continuing though reduced presence east of Suez and in South-East Asia, and not least, a re-assertion of British influence in the Middle East.

Like their Labour predecessors, the Conservatives after 1951 saw a major role for Britain in the Middle East.[21] Strategic and oil interests and fear of Soviet influence gave Britain significant ambitions in the region in the 1950s. The network of air and sea bases and political clients built since the interwar years, made the British determined to continue their role as the dominant power in the area and to use it as a lynchpin of a revitalised empire. In one respect this was successfully maintained; the

Baghdad Pact with Iraq and Turkey in 1955 was designed, albeit more in the sense of political support than as a military alliance, to underpin British ambitions in the region, being the centrepiece of a network of bases and influence that included Aden, the Persian Gulf, Cyprus, the Suez Canal and Jordan and that stretched from Libya to Iran and Pakistan, and arguably included Kenya too. Relations with Egypt were less happy in these years, however, and the revolution of 1952 that eventually brought Gamal Abd al-Nasser to power was but part of a longer process that prompted Britain to re-negotiate its position concerning the Suez Canal and to put a renewed emphasis on Cyprus's strategic role. Churchill at least, was determined for Britain to stand its ground, but the new Canal agreement, signed in 1954 and involving British withdrawal from the Canal Zone by 1956 (though Britain obtained a right of return in a crisis), was designed to improve Anglo-Egyptian relations.[22] It was apparent that by the mid-1950s Britain's ambitions for a central role in the Middle East were on the road to being achieved.

The idea of the Commonwealth played a central part in these ambitions for a reshaped empire in the 1950s. The Commonwealth in this period was much more than simply a means of massaging Britain's *amour propre* in the face of a diminished empire. Its function was more ambitious and the British government was determined, in these years, to develop and even extend its role in providing resources and allies as well as providing a positive image before the court of world opinion.[23] There was talk of imperial preference, and of developing the Commonwealth link to sustain the British economy, as did occur through the Sterling Area.[24] This showed how seriously the British still took their overseas economic interests. Equally seriously, there were strenuous efforts to develop its defence capability, by binding in the Australians and New Zealanders to aid the British in the Middle East and elsewhere, and by developing a Commonwealth Strategic Reserve; Australia also provided facilities for nuclear testing in these years.[25] It was only with the accession of former African and Asian colonies upsetting the 'balance' within the Commonwealth and generating increasing disputes involving the South Africans, that this ambition came to be abandoned. Nonetheless, there was talk of circumventing this by developing a two-tier (or more correctly, an inner circle–outer circle) Commonwealth, an idea that eventually proved unworkable.[26]

That the Conservative governments could conceive of such a revitalised empire after 1951 derived in great part from the recovery of Britain's economy and the sharply rising standard of living within Britain in these years, a process that was marked by the convertibility of sterling from 1958. The imperial economy remained significant for Britain in the early 1950s, less so than in the past as a source of dollars, but Britain still valued imperial markets and resources and still saw the role of imperial trading privileges as central to its economic future.[27] Recognition of the possibilities offered by the moves towards a European Common Market in the 1957 Treaty of Rome remained for the future. Nonetheless the defence burden that empire imposed on Britain was huge and by the mid-1950s questions were being asked both as to whether Britain could afford such expenditure and as to whether it was, in a nuclear age, entirely necessary. It was only in the late 1950s that the declining share of British trade coming from the empire and the declining relative significance of the sterling balances in London, began to suggest that the answer to both these questions was no.

Clearly the imperial policy of the Conservative governments of 1951–57 was even more positive and ambitious than suggested by Goldsworthy's celebrated description of a Britain aiming to 'keep change within bounds' in these years.[28] The aim of the policy after 1951 was certainly to hold the line against imperial retreat, but it also went beyond that to a determined attempt at imperial re-assertion. It represented an effort to use the empire as part of an ambitious vision of a revitalised Britain, economically recovered from the ravages of the War, playing an active and interventionist role across the globe in defence of British interests. Britain was to be a member of the Big Three, as the Labour government had intended in the post-War years, but a member on its own terms, able once more to act unilaterally and independently of the United States.[29]

To act as one of the Big Three patently required a nuclear capacity. The Conservatives' determination – inherited, to be sure, from the Labour government's decisions following the War – was to maintain an independent nuclear deterrent and 1952 saw the testing of Britain's first atomic bomb. Behind this determination for an independent nuclear deterrent however was the central imperial and strategic policy of the Conservative governments of 1951–57, namely, the desire to assert independence of the United States and the determination to utilise the empire (as part of Churchill's renowned 'three circles' of British interests) to achieve this. Given the power of the United States and given the experience of 1939–45 (or more precisely, 1941–45), relations with Washington were unquestionably at the heart of Britain's strategic future in the post-War world.[30] What Britain needed was US support, not least in Europe against the Red Army, something by no means guaranteed in 1945 but which she had achieved by the time of the signing of the NATO pact in 1949. American reinforcement in Europe allowed Britain to turn to its wider, world interests. Equally, the success of Britain in asserting those wider interests against putative Soviet subversion, enabled her to show her value to the transatlantic relationship, a process reinforced by Britain's continuing commitment in the Korean War. But this relationship was never a one-way street, as could be seen in British determination to take its own line over communist China and over the Vietnam negotiations of 1954; having secured an American commitment to Europe, the British in the 1950s were determined to assert their independence from Washington.[31] The Big Three meant precisely that as far as the British were concerned. A revitalised empire was necessary for the 'imperial unilateralism' that was seen as central to Britain's continuing role as a Great Power.

The ambition to maintain independence of Washington played its part in Britain's intervention in Suez in 1956.[32] This is not the place to outline in detail the events of this well-known story. It was ultimately the miscalculation by Britain over what the American reaction would be which explains the disaster that ensued when the British and French, in collusion with the Israelis, invaded Egypt in October 1956. A military success, it was a political catastrophe once the United States showed its anger by refusing to support sterling on the world money markets; a process that led to an ignominious British retreat. It was, as Anthony Nutting said, 'No end of a lesson', but not just for Britain's role in the Middle East.[33] It also marked the beginning of the end for Britain's hopes to maintain an independent and unilateral foreign policy. While the role of the Suez crisis as a watershed in British imperial policy can be greatly exaggerated, clearly it marked a major turning point in British hopes of maintaining an independent role, indeed any significant role, overseas.

The lesson of Suez indeed, was that it showed that Britain did not have the capacity to act overseas independently of the United States. This failure of imperial unilateralism effectively undermined the whole thrust of Conservative imperial policy since 1951. Yet it took time for this lesson to be absorbed in London. The central figure in this re-evaluation of British policy after Suez was the new Prime Minister, Harold Macmillan (1957–63), who came to power, with US approval, following Eden's resignation. His time in office was characterised by his recognition of the need to maintain closer relations with the United States.[34] The fall-out from Suez was but part of the reassessment of imperial policy generated in these years. Of key significance was the defence review begun in 1956 and that resulted in the White Paper of

1957. This review, driven by concerns at the cost of defence, stressed the financial necessity of moving towards a nuclear strategy and away from large conventional forces, a policy that in turn prompted Britain's need to approach the United States for nuclear weapons systems and one which led to the Nassau meeting of Macmillan and President Kennedy in 1962.[35] However this reshaping of Britain's defence capabilities in the late 1950s clearly raised the question as to whether the empire was now obsolete. Also significant in generating this reassessment was an awareness of the underlying fundamental problems in the British economy, as seen in the balance of payments difficulties of these years. This, together with the realisation of the growing importance of the European economy to British trade in the late 1950s, and the relatively declining significance of the Sterling Area, led to Britain's first application to join the European Common Market in 1961.[36]

Moreover changes were occurring in the late 1950s in the areas in which Britain had hoped to maintain an imperial presence, whether the Middle East, east of Suez or Africa. This was obviously so in the Middle East, where the Suez crisis was followed by the effective collapse of the Baghdad Pact and, in 1958, the revolution in Iraq that overthrew both the monarchy and the pro-British Prime Minister, Nuri al-Said.[37] While Britain was still prepared to intervene in the region, as in Oman after 1957, in Jordan in 1958 and Kuwait in 1961, was keen to maintain its influence throughout the Persian Gulf states, and fought a long drawn out counter-insurgency campaign in Aden in the mid-1960s, it was clear that British influence in the Middle East was waning. The decision to withdraw from Aden in 1967 and the following year to announce withdrawal from the Gulf brought this process to conclusion. Although Britain continued, with US encouragement, to maintain ambitions east of Suez and not least in South-East Asia through SEATO (the South-East Asia Treaty Organisation, signed in 1954), the granting of independence to Malaya in 1957 and the ending of the emergency there in 1960 were signs of changing priorities.[38]

As far as the African colonial territories, were concerned, Macmillan can be said to have initiated a re-assessment of Britain's role with the 'cost-benefit analysis' of the value of colonies in early 1957, an analysis suggesting that Britain could safely withdraw from much of the empire with little economic loss to herself.[39] It was the arrival of Macleod in the Colonial Office in 1959, coinciding with the policy paper 'Africa: the next ten years' from the Cabinet Office Africa Committee, that saw this re-assessment given full rein and culminated in fresh moves towards decolonisation.[40] In Louis' words, Macleod was to be to the African

Empire 'what Mountbatten had been to India'.[41] Patently, from 1959 onwards, the pace of decolonisation picked up speed across the continent, driven by heightened concerns at possible Soviet influence and the desire to build up collaborative elites sympathetic to British economic interests. The revelation of the Hola camp atrocities in Kenya in 1959 when 11 camp inmates were beaten to death by their guards, and the realities of politics in the Central African Federation revealed by the Devlin Report, also in 1959, reinforced this.

It is certainly true that this re-assessment did not mark an end to Britain's ambitions as a world power. Even in the late 1950s there was still a vision in London of Britain as a global power relying on what some termed 'an empire of points' or strategic bases – Aden, Cyprus, Gibraltar and Singapore to name but few – that could continue to provide, in a nuclear age, the framework for an ambitious and assertive world role.[42] Indeed there were attempts to find new strategic bases, such as in Nigeria and Kenya, in this period.[43] Equally Britain continued to play a significant role east of Suez for long after this, as seen in 'Confrontation' with Indonesia in 1963–66. Nonetheless it was also clear that there was a much greater willingness to resolve colonial problems by contemplating withdrawal. Macmillan's renowned 'Wind of Change' speech to the South African Parliament in February 1960 reflected the new realities in Africa. The Gold Coast (as Ghana) had gained its independence in 1957, while Nigeria, Britain's largest colonial territory after 1947, was to gain its independence in 1960.[44] In the case of Kenya, the Lancaster House conference in 1960 saw significant moves towards majority rule and ultimate independence.[45] Simultaneously moves were being made towards independence in Tanganyika and Uganda; the three East African territories were to get their independence in 1963, 1961 and 1962 respectively. In Central Africa, the outcome of the 1959 emergency led to the London conference of 1960 and the break-up of the Federation in 1963; Nyasaland (as Malawi) and Northern Rhodesia (as Zambia) gained their independence the following year. Elsewhere, the collapse of the Federation of the West Indies led to independence for Jamaica in 1962 followed by Trinidad and Tobago in the same year and Barbados in 1966.[46]

It is wrong however to exaggerate the impact of these changes before 1959, and indeed during the 1950s more broadly. The Conservative governments of this period still had a realistic vision of the future that saw Britain as a world power playing an assertive role across the globe in defence of British interests; the empire was central to this ambition. This was not a reactionary, last-ditch attempt to stave off the inevitable, except in hindsight. Rather it was a coherent and rational attempt to re-assert Britain's role as a Great Power in the defence of British economic and strategic interests. It was, in Porter's assessment, 'not unsuccessful' as well, given the changes that were occurring in the world and within Britain in these years.[47] In 1959 Britain still held a significant empire overseas and, arguably, a larger one than many might have predicted in 1945. Both in terms of its formal holdings in Africa and its residual influence in the Middle East and South-East Asia in 1959, this was an empire that still reflected a Britain with a global reach and a presence on all continents and in all oceans. With the continuing vision of a possible 'empire of points', shaped to the needs of a nuclear world, this was an empire that still had potency as the decade came to an end.

This is not the place to speculate on the 'what if' of history, and what might have happened if the Conservatives had followed a different line in 1951, adjusting more quickly to the changes facing the empire. But what is clear is that the years 1951–59, defined as the period between the Labour governments and the moves towards the rapid decolonisation of the empire after 1959, have coherence as a distinctive era in the history of Britain's withdrawal from her empire. It was a period begun with dreams of imperial re-assertion by the Conservatives but one that ended with the retreat from colonies in Africa and effective withdrawal from the Middle East. Even the putative 'empire of points' proved, in the longer term, of limited durability. It saw a determined attempt to build an overseas policy that would allow Britain to use the empire to act independently of the United States, but ended with the realisation that such unilateralism was not feasible. Both revival *and* retreat, arguably, characterise British policy in these years therefore. Ambiguity, contradictions, 'conflicting aims and objects', all, as the chapters that follow in this volume suggest, characterise this period.[48] But its significance in the history of Britain's withdrawal from empire as a moment when an assertive attempt to reshape Britain's imperial future occurred, can hardly be gainsaid.

Notes

1. From the general historiography on British decolonisation the following works may be consulted with particular profit: J. Gallagher, *The Decline, Revival and Fall of the British Empire* (Cambridge: 1982); J. Darwin, *Britain and Decolonisation: The Retreat from Empire in the Post-war World* (Basingstoke: 1988); J. Darwin, *The End of the British Empire: The Historical Debate* (Oxford, 1991); D. Reynolds, *Britannia Overruled: British Policy and World Power in the Twentieth Century* (Harlow, 1991); Wm.R. Louis and R. Robinson,

'The imperialism of decolonization', *Journal of Imperial and Commonwealth History* (hereafter *JICH*), 22 (1994), 462–511. W.D. McIntyre, *British Decolonization 1946–1997: When, Why and How did the British Empire Fall* (Basingstoke: 1998); N.J. White, *Decolonisation: The British Experience since 1945* (Harlow: 1999); J. Darwin, 'Decolonization and the end of empire', in R.W. Winks (ed.), *Oxford History of the British Empire,* volume 5, *Historiography* (Oxford: 1999), pp. 541–57; J.M. Brown and Wm.R. Louis (eds), *Oxford History of the British Empire,* volume 4, *The Twentieth Century* (Oxford: 1999), passim and L.J. Butler, *Britain and Empire: Adjusting to a Post-imperial World* (London: 2002).

2. This point is made persuasively by J. Darwin, 'British decolonization since 1945: a pattern or a puzzle?', *JICH* 12 (1984), 187–209.

3. W.R. Louis, 'The dissolution of the British Empire', in Brown and Louis, *The Twentieth Century,* p. 340; McIntyre, *British Decolonisation,* p. 38.

4. The domestic dimension to these years is covered in: D. Goldsworthy, *Colonial Issues in British Politics, 1945–1961: from 'colonial development' to 'wind of change'* (Oxford: 1971); S. Howe, *Anticolonialism in British Politics: The Left and the End of Empire* (Oxford: 1993); P. Murphy, *Party Politics and Decolonisation: The Conservative Party and British Colonial Policy in Tropical Africa, 1951–64* (Oxford: 1995).

5. D. Goldsworthy, 'Keeping Change within Bounds: Aspects of Colonial Policy during the Churchill and Eden Governments, 1951–57', *JICH* 18 (1990), 81–108. These issues are covered in greater depth in D. Goldsworthy (ed.), *The Conservative Government and the End of Empire 1951–57: British Documents on the End of Empire* (3 parts, London: 1994) and R. Hyam and Wm.R. Louis (eds), *The Conservative Government and the End of Empire 1957–64: British Documents on the End of Empire* (2 parts; London: 2000).

6. The way developments that began in the 1950s could continue to consume British energies through to the 1970s is examined in Chapter 9 by Wm. Roger Louis in this volume.

7. McIntyre, *British Decolonization,* p. 38.

8. Louis and Robinson, 'Imperialism of Decolonization', pp. 471–2. This can also be seen in the way US policy to the Caribbean changed during this period towards support for a continuing British presence, largely due to fears of political instability in the event of a precipitate British withdrawal, Sutherland to Thomas, 7 January 1964 in S.R. Ashton and D. Killingray (eds), *The West Indies: British Documents on the End of Empire* (London: 1999) document 220.

9. Louis, 'Dissolution of the British Empire', p. 339.

10. Goldsworthy, 'Change within Bounds', pp. 83–4. Eden famously described changes in the Gold Coast as proceeding at a 'pretty dangerous political gallop'.

11. Chapter 1 by John Darwin in this volume deals with the idea of a fourth British Empire.

12. Goldsworthy, 'Change within Bounds', p. 100; Darwin, 'Decolonization since 1945', p. 200.

13. Certainly the Gold Coast received its independence two months after Eden's resignation, but this was the culmination of decisions taken under the post-war Labour governments.

14. Other methods used to 'pick' nationalists are outlined for the case of Nigeria, in Chapter 7 by Martin Lynn in this volume. The EOKA movement had as its aim a union of Cyrus with Greece.
15. M. Lynn, 'The "Eastern Crisis" of 1955–57, the Colonial Office and Nigerian Decolonisation', *JICH*, 30 (2002), 91–109.
16. For the negotiations that led to independence see K. Kyle, *The Politics of the Independence of Kenya* (Basingstoke: 1999). For the methods Britain used to suppress Mau Mau see D. Anderson, *Histories of the Hanged: Britain's Dirty War in Kenya and the End of Empire* (London: 2005) and C. Elkins, *Britain's Gulag: The Brutal End of Empire in Kenya* (London: 2005).
17. The origins of the Federation are discussed in Chapter 3 by Philip Murphy in this volume.
18. Darwin, 'Decolonization since 1945', 200. The process of decolonisation in Africa is covered in J.D. Hargreaves, *Decolonization in Africa* (Harlow: 1988).
19. Darwin, 'Decolonization since 1945', p. 199.
20. Darwin, 'Decolonization since 1945', p. 200.
21. E. Monroe, *Britain's Moment in the Middle East, 1914–71* (London: 1981); Wm.R. Louis, *The British Empire in the Middle East 1945–1951* (Oxford: 1984); Louis and Robinson, 'Imperialism of decolonization', p. 477.
22. Wm.R. Louis, 'The tragedy of the Anglo-Egyptian settlement of 1954', in Wm.R. Louis and R. Owen (eds), *Suez 1956: The Crisis and its Consequences* (Oxford: 1989), pp. 43–71; G. Balfour-Paul, 'Britain's informal empire in the Middle East', in Brown and Louis, *The Twentieth Century*, p. 509; R. Ovendale, *Britain, the United States and the Transfer of Power in the Middle East 1945–62* (London: 1996); N.J. Ashton, *Eisenhower, Macmillan and the Problem of Nasser: Anglo-American Relations and Arab Nationalism, 1955–59* (Basingstoke: 1996). British policy towards Egypt can be traced in J. Kent (ed.), *Egypt and the Defence of the Middle East: British Documents on the End of Empire* (3 parts, London: 1998).
23. British views of the role of UN opinion during the decolonisation process are developed in Chapter 9 by Wm. Roger Louis in this volume.
24. A.E. Hinds, 'Sterling and imperial policy, 1945–51', *JICH*, 15 (1987), 148–69; A.E. Hinds, 'Imperial policy and colonial sterling balances, 1943–56', *JICH*, 19 (1991), 24–44; Butler, *Britain and Empire*, 104; C.R. Schenk, *Britain and the Sterling Area: From Devaluation to Convertibility in the 1950s* (London: 1994).
25. Butler, *Britain and Empire*, pp. 102–4.
26. Goldsworthy, 'Change within bounds', pp. 96–9.
27. These ideas are developed in Chapters 4 and 5 by Sarah Stockwell and Nicholas J. White in this volume.
28. Goldsworthy, 'Change within bounds', p. 84; the idea is discussed in Chapter 2 by S.R. Ashton in this volume.
29. R.F. Holland, 'The imperial factor in British strategies from Attlee to Macmillan, 1945–63', *JICH* 12 (1984), 165–86; R.F. Holland, *The Pursuit of Greatness: Britain and the World Role, 1900–70* (London: 1991), pp. 269–70.
30. I. Clark and N.J. Wheeler, *The British Origins of Nuclear Strategy, 1945–55* (Oxford: 1989); Holland, *Pursuit of Greatness*, pp. 241–58.
31. Holland, 'Imperial factor', p. 183; Louis and Robinson, 'Imperialism of decolonization', pp. 476–81.

32. The story is outlined in the various articles in Louis and Owen, *Suez 1956*.
33. A. Nutting, *No End of a Lesson: The Story of Suez* (London: 1967).
34. Holland, 'Imperial factor', 179; Louis and Robinson, 'Imperialism of decolonization', pp. 483–92. This issue is examined in Chapter 8 by N.J. Ashton, in this volume.
35. Butler, *Britain and Empire*, pp. 99–101; N.J. Ashton, *Kennedy, Macmillan and the Cold War: The Irony of Interdependence* (Basingstoke: 2002).
36. The argument that the empire became economically less important to Britain in these years is developed by P.J. Cain and A.G. Hopkins, *British Imperialism: Crisis and Deconstruction, 1914–1990* (Harlow: 1993), pp. 286–91. But see also N.J. White, 'The business and the politics of decolonization: the British experience in the twentieth century', *Economic History Review*, 53 (2000), 544–64.
37. Darwin, *Britain and Decolonisation*, 231; R. Khalidi, 'Consequences of the Suez Crisis in the Arab world', in Louis and Owen, (eds), *Suez 1956*, pp. 377–92.
38. A.J. Stockwell (ed.), *Malaya: British Documents on the End of Empire* (3 parts, London: 1995); N.J. White, *Business, Government and the End of empire: Malaya 1942–57* (Oxford: 1996); A.J. Stockwell, 'Imperialism and nationalism in South-East Asia', in Brown and Louis (eds), *The Twentieth Century*, pp. 465–89; W.R. Louis, 'The dissolution of the British Empire in the era of Vietnam', *American Historical Review*, 107 (2002), 1–25; N.J. White, 'The survival, revival and decline of British economic influence in Malaysia, 1957–70', *Twentieth Century British History*, 14 (2003), 222–42.
39. P.E. Hemming, 'Macmillan and the end of the British Empire in Africa', in R. Aldous and S. Lee (eds), *Harold Macmillan and Britain's World Role* (Basingstoke: 1996); A.G. Hopkins, 'Macmillan's Audit of Empire, 1957', in P. Clarke and C. Trebilcock (eds), *Understanding Decline*, (Cambridge: 1997), pp. 234–60.
40. R. Ovendale, 'Macmillan and the Wind of Change in Africa, 1957–1960', *Historical Journal*, 38 (1995), 455–77. 'Africa: the next ten years' was produced by a committee of officials chaired by the Cabinet Secretary and can be found in Hyam and Louis, *Conservative Government and End of Empire* part 1, document 20.
41. Louis, 'Dissolution of the British Empire', p. 351.
42. Goldsworthy, 'Change within bounds', pp. 99–100; Holland, *Pursuit of Greatness*, p. 262.
43. O. Ojedokun, 'The Anglo-Nigerian entente and its demise, 1960–62', *Journal of Commonwealth Political Studies*, 9 (1971), 210–33; Louis and Robinson, 'Imperialism of decolonization', 483.
44. British concerns about the consequences of Ghanaian independence are outlined in Chapter 6 by Richard Rathbone in this volume. An important dimension of this is covered in S.E. Stockwell, *The Business of Decolonisation: British Business Strategies in the Gold Coast* (Oxford: 2000). The story of Ghana's move to independence can be followed in R. Rathbone (ed.), *Ghana: British Documents on the End of empire* (2 parts, London: 1992), and Nigeria's equivalent in M. Lynn (ed.), *Nigeria: British Documents on the End of Empire* (2 parts, London: 2001).
45. The story of Kenya's move to independence can be followed in B.A. Ogot, 'The Decisive Years, 1956–63', in B.A. Ogot and W.R. Ochieng (eds),

Decolonization and Independence in Kenya 1940–93 (London: 1995) and Kyle, *Independence of Kenya*.
46. Ashton and Killingray, *The West Indies*.
47. B. Porter, *The Lion's Share: A Short History of British Imperialism, 1850–1995* (Harlow, 3rd edn, 1996), p. 337. For the interrelationship between the empire and domestic British politics and culture in these years, see Chapter 10 by Stephen Howe in this volume.
48. Darwin, 'Decolonization since 1945', p. 198.

1
Was there a Fourth British Empire?

John Darwin

It is tempting to reply with an expression of horror: a fourth British Empire is surely a concept too far. At least the 'third British Empire' carried the imprimatur of Alfred Zimmern,[1] but did contemporary usage extend to a fourth? Perhaps surprisingly the answer is yes. He was looking forward to an active association 'with the Fourth British Empire', John Curtin told a wartime conference of the Australian Labour Party in December 1943.[2] Taking his cue, the historian Wayne Reynolds has applied the term to Britain's post-war effort to maintain her global power through a nuclear weapon developed in partnership with the Australian government.[3] But perhaps a case can be made for its wider application in Britain's post-war history. The justification would have to be that there were unmistakable differences between the British Empire that emerged from the Second World War and the empire that had gone to war in 1939. Unmistakable differences not so much in the sense that after 1945 the old structure had been weakened and was in decline. Rather, that after the war, and the huge imperial crisis that followed, the British and their imperial friends set out to construct yet another system of global power, fashioned for a new world order, dependent on different sources of strength, avowing a new ideology and vulnerable to different kinds of wasting disease. That is the claim that this chapter advances.

A supplementary case might also be made that the resort to numbers is not merely an example of gratuitous labelling. It is meant to signal a view of British imperial history that deserves fresh emphasis. It is all too easy to write about empire in what might be called the introverted mode, as if all that mattered were the internal squabbles of its interests and factions, rulers and ruled. The missing dimension is the constant pressure exerted by global conditions: the rollercoaster ride of the world economy; the sudden conjuncture of geopolitical change; the intrusive presence of new information and knowledge. From this point of view the most powerful motor in the empire's history was the constant struggle to adapt its internal politics to the relentless demands of exogenous change. The numerical sequence denotes in rough and ready fashion the successive attempts to devise an imperial system that could exploit the opportunities and contain the disruptions of the wider world. It may serve to remind us that even an empire as grand as the British was an epiphenomenon of the course of world history.

I

This point may be clearer if we consider the conditions that permitted the rise of a British world-system in the nineteenth century. After the experimental phase in global (as opposed to Atlantic) empire between 1830 and 1870 (what Robinson and Gallagher called 'mid-Victorian imperialism'), the modern British world-system really crystallised around four central elements: the naval and economic power of Britain as a great European state; British India as the grand auxiliary of British power in Asia; the settler countries as the dynamic vanguards of a 'British world'; and the City's commercial empire of overseas property and transport infrastructure, which bonded the system together and met some of the cost of its extensive superstructure. It was this world-system that British leaders were so anxious to defend by annexation, diplomacy and war before 1914.

They did so with remarkable success largely because global conditions – especially in Eurasia – were so favourable to their enterprise, and allowed them to turn their combination of resources to maximum advantage. These conditions may be summarised as follows. First, the geopolitical situation at each end of Eurasia was remarkably benign. Despite the historical ink that has been spilt in rivers on the great power rivalries of 1880–1914, the striking feature of the politics of Europe throughout most of this period is the uniformly conservative outlook of the great power governments. None of them dared risk their domestic order by courting a war that would repeat the catastrophe of 1792–1815. This was especially true of the eastern powers. German rule over Western Poland was of far greater moment than German rule in Western Africa or the Western Pacific. A European upheaval was more than likely to release the pent-up energies of submerged nationalities and wreck the dynastic *imperia* that kept them in check.

The result was that despite the urgings of hyperactive proconsuls, promotion-seeking soldiers and market-seeking merchants, none of the

Continental great power governments was ready to pursue its destiny to the point of war. This worked hugely to Britain's advantage since of the powers her local agents had staked the largest claims and usually disposed of the best resources – leaving the Gallic cockerel (in Salisbury's sardonic phrase) to scratch in the sand. This was why the African partition spilt almost no white blood and why the imperial rivalry of the late nineteenth century was more stressful than threatening to the British world-system.

The conservative outlook of European statesman was matched by the 'passive' state of East Asian politics. We should not exaggerate. Even in the era of Qing decline, Chinese self-assertion in Inner Asia could ruffle the feathers of the Government in Simla.[4] By the 1890s, Japan's aspiration to great power status could no longer be dismissed as an oriental dream. Nevertheless, before 1914 there could be no question of an East Asian power having the nerve, let alone the means, to assault British interest in Asia. The external threat to British rule in India came from the European power to the north not the Asian power to the east. The paranoid fantasists of the White Pacific feared a stealth invasion of 'Asiatic' migrants not a military conquest. For the British this pattern of politics in Eastern Eurasia was especially convenient. It let them guard their Asian interests by diplomacy in Europe and a naval concentration in European waters. It made the costs of defending an absurdly elongated empire politically manageable even to governments that were committed to higher welfare spending at home.[5]

The shape of the British world-system in the late nineteenth century reflected the influence of these highly favourable conditions. British governments could station nearly half their army 6000 miles away in India where it could fulfil a double purpose: as the strategic reserve for an Afro-Asian world stretching as far south as Cape Town,[6] as far east as Tientsin; and as a colossal counterweight in Indian politics, loading the scale of collaboration in Britain's favour. Two further consequences flowed from this. London was able to charge as much as two-thirds of its total standing army (180,000 British, 140,000 Indians) to the Indian budget – a political convenience of immeasurable value. Second, by loading the burden of imperial defence on the voteless Indian taxpayer, they could relieve both the taxpayer at home and the settler taxpayers of the white dominions. Responsible government in the settler countries could not have survived any attempt to extract more than nominal payment for the costs of defence – not at least before the naval scares after 1900. Nor could the colonies have pressed so rapidly ahead with their economic development had their budgets been loaded with military estimates. The whole pattern of their demographic, political and economic progress would have been very different.

Geopolitical conditions were powerfully reinforced by the rapid evolution of a world economy. By the 1880s the rapid spread of modern communications had created an all but global system of economic exchange. As Cain and Hopkins have reminded us, the greatest beneficiaries of this were the British; the purveyors of shipping, insurance, exchange facilities, commercial credits and foreign investment.[7] The years after 1880 saw the huge extension of London's commercial empire in the form of banks, insurance companies, shipping lines, telecommunications providers, news services, and railway companies, as well as extractive enterprises like mining and oil. In the boom conditions that set in from the mid-1890s, Britain maintained a huge balance of payments surplus from invisible exports, funding an ever-growing outflow of overseas investment.[8] It was this prosperity that allowed the great naval rearmament before 1914 to be achieved with so little sign of economic strain. It was the scale and scope of their commercial empire that fortified British confidence in their constrictive power against any would-be foe. It was the great guarantee, alongside naval power, that Britain's intermediate place between continental Eurasia and the Open Sea would be safe from encirclement or economic attrition.

II

Nevertheless, the British world system consolidated between 1880 and 1913, for all its scale and wealth, had depended upon a set of transient international conditions for its economic and geostrategic stability. It was the fragile equilibrium which these permitted that had largely determined the pattern of its internal relations and tilted them in favour of imperial cohesion rather than fragmentation or centrifugalism. This fragile equilibrium was violently disrupted between 1914 and 1923 by war and the revolutionary upheavals that accompanied and followed it. Amid the post-war turmoil in India, China, Turkey, Egypt, Iraq and Ireland as well as in Britain's domestic politics, it is easy to see why some faint-hearts were willing to believe that the British empire had become a 'lost dominion'.[9] These obituaries were premature. By 1924–25, the return of a modified 'normality' had turned the tables against those who hoped for the drastic devolution of British power or its disappearance altogether.

The result was not the restoration of the old British system but a new set of imperial relations and spheres. The most striking feature seemed

to be the acknowledgement of the full sovereignty of the white dominions and Ireland (under the Balfour formula and the Statute of
Westminster 1931) and of the right of India to attain full internal self-
government as a 'dominion' (under the Montagu declaration of August
1917, supplemented by the promise of Lord Irwin in October 1929). It
was this new constitutional relationship that encouraged Alfred
Zimmern to write of a 'third British empire'.[10] The third British Empire
was to be an empire of free association, bound together by mutual interests and common values. This more voluntarist approach seemed to be
echoed in the pragmatic acceptance that in other parts of the formal and
informal empire British interests had to come to terms with local
nationalisms and make concessions to their 'amour-propre' (in the
phrase of Lord Milner) at least.[11] Towards Egypt, China, Turkey and
Persia, British policy in the 1920s showed a guarded willingness to
retreat from the high-water mark of past imperial claims and extraterri-
torial privilege.[12] But too much emphasis should not be given to this
new rhetorical superstructure. Just as striking was the huge extension of
British power in the Middle East that remained even after the local dust
had settled in 1922. Across much of the British colonial world in Africa
and Asia, their imperial will (or its local agents) seemed as hard to
challenge as before 1914. Imperial benevolence towards Afro-Asian
nationalism – whether in Egypt or China – was quick to shrivel when
the pressures eased. And it was highly arguable whether the ambiguities
of 'dominionhood' had done much to change the realities of Indian and
white dominion inequality in the face of British military and economic
power.[13]

Nevertheless, some fundamentals *had* changed. At the geopolitical
level, the British had been forced to acknowledge naval equality with
the United States, and to engage for a crucial period in the diplomacy
of naval disarmament.[14] Second, they were forced to recognise that
the century-long 'passivity' of East Asia was over and to re-think the
strategic consequences for their eastern (and Australasian) empire.
Third, there was no escape from the painful fact of economic weakness.
The pre-war age when London's commercial empire was global, when it
piled up a huge balance of payments surplus and financed an ever-
increasing portfolio of overseas property had gone for good. Although
there had been a limited recovery by 1925, when Britain went back on
gold, it was partial at best. Foreign investment was rationed and very
little went outside the sterling countries.[15] The real value of Britain's
overseas property had fallen by 40 per cent by 1929 and her dollar
holdings by more than 90 per cent.[16] The burden of foreign (mainly

American) and domestic debt drove up interests, squeezed the supply of capital and put heavy pressure on the balance of payments. 'Sticky' wages and the need for domestic peace stopped the downward 'adjustment' of manufacturing costs and weakened the competitiveness of industrial exports. It was in this vulnerable position that London confronted the economic blizzard that set in after 1929, and drove it off gold in 1931. Thus the economic magnetism that helped to integrate a decentralised empire had slackened just as the geostrategic advantages conferred by naval superiority before 1914 were made obsolete by American rivalry and Japanese imperialism. When the world economy 'deglobalised' after 1930, commodity prices collapsed, foreign markets imploded, emigration tailed off and then went into reverse, and colonial nationalisms were supercharged with socio-economic resentments, it was little wonder that many thoughtful observers concluded that the British variety of imperialism had entered its final – if not highest – stage.[17]

But before 1937–38 there was little evidence that these symptoms of 'decline' presaged the general collapse of the British system of global power. On some criteria, the British might have been 'weaker' than in their Victorian 'heyday'. But the test they faced was not some absolute standard of imperial power but one of relative capacity in the contemporary world. On this realistic basis, their prospects were much less gloomy. In a world that had broken up into trading blocs, the sterling empire was the largest and most stable. Its reconstruction under the Ottawa agreements of 1932 signalled the mutual dependence of its largest units and the continuing attraction of the British market. The economic power of the United States, that had mesmerised British observers in the 1920s,[18] looked much less impressive, its economic policy seemed clumsy and American recovery was slower. Second, the United States and the Soviet Union, the two 'big beasts' of the revolutionary era of 1917–23, had retreated into isolation by 1930, America after performing the useful service of helping to discipline a recalcitrant Japan. Third, after Locarno in 1925, it looked as if the balance had been restored in European politics, or at least in that part of it that was likely to threaten another security crisis of the kind that had dragged Britain into war in 1914. The admirals might have grumbled (as they usually did), but before the mid-1930s, reversing the trend towards naval disarmament seemed a sensible precaution rather than an immediate emergency. Thus the 'third British empire', with its characteristic compound of political devolution and economic coordination, its new 'imperial oasis' in the Middle East, and its new strategic frontier in the Asia Pacific, looked more than capable of dividing and defeating any plausible set of rivals or enemies. While that held true, the ability of its internal foes – Gandhians, Wafdists, Anti-Treatyites, Purified Nationalists or Husseinis – to force it into 'immoderate' concession, let alone abdication, was likely to be small.

Events belied the reasonable expectations of sensible men. British leaders assumed that they were living in an age of liberalism, even if temporarily suspended by an economic emergency. In fact they were living through an age of revolution in the Eurasian heartlands on whose complex politics their empire's survival was mysteriously dependent. The first round of revolution between 1914 and 1923 had been checked. The second after 1930 was turbocharged by economic catastrophe and the revolutionary ideology of left and right. International politics were no longer ruled by the chessboard diplomacy of limited ends, but by the ruthless search for unlimited power. At both ends of Eurasia, the vital pre-conditions that allowed the strategic defence and political cohesion of the British imperial archipelago, were eroded at terrifying speed. Without the means (or perhaps the will) to construct a balancing coalition in Europe, or the mutual trust that was needed to revive the Anglo-American front against Japan in 1921–22, they fell back on comforting illusions of economic power: Britain would win the 'long war' against the brittle economies and social structures of the aggressor powers.[19] But in the Eurasian *Blitzkriegs* of 1940–42, they lost the short war and spent most of the resources they might have used for the longer one.[20] In three terrible years, the key components of their pre-war world-system – political authority in India (and all its benefits), the strategic partnership of the white dominions and the magnetic force of their commercial empire – were fatally compromised. The mainsprings of their strength as an independent world power had been blasted away.

III

It was thus Churchill's fate to preside if not over the liquidation of the British empire, then over its impending demise as an autonomous world-system. It is not clear how far his ideas for an imperial revival went beyond the frantic cultivation of the 'special relationship', the full recovery of Britain's lost colonies and the vigorous assertion of British claims to great power equality alongside the United States and the Soviet Union. Certainly, his championing of the 'Monster of Hampstead' suggested a keen appreciation of the vital importance of the European balance of power. Before he could turn his mind to imperial renovation, he was swept away by an electoral earthquake. Over the next three years, the price of imperial defeat between 1939 and 1942, delayed or concealed by the conduct of the war, became painfully visible. In India and Burma, the British forfeited all real control over the timing and terms on which independence was granted, surrendering in the process any surviving claim to the strategic benefits on which their Asian influence had depended heavily. Their humiliation in Palestine – the side effect of the European catastrophe and economic dependence on the United States – was a vital, perhaps decisive, factor in the failure to reconstruct their Middle East primacy in alliance with Egypt, and the descent of Anglo-Egyptian relations towards a nadir of violence and mutual recrimination. Their wartime partnership with Canada – the 'arsenal of empire' – with its economic, military and (latterly) nuclear benefits, had all but dissolved by 1947 as Canadian dependence on its southern neighbour (formalised in the *permanent* agreement of August 1940) revised the shape of the North Atlantic Triangle.[21] In South Africa, the gloomy predictions of *When Smuts Goes*[22] became even gloomier when Smuts (unexpectedly) went in 1948. The real extent of Britain's economic losses was made brutally clear when dollar convertibility brought about a sterling collapse in 1947 and imposed an austerity regime in domestic consumption even more severe than that enforced in wartime. Nor, despite its terrible price, had victory over Germany and Japan yielded any lasting security. The onset of Cold War in Europe and East Asia promised years if not decades of a virtual war economy with all its risks and political consequences.

The parochial outlook of British political historians has made the international outlook of the Attlee government much more puzzling than it really was. In fact, it was Attlee's ministry that took up the challenge of imperial renovation in a remarkable display of pragmatic imperialism. They were driven by geostrategic, economic and welfare necessities, but they conceived instinctively of solutions that would exploit and improve on Britain's pre-war system as far as possible. In historical memory, it is their negative calculations that have attracted the most attention: the blunt acknowledgement that British rule in India had become untenable; that staying in Palestine would only worsen Anglo-Arab relations; that nothing would be gained by refusing Irish and Burmese demands to leave the Commonwealth; that the price of keeping India in was to accept the principle of republican membership; that the momentum for self-government (not yet independence) in Colonial Ghana had become irresistible. But the imperial thinking of the Attlee government went far beyond the policy of 'scuttle' that they

were so anxious to repudiate.[23] Its starting point was the secret decision
to build an atomic weapon, the independent deterrent that would
guarantee British survival as an independent world power. Until it was
available, they decided to keep peacetime conscription to provide the
military manpower for their global commitments. They also decided
that for all its political inconvenience, the strategic value of their military presence in the post-war Middle East (as the base from which Soviet
aggression could be punished) was much too great to give up, prolonging indefinitely Britain's regional imperium, and promising collateral
benefits in the supply of oil. Third, their response to the crisis of sterling
might have been desperate: suspending convertibility. But it hardened
into an iron programme for the medium-term recovery of sterling's status
as a master currency by prolonging the wartime system of exchange controls in the sterling area. Fourth, they planned to bolster sterling and
rebuild its strength by exploiting as quickly as possible the productive
capacity of the non-self-governing empire, especially in dollar-earning,
dollar-saving goods as well as strategic commodities like copper and
uranium.[24] This meant the rapid upgrading of the colonial machine in
tropical Africa and Southeast Asia. Lastly, they took seriously the need
for a new imperial ideology identified in wartime. The language of
'development', 'modernisation' and 'partnership' originally fashioned to
lull the political sensibilities of Middle America,[25] became key components
of the redescription of empire as the schoolroom of Commonwealth, the
permanent association of voluntary members through which Britain's
global influence would be maintained indefinitely.

This was the sketch (to use a term favoured by imperial historians) for
a fourth British Empire, quite distinct in its geopolitical circumstances,
geostrategic concerns, economic methods, collaborative partnerships
and avowed ideology from its pre-war counterpart. Given the magni-
tude of imperial disaster in 1940–42, even to have contemplated such a
neo-imperial future might seem *folie de grandeur* on an epic scale. But to
a surprising extent, Bevin, Cripps and Attlee – its major architects – were
vindicated by circumstances. Geopolitics were crucial. Anglo-American
relations fell some way short of the intimate partnership dreamt of by
Churchill and Keynes. The MacMahon Act, the terms of the American
Loan and the disaster of aborted convertibility reflected the post-war
suspicion that the British would regain by some sleight of hand the
rough equality of power they had enjoyed with America in the interwar
years, and use it to frustrate the international economic changes on
which American prosperity was thought to depend. However, the slide
towards the covert antipathy of the interwar years was stopped in its

tracks by the overt antagonism towards the Soviet Union and the domestic crusade against communist subversion. In the Cold War struggle in Europe and Asia, Britain became the indispensable ally to be aided and comforted – especially in the critical phase from 1948 to 1953. Second, for all the anxiety provoked by their suspected bid for global mastery, neither the Soviet Union nor Communist China possessed the will or resources in the post-war decade to mount a direct assault on the regions most vital to Britain's national defence or imperial influence. Third (and partly in consequence), America's strategic guarantee under the North Atlantic treaty secured the European balance at a bearable cost – in striking contrast to the appeasement era. Nor were global economic conditions entirely unfavourable. For all the strain upon Britain's depleted reserves, exhausted manpower and run-down plant, the early post-war years saw a strange Indian summer of the old imperial economy – once Washington had been reconciled to a closed sterling bloc. The dollar shortage, the sterling balances, the scarcity of industrial goods and the inflated demand for raw materials and commodities tightened the commercial bond between Britain and the sterling empire to a pitch that would have gratified the ghost of Joseph Chamberlain. Lastly, the vital bias of Britain's own war economy had been tilted sharply towards aerospace technology and the massive expansion of overseas air power. Upon the base created by this huge investment in cutting edge weaponry, it seemed possible to build not only a great new system of air communications (the project for a commercial jet liner) but the war heads and rocketry that would carry Britain into the nuclear age.

But who would be the partners in this new imperial enterprise? It was soon apparent that India's participation in 'Commonwealth defence' was a blimpish daydream. In fact its strongest axis was not to be Anglo-Indian but Anglo-Australian. A whole series of circumstances conspired to make Anglo-Australian relations closer and more compatible than at any other time in the imperial past. In the uneasy aftermath of the Pacific War, Australian leaders were all too aware that it was on British help that they would have to rely if a new threat loomed out of the Near North. The reinforced British presence in Singapore and Malaya was a welcome sign that the British meant to stay. Australian governments were even more anxious than before the war to fill up Australia's empty spaces against a stealth invasion of Asian immigrants. 'Populate or perish' became the post-war slogan, with ten British migrants for every one from Europe.[26] Third, the urgent need to swell Australia's numbers created an even more urgent need to expand the economy. The easiest way was by selling more to Britain as the empire's 'food arsenal'. In all these ways, there was close complementarity with Britain's post-war needs. There was a fourth dimension. Australia became Britain's principal partner in the project to build an independent deterrent. It supplied the test ground (at Maralinga) for Britain's atomic bomb, and the rocket range (at Woomera) for its delivery mechanism. An ancillary industry sprang up to service this new weapons industry. On the Australian side the motive for partnership was extremely powerful. It strengthened Canberra's leverage on London's policy and promised sooner or later that Australia would obtain its own deterrent – the absolute guarantee for a white Australia that Australian leaders had wanted even before federation. Thus sentiment and calculation (the twin components of settler nationalism) not 'blind loyalty' pushed Chifley and Menzies into the British embrace: offering Australian troops for Middle East defence (in the event of war); entering (with New Zealand) into the Australia, New Zealand and Malaya (ANZAM) arrangements for the defence of Malaya; backing London to the hilt at the time of Suez.[27] It looked indeed like a perfect marriage: the stronger and richer that Australia became, the larger its role in promoting the pan-British interest in the Asia Pacific.

London might have liked a similar partnership in South Central Africa, a region whose economic and strategic significance had expanded greatly under post-war conditions. But with the fall of Smuts (who died in 1950) there was no South African Menzies with whom to do business: only Malan and Strijdom. Partly in consequence, London withdrew its veto on the political union of the Rhodesias and assisted at the birth of the Central African Federation. The Federation was to be a Central African Australia, dynamic, stable and '100% British'.[28] It would help the rapid growth of Northern Rhodesia whose settler population increased by leaps and bounds. It would offer a middle way between the rival poles of white supremacy and 'extreme' black nationalism, and might even influence the political development of British East Africa. But the Federation's first decade was less than half over before the doubts began.

Further afield durable allies for the imperial project were in short supply, though just how short it took time to reveal. In the Middle East, the British bit the bullet, and made an agreement with Egypt's new military regime to evacuate the Canal Base, but with a right of return. The hope was that Nasser would prove an Egyptian Ataturk, a domestic reformer who would welcome the promise of strategic defence and respect Egypt's delicate international status. In much of tropical Africa, the British also looked for reformers and modernisers who would preach 'moderate' nationalism in return for a dribble of concessions from the colonial state. In colonial Malaya, where the economic stakes were higher, and political conflict had an ethnic base, the best British hope was to build a coalition of moderates behind a costly barrier of internal security. Common to all three regions was a worrying pattern of costs and benefits. Each had become more important than ever to British world power. Each was exposed to hostile political pressures, inside and outside, corroding the will and the means to collaborate. Each was likely to impose an open-ended burden if anything went wrong.

IV

It was the fragility of its partnerships that made the fourth British Empire so vulnerable to change. In the early 1950s it seemed fair to hope that global conditions would raise the value of Britain's residual assets and discourage recalcitrance among her partners and clients. But by the end of the decade the roof was falling in. Suez was symptomatic. It showed that the post-war hiatus in the superpowers' advance had run its course. In the new competition for influence, the old-style colonialism of the fourth British Empire had become an embarrassment – as the American response to Eden's invasion made brutally clear. Suez also showed just how difficult it was to manage the politics of local collaboration. Part of Nasser's grounds for complaint against Britain was the close British friendship with his local rivals in the Hashemite states. The Middle East was an exceptionally volatile salient in which to conduct semi-imperial diplomacy without more physical power. But by the later 1950s even the jerry-built colonial states that the British were using to 'modernise' Africa were finding it increasingly difficult to channel local discontent into the 'moderate' grooves approved by official policy. An under-engined colonialism with few gifts to distribute could only fall back on expensive coercion – for which its rickety apparatus was even less well adapted. In the third case, Southeast Asia, the British achieved a smooth political transition only to find that their regional solution was violently challenged by a local power. The costs of *konfrontasi* showed that even liberated colonies could impose an intolerable burden on their former masters.[29]

Each of these examples shows that without the support of the old commercial empire and the manpower tribute that India had paid, the imperial project would levy a massive toll on Britain's industrial output and depend disproportionately on her great power leverage. By 1960 neither was equal to the task. Britain's brief post-war primacy as the dominant West European power had come to an end with the treaty of Rome and what Harold Macmillan saw as the satanic alliance between Paris and Bonn. At the same time, it was becoming increasingly clear that if sterling's return to convertibility (essential if its master status were to be recovered) were not to induce an endless succession of financial crises, drastic efforts must be made to boost the export economy and the civilian sector. In the face of these obstacles, the Macmillan government all but abandoned the fourth British Empire as an obsolete vehicle for Britain's great power influence. The application to enter the European Economic Community (EEC) signalled the end of the Commonwealth trading system – and of Anglo-Australian economic partnership.[30] With the abortion of Blue Streak, in favour of practical dependence upon American weapons, London gave up the ambition to be an independent nuclear power. This too struck heavily at the central axis of the post-war empire.[31] With the public repudiation of South African *apartheid* and the closing down of the Central African Federation, London signalled its belief that such disreputable allies would undermine its claim to the friendship of the new Afro-Asian nations. Freed from the lumber of Attlee's post-war empire, Britain would exert a dominion of influence. With a new special relationship with the United States, a revived authority in Europe, and a post-imperial Commonwealth, Britain's global power would have a streamlined modernity. In fact of course what lay ahead was the stony road to the Gaullist *non*, UDI, devaluation and the nadir of power in the 1970s.

V

It is now a very old commonplace that the British Empire is best understood not as a territorial phenomenon but as the grand project for a global system. Its coercive deficit made it dependent upon its local partnerships and the universalist appeal of its main ideology. Its strategic safety rested on Britain's ability to shuffle military resources along a maritime corridor that stretched from Quebec to Shanghai and via Suez and the Cape. Its economic cohesion required the free movement of goods and capital across regions large enough to sustain the division of labour and the returns to scale that commercial prosperity demanded. Since the 1830s, each condition had argued strongly in favour of territorial expansion well away from the power concentrations at each end of Eurasia. In geopolitical terms, the British system was a chain of islands (even India was a quasi-island[32]) occupying an intermediate position between the

Old World of Eurasia and the Outer World beyond. From first to last its survival and growth depended upon the reluctance or inability of the great Eurasian states to disrupt its far-flung lines of security and commerce.

For that reason it was always a work in progress, forced into continuous adjustment by economic or political change at each end of Eurasia, and, in the twentieth century, by the shifting balance of power between Eurasia and America. In the supreme crisis of 1918, the British had been forced into their boldest step: the attempt to annex almost the whole Middle East. But over the central period of their global success, between 1870 and 1940, their resilience had been based upon four vital assets. The first was the strength conferred by the military and industrial power of the Home Islands, and the leverage this conferred in the diplomacy of Europe. The second was India. The third was the loyalty (more or less conditional) of the neo-Britains overseas. Last was the property portfolio managed from London, the City's commercial empire of shipping, services, installations and enterprises. These had been enough to make the British system the great survivor in the holocaust of empires after 1916. But (in their depleted state) they were far too little to guarantee its safety once revolution set in at each end of Eurasia in the 1930s.

That was why the great Eurasian war of 1940–42 marked the real end of an independent world-system under British control. The 'fourth British Empire' constructed in haste after 1945 was a last attempt to turn global politics to Britain's advantage and build a new British system to insure against the uncertainties of the post-war world. Its surviving assets enjoyed a brief scarcity value in a ruined landscape. But it had little prospect of even medium-term survival, except as the client of a greater power, and its internal stresses soon reduced its value as a global ally. When its crisis came after 1960, the end was swift, even if the pain of breaking the 'status barrier'[33] left a dull ache in the body politic, and a sense of displacement that extends far beyond Britain.

Notes

1. A. Zimmern, *The Third British Empire* (Oxford: 1926).
2. W. Reynolds, *Australia's Bid for the Atomic Bomb* (Carlton, Vic.: 2000), p. 2.
3. Ibid.
4. See Alistair Lamb, *The MacMahon Line: A Study in the Relations Between India, China and Tibet 1904–1914* (London: 1965).
5. This argument can be found in G. Monger, *The End of Isolation* (London: 1963).
6. As laid down by the Royal Commission on the Administration of the Expenditure of India 1899–1900 (The Welby Commission).

7. P. Cain and A.G. Hopkins, *British Imperialism*, 2nd edn (London: 2002).
8. By 1913, Britain was accumulating an annual surplus on its balance of payments of around £200 million.
9. The jeremiad by Al.Carthill (pseud.) on the post-war *Raj* was entitled *The Lost Dominion* (Edinburgh: 1924). For a similar polemic by an 'Old China Hand, J.O.P. Bland, *China, the Pity of It* (London: 1931).
10. See note 1.
11. 'In dealing with an Oriental people', wrote Milner of the Egyptians in February 1920, 'the question of form is of capital importance'. J. Darwin, *Britain, Egypt and the Middle East* (London: 1980), p. 97.
12. The Foreign Office 'Christmas memo' of December 1925 urged the accommodation of Chinese nationalism by the abandonment of territorial rights and conceding China tariff autonomy. See E.K.S. Fung, *The Diplomacy of Imperial Retreat: Britain's South China Policy 1924–1931* (Hong Kong: 1991), pp. 101–4.
13. For these arguments, J. Darwin, 'Imperialism in decline?' *Historical Journal*, 23, 3 (1980), 657–79.
14. For the Anglo-American diplomacy of naval disarmament, B. McKercher, *Transition of Power: Britain's Loss of Global Pre-eminence to the United States 1930–1945* (Cambridge: 1999), ch. 1.
15. The best study of this is J.M. Atkin, *British Overseas Investment 1918–1931* (New York: 1977).
16. By 1931, British dollar holdings had fallen to around £100 million from their 1913 level of £800 million. Allowing for the fall in money values (perhaps 35 per cent) reduces the figure even more.
17. See M.J. Bonn, *The Crumbling of Empire* (London: 1938).
18. G. Peel, *The Economic Impact of America* (London: 1928), for an example.
19. Official policy in the late 1930s assumed that the high levels of defence spending in Germany and Japan could not be sustained without creating a huge inflationary crisis with its social and financial consequences.
20. By March 1941, British holdings of dollars and gold approximated to a month's worth of spending on essential supplies from the United States.
21. See B.W. Muirhead, *The Development of Post-War Canadian Trade Policy: The Failure of the Anglo-European Option* (Montreal and London: 1992).
22. See Arthur Keppel-Jones, *When Smuts Goes* (London: 1947).
23. The one aspect of its India policy on which the Attlee Cabinet was agreed was that it should not appear as 'the first step in the dissolution of the British Empire'. J. Darwin, *Britain and Decolonization* (Basingstoke: 1988), p. 94.
24. For this policy, Alistair Hinds, *Britain's Sterling Colonial Policy and Decolonization 1939–1958* (Westport, CT: 2001).
25. See Suke Wolton, *Lord Hailey, the Colonial Office and the Politics of Race and Empire in the Second World War: The Loss of White Prestige* (Basingstoke: 2000).
26. The phrase was Billy Hughes' in 1937. See James Jupp, *From White Australia to Woomera* (Cambridge: 2002), p. 11. Official policy after the war aimed at an immigrant intake of which the British element would form 50 per cent. See minutes of Cabinet, 22 July 1952, National Archives of Australia [NAA] A 11099, 1/15, p. 34.
27. Australian policy can followed in A.W. Martin, *Robert Menzies: A Life*. Vol. 2 (Carlton, Vic.: 2000); P.G. Edwards, *Crises and Commitments* (North Sydney: 1992); H.Donohue, *From Empire Defence to Long Haul*. Papers in Australian Maritime Affairs No. 1 (Canberra: 1996).

28. The best account of the making of the federation remains, J.R.T. Wood, *The Welensky Papers* (Durban: 1982). For British official documentation, see Philip Murphy, ed., *Central Africa* (London, 2005) in the British Documents on the End of Empire series.

29. See J. Subritzsky, *Confronting Sukarno: British, American, Australian and New Zealand Diplomacy in the Malaysian-Indonesian Confrontation, 1961–1965* (Basingstoke: 2000).

30. For this phase, Stuart Ward, *Australia and the British Embrace: The Demise of the Imperial Ideal* (Carlton, Vic.: 2001).

31. For the Australian reaction to the cancelling of Blue Streak in 1960, see the correspondence in the National Archives of Australia, NAA A 1209/64.

32. For this view of India, K.M. Pannikar, *India and the Indian Ocean* (London: 1945).

33. This phrase was Richard Crossman's.

2
Keeping Change Within Bounds: A Whitehall Reassessment[1]

S.R. Ashton

Sir Charles Jeffries was the institutional memory and historian of the Colonial Office (CO) and the Colonial Service. He joined the CO in 1917 and retired in 1956 as Joint Deputy Under-Secretary of State. A year before retirement he published an introduction to the CO as part of a new Whitehall Publishing Series intended to provide 'authoritative descriptions' of the major departments of central government. His account revealed that in 1953 a total of 1227 first appointments had been made to the Colonial Service. As well as 108 administrative officers, the total included 62 agriculturalists, 252 engineers, architects, and town planners, 222 education officers, 133 doctors and dentists, 47 police, 43 surveyors, 36 veterinary surgeons, 50 barristers and solicitors, 211 geologists, and 14 forestry officers. Paradoxically, according to Jeffries, while its indirect administrative responsibilities overseas had diminished, the CO's own direct administrative and executive responsibilities had greatly increased over the past 15 years. The management of funds allocated under the Colonial Development and Welfare Acts, the work of the Colonial Research Council, and the training courses for the Overseas Civil Service were cited as examples. Even if some colonial territories became independent in the near future, Jeffries believed the CO would still have 'immense continuing responsibilities for as long as any planner can usefully look ahead'. He could not envisage a return to the pre-1925 arrangement under which a single Secretary of State dealt with the Commonwealth as well as the colonies.[2] This was hardly an obituary for the CO, still less the sounding of a retreat. On the contrary, the whole tone of Jeffries' account was of a department just getting into its stride.

Senior ministers in the incoming 1951 Conservative government echoed these sentiments. Churchill in December 1954 dreamt of a redesigned Parliament Square 'as a truly noble setting for the heart of the British Empire'.[3] This was not as fanciful as it now seems. Originating under the Attlee government but failing for financial reasons, the intention was that the old Westminster Hospital would make way for a new CO building. Jeffries delivered his own verdict: 'It will be clearly be some considerable time – though, one may hope, not forty years in the wilderness – before the Office can move into the promised land.'[4] More practical were the views of the Minister of Housing and Local Government, Harold Macmillan. Reflecting in June 1952 on the parlous state of the nation's finances, Macmillan wanted priority given to strengthening trade within the Sterling Area. This would involve sacrifices at home (cuts in capital social programmes) and abroad (further restrictions on dollar imports). The 'choice', as Macmillan put it, was either 'the slide into a shoddy and slushy Socialism, or the march to the third British Empire'.[5]

In 1951, however, CO officialdom was alert as never before to international opinion on colonial issues. Oliver Lyttelton, the Secretary of State, accepted his officials' advice that a statement was needed to make clear that the Conservative government intended no break with the initiatives, particularly in the context of West African political progress, established by the wartime coalition and developed further by the Attlee administration. In a statement to the House of Commons on 14 November 1951, Lyttelton reiterated self-government within the Commonwealth as the main aim of policy; in furtherance of it the government intended to ensure economic and social development in colonial territories kept pace with political change.[6] Civil servants, even more than ministers in office, are generally reluctant to recommend policy statements involving commitments which are too specific. Lyttelton's parliamentary statement was no exception. Two observations might be made in explaining what it actually meant.

First, by linking economic and social development with the pace of political change, Lyttelton was in fact saying Britain would not grant independence to a colonial territory which did not possess means of its own to sustain it. The expectation in the Caribbean that Britain might provide budgetary assistance as well as development capital beyond independence obliged the government to make the position clear. In June 1956, in the context of negotiations to establish a federation in the West Indies, Alan Lennox-Boyd, Lyttelton's successor, explained to Jamaica's Governor, Sir Hugh Foot: 'I do not see how it is possible for real political independence to be attained and maintained when the Government of the country concerned is unable to maintain itself without financial assistance from outside'.[7] Second, the reference to self-government within the Commonwealth was deliberately intended to be vague. In answer to the Foreign Office (FO) which wanted clarification of how Lyttelton's statement might affect Sudan, the CO replied it 'meant no more and no less than it said'. Self-government within the Commonwealth had been set as the objective 'without defining exactly what was meant'. While Britain alone could grant independence to a colonial territory, admission to the Commonwealth was a decision for all members. To suggest some colonies might be offered something less than Commonwealth membership would be damaging. There could be no surer way of driving them out of the Commonwealth; hence 'we have to speak in general terms and must continue to do so'.[8]

But there were other reasons for the lack of transparency about colonial policy at the beginning of the 1950s. The CO was no longer primarily concerned, as it had been before the war, with good government, law and order, and sound finance. Political management over a much wider area formed a significantly larger part of the CO's brief. Hitherto largely confined to Ceylon, Palestine, Cyprus and Malta, since the end of the war the management of political change had extended to Africa, the Caribbean, and South-East Asia. And as Philip Murphy reminds us, with colonial rule in this sense the subject of a constantly changing process of locally struck bargains, long-term planning or detailed policy statements for any particular territory served little purpose.[9] Equally, however, colonial policy was never the exclusive preserve of the CO, not even in the contexts of constitutional reform or development and welfare. Colonial policy reacted with and was influenced by much wider considerations of defence, international relations, and Britain's own economic management. It concerned all Whitehall departments – the FO, Ministry of Defence (MoD) and Commonwealth Relations Office (CRO) – with interests and responsibilities overseas, as well as the Treasury. Each of these departments brought to colonial policy a different perspective. Collectively, these differences made it all but impossible to define colonial policy in a way generally acceptable throughout Whitehall.

Differences between the CO and FO extended to the most basic of issues. An FO paper on colonial nationalism in 1952 was variously described by CO officials as 'a jejune, misguided and in places slightly horrific document', and as little better than a 'Sixth Form essay'. To the FO call for further study of the issues raised the CO responded with condescension. The problems arising from colonial nationalism were 'a primarily daily concern' in the CO; hence 'we are not convinced that any new and comprehensive examination of the subject is necessary'.[10]

For its part the FO observed in 1956 it was having difficulty persuading both the CO and CRO to take seriously the threat of communism in Africa.[11] This was odd, given the amount of time the CO spent in 1953–54 in correspondence with British officials in the Gold Coast on measures to counteract communist influence in the colony's trade unions.[12] International factors were involved in West Africa. FO officials shared the view of Anthony Eden, the Foreign Secretary, when he observed in 1951 that political developments in British West Africa (the Gold Coast and Nigeria) were moving 'at a pretty dangerous gallop'.[13] Part of the problem for the FO was the unsettling effect on neighbouring French territories. It was therefore wholly ironic that when, in October 1952, Eden announced in parliament proposals to give the Sudan (a charge not of the CO but the FO) an 'all-Sudanese Cabinet, responsible through an all-Sudanese Parliament to the Sudanese people', the reaction of the CO was to fret about the impact this would have on the Gold Coast. Had the CO been consulted about Eden's statement it would have suggested alternative wording which did not 'splash' this feature of the Sudan's draft constitution.[14]

The views of the MoD on colonial policy were expressed in 1954 by the Permanent Secretary, Sir Harold Parker, in the context of an idea occasionally floated that forces from the colonies might form the nucleus of a colonial army to replace the Indian army. It was never taken seriously because, as in the case of the Indian army prior to India's independence, Britain would have to pay the costs. Parker believed many colonies needed better intelligence and more effective local security forces. Against a backdrop of emergency operations in Malaya and Kenya, a looming emergency in Cyprus, and troop landings in British Guiana, he complained about an apparent tendency in certain colonies to simply 'drift into trouble'. As he told Macmillan, now Minister of Defence, in November 1954, 'the Army argues that the Colonial Office gets into a mess and then asks the Army to help it out. Experience shows that this is a long and expensive business.'[15] Colonial expenditure raises the question of relations between the CO and Treasury. These were not as strained as might sometimes be assumed. Bargaining over the next colonial development and welfare allocation was part of the normal process of government, and the CO never complained it had been treated unjustly. More noteworthy was the 'epic' tussle between the two departments in 1954–55 over CO concerns to put in place mechanisms to persuade expatriate civil servants to remain in post in colonies approaching independence. In eastern Nigeria especially the CO believed civil service resignations would lead to what it feared most – independence accompanied almost immediately by administrative collapse. To avoid it Her Majesty's Overseas Civil Service was set up in 1954, and in the following year the Treasury reluctantly agreed that officials made redundant would be maintained on an unattached list at the expense of the British taxpayer until they found alternative employment.[16]

The major differences in Whitehall were between the two sister departments, the CO and the CRO. Both were uneasy as the Gold Coast approached independence in 1957. Corruption and a drift towards authoritarianism were identified as key problems. William Gorell Barnes, Assistant Under-Secretary of State at the CO, thought 'fascist tendencies' were at work.[17] The ruling Convention People's Party was indicted, and CO officials wondered if Kwame Nkrumah should be asked to stand down as Prime Minister. Their CRO counterparts did not relish the prospect of having to deal with an independent Ghana as the first African member of the Commonwealth. Fed information by Francis Cumming-Bruce, their own appointee as external affairs adviser to the Gold Coast government, CRO officials believed that the Governor, Sir Charles Arden-Clarke, and the CO were deliberately concealing what was happening in the Gold Coast. Cumming-Bruce wrote in July 1956: 'The days when Governors on the Guinea Coast lived in slave castles, and did not correspond with the Colonial Office for six months at a time, seem very close here.'[18]

Too much should not be made of these differences over the Gold Coast. Ghana was, after all, a test case for both departments, and subsequent acts of decolonisation in Africa found the CRO, if not entirely comfortable then at least considerably less agitated. Rather more important were their differences over Central Africa and South-East Asia. Philip Murphy has described Whitehall's policy-making structure for Central Africa in the 1950s as a recipe for conflict and confusion.[19] While the CRO conducted relations with Southern Rhodesia and the federal government established in 1953, the CO remained administratively responsible for the two other territories in the federation, Northern Rhodesia and Nyasaland. The CRO was concerned primarily to advance the interests of the European settlers. African political aspirations were the priority for the CO. In effect, according to Murphy, the two departments were defending virtually incompatible principles, and different perspectives continued to inhibit policy-making until March 1962 when a new Central Africa Office was created in Whitehall, with R.A. Butler, the Home Secretary, in charge. A similar picture emerged over South-East Asia where, following Malaya's independence in 1957, government policy aimed to complete decolonisation through a Malaysian federation by adding Singapore and the Borneo territories. Like the FO, the CRO wanted to press ahead. Malaysia would provide military savings, rationalise regional defence, and create stability for Australia and New Zealand in an area they regarded as their northern frontier. By contrast, the CO was concerned with the welfare of the Borneo peoples. It wanted slower progress, arguing for delay in the creation of Malaysia until conditions were right. As late as August 1963 an FO official believed these different approaches left 'quite a lot of room for doubt as to what Her Majesty's Government want'.[20]

An assumption is sometimes made of the CO as a lightweight department, easily thrown off course or sidelined if it encountered opposition from departments considered of higher rank. There is no evidence for this. Closer to the mark was a contemporary view elsewhere in Whitehall that while not necessarily secretive, the CO was never particularly forthcoming when it came to sharing information. In recommending to Eden (now Prime Minister) in August 1955 the setting up of a Cabinet Committee on Colonial Policy, Sir Norman Brook, the Cabinet Secretary, observed how the CO was less efficient than the FO in the 'prompt' circulation of telegrams. Other ministers and departments had the feeling of being confronted by situations of great urgency because the CO failed to provide them with advance information about developments 'which they knew or suspected to be taking place'.[21] The CO was sensitive to the criticism. A year earlier governors had been instructed to submit periodic dispatches – for circulation outside the CO – explaining the latest happenings in their territories.[22] There were certain cards the CO wanted to play close to its own chest. In 1958 the Office contemplated for the first time what action might be taken against the government of the Federation of Rhodesia and Nyasaland in the event of a unilateral declaration of independence and the use of force to take over the two northern territories. CO views on the subject were not to be shared with other departments, least of all the CRO.[23]

If policy was not carefully planned or too closely defined there were none the less guiding principles. At the beginning of the 1950s the CO was still enthused by the sense of mission and purpose with which it had emerged at the end of the war. The intention was to revitalise the empire in order eventually to be able to liquidate it in an orderly manner beneficial both to the countries concerned and Britain. What the CO wanted as models were 'more Ceylons and fewer Burmas'.[24] The long-term aim was to transfer power to moderate nationalists who valued the Commonwealth association, provided continuing defence facilities where necessary, and offered no threat to British commercial interests. How long the process would take was open ended. Assumptions were made about dates but there was never a timetable.

The Gold Coast in 1947 was assumed to be a generation away, not from independence but internal self-government. In 1952 the earliest possible date for Malayan self-government was said to be 1960. More considered thought was given to the timescale in the context of how the Commonwealth might evolve. The remote possibility of Sudan seeking membership, the more immediate prospect that the Gold Coast would want to join, and a further proposal that responsibility for both the Gold Coast and Malta might be transferred from the CO to the CRO, led to the appointment of an official committee on Commonwealth membership chaired by Brook. In a report for the Cabinet in October 1954 the colonies were divided into three groups.[25] The Gold Coast, Nigeria, the Central African Federation, the Malayan Federation and possibly a West Indian Federation were placed in the first group for which independence and full Commonwealth status were envisaged 'over the next ten or twenty years'. Kenya, Tanganyika, Uganda and Sierra Leone were placed in a third, intermediate group for which the course of political development was uncertain. Every other country else was placed in the second group. These were mostly small territories, some strategically important, for which internal self-government might one day be possible but never full independence and Commonwealth membership. To deal with ministerial concerns that an expanding Commonwealth would impair intimate relations maintained between the older members, officials examined a proposal for a two-tier Commonwealth. To qualify for the upper tier, not only would a country have to be financially self-supporting, it would also be required to show it was effectively conducting its own foreign policy. Officials rejected the idea. Countries consigned to a lower tier would almost certainly leave the Commonwealth. In which case Brook told Churchill the empire would be condemned to 'death by a thousand cuts'.[26] The tests for the upper tier were not absolute but matters of judgement. Although India, Pakistan and Ceylon were full members, to apply the tests would give the impression, according to Brook's committee, 'that the second tier had been invented to prevent any further countries with coloured populations from entering the inner circle'. Reluctantly Conservative ministers accepted this advice. They thought it 'unfortunate that the policy of assisting dependent peoples to attain self-government had been carried forward so fast and so far'. So concerned were they that at the end of 1955 they thought it desirable, in a Commonwealth context, to substitute 'full self-government' for 'independence'.[27]

CO officials doubted the practicability of this particular suggestion. They could not envisage the Gold Coast celebrating 'Ghana Full-Self-Government Day', and there was the UN reaction to consider.[28] Yet in other respects they shared ministerial reservations. Political change in West Africa and South-East Asia had happened much sooner than they had intended or thought desirable. The pace accelerated in Malaya because of the emergency. Draconian security measures were introduced but there were also hearts and minds to be won. Malaya's independence in August 1957 conformed to the Ceylon model. The political leaders were moderate and co-operative. West Africa was more worrying. In Africa the CO wanted to build political experience from below, starting with local government. The Accra riots of 1948, and the subsequent Watson and Coussey Reports, undermined what the CO wanted to achieve. By 1952 Nkrumah was Prime Minister, and in 1954 there was an all-African Cabinet. Progress in the Gold Cost influenced neighbouring Nigeria where the stakes were much higher. The CO delivered its own verdict in March 1957:

> The pass in British West Africa was sold when the Watson Commission Report on the Gold Coast was published in 1948. The recommendations of that Commission were very radical. They set the pace in the Gold Coast and by so doing they lost us a vital fifteen to twenty years in Nigeria. Successive Governments since have taken the line that the risks of going too slow were probably greater than the risks of going too fast; and it remains true that a slow pace will lose us that goodwill we have at present and cause much friction. But in West Africa the pace set by the fastest (Ghana) is certainly more than the vast and unwieldy Nigeria looks like being able to take.[29]

In both cases, the CO bowed to the inevitable, pausing only fleetingly to consider whether the brake should be applied, and the process put into reverse. In 1955, as a response to a financial and administrative crisis in the Eastern Region of Nigeria involving the regional Premier, Nnamdi Azikiwe, the CO contemplated suspending the regional constitution. When it became clear British troops would be needed from outside West Africa to deal with any opposition, the CO drew back from this particular precipice.[30] Similarly, in the Gold Coast, the CO could not force Nkrumah's resignation in 1956 because there was no alternative to him. As Arden-Clarke had advised in May 1951, there was 'only one dog in our kennel'.[31] Rather than block political change in West Africa, the CO attempted to control it. In February 1953, in the context of preparations for internal self-government in the Gold Coast, Lyttelton defined what this meant. The Governor's reserve powers had to be kept intact, the police had to be outside political control, there had to be safeguards for the public service, and all questions of external affairs had to be referred to London. [32]

The Secretary of State described these as 'the bare essentials' which 'on no account' could be conceded. But it was not possible to maintain controls indefinitely. Jeffries argued at the end of 1955 that the Gold Coast was no more ready for independence than a teenage daughter was ready for the 'proverbial latch key'. Nor would the Gold Coast be more ready in five or ten years. The British response to local pressure was 'to continue doling out small doses of additional responsibility, keeping if possible one step ahead of this demand'. This was the traditional line, but the main argument against it was that at best 'it can only maintain a state of uneasy equilibrium'. Nationalist politicians concentrated on securing the next constitutional change, 'instead of getting on with the job'. Constitutions were 'in a state of continual flux and there is no stability'.[33] R.J. Vile from the CO's West Africa Department made much the same point when he argued: 'The choice before us may well then be one of accepting independence at a certain date because its refusal would create worse conditions than its acceptance.'[34] And so it proved over Ghana in 1957 and Nigeria in 1960. Neither was considered ready for independence but Lennox-Boyd argued in the case of Nigeria in October 1958:

> I would certainly not like to assert that self-government will in Nigeria be good government. There is a heavy responsibility on us therefore in taking a decision committing us to a definite date for Nigerian independence as much as two years ahead. ... Relations between this country and Nigeria could not be better than they are at present. To refuse the request would undoubtedly create an atmosphere of bitterness and distrust which would prejudice our future relations with an independent Nigeria and even if we were to refuse the request now we could not delay independence much longer. ... To continue to govern a discontented and possibly rebellious Nigeria would also present well nigh insoluble administrative problems in view of the transfer of effective power that has already taken place in the domestic field. It might even need substantial military forces.[35]

Time was one commodity the CO never had in sufficient quantity. Another was adequate finance for colonial development. In 1957 the cost of the colonies to Britain through colonial development and welfare expenditure, the Colonial Services vote, and the Colonial Development Corporation, was £51 million. This figure paled into insignificance in comparison with defence expenditure in the same year of £1,550 million.[36] In a West Indian context and going back to the beginning of the 1950s, CO officials had begun questioning the order of priority in the allocation of development and welfare funds. Too much emphasis, it was suggested, had been placed on social improvement in advance of economic development. Some of the smaller Caribbean islands were burdened by recurrent budgetary costs they could not sustain. Over the empire as a whole, the private sector seemed reluctant to become involved in colonial development. Potential investors in the colonies wanted a quicker rate of return, and they were troubled by political uncertainties. Surveying the prospects for, and sources of, development capital in 1956, Sir Hilton Poynton, Joint Deputy Under-Secretary of State at the CO, alluded to 'a school of thought' within Whitehall maintaining that 'if the available resources are too small to go round, we may have to begin a deliberate policy of shedding some of our Colonial burdens'.[37]

It did not come to this. Instead what had to be relinquished was the principle that colonies could not become independent unless they were financially self-supporting. The line was held when Ghana became independent in March 1957, and the Ghana Independence Bill expressly excluded the Colonial Development Corporation from operating in the country. Malaya was treated more generously at independence in August 1957, primarily because of the military costs incurred during the emergency. But the line could not be held in the West Indies. An independent federation of the West Indies was deemed incapable of survival without outside financial assistance. In theory, the decision taken at the Montreal Commonwealth Trade and Economic Conference in 1958 should have eased the financial problem in the West Indies. It was agreed that independent Commonwealth countries would be eligible for Commonwealth assistance loans. But Britain and the West Indian dependencies could never agree how much a Caribbean federation should receive. West Indian politicians thought they were entitled to far more than Britain considered it could afford. CO officials accused Caribbean politicians of having a mendicant mentality. These politicians in turn were suspicious of British attempts to involve other countries (Canada and the United States) in a financial package because they viewed this as an attempt to escape the obligations Britain owed the Caribbean because of slavery. A federation in the West Indies was established in 1958 but it never achieved independence and collapsed in 1962 when Jamaica seceded, followed swiftly by Trinidad, leaving Britain with responsibility in the East Caribbean for the small islands which preferred dependent status if independence meant being cast financially adrift.[38] Elsewhere, however, the prospect of Britain having continuing financial responsibilities for former colonies after they became independent was accepted as the lesser of two evils. In a Ugandan context Macmillan told the Cabinet in February 1962 that 'while the cost of relinquishing colonial rule was proving to be high, it was probably better to accept definite, if large, financial commitments on independence than to risk the indefinite and larger expenditure in prolonging Colonial rule against a risk of collapse of law and order'.[39]

Whether Britain could afford its colonies, or alternatively, whether it could afford to give them up, lay at the heart of the CO input into the various inquiries undertaken throughout the 1950s about Britain's increasing inability to sustain an extensive range of commitments overseas from a shrinking resource base. A report in June 1956 on 'The future of the United Kingdom in world affairs', commissioned by Eden and prepared by officials from the FO, Treasury, and MoD, concentrated primarily on the maintenance of the international value of sterling. Success in this aspect of policy was described as 'a matter of life and death to us'.[40] The report made only two brief references to the colonies, first in the context of development and welfare expenditure, and second in the context of the need in Africa to counter communist subversion and 'extreme' nationalism. There was no suggestion that any colonial territory might be relinquished. The 'profit and loss' account of the colonies – how much they cost and what Britain gained by having them – called for by Macmillan when he became Prime Minister in January 1957 was the next logical step in the government's efforts to square commitments with resources. This stocktaking of the colonial empire was undertaken by the CO and generated an enormous quantity of documentation. It reached the overall conclusion that the economic costs involved in having the colonies were finely balanced, and should not be a factor in deciding whether to dispose of them.[41] More important to Britain economically was how countries behaved after independence. The key criteria were that they should remain in the Sterling Area, respect British commercial interests and preserve administrative stability by retaining expatriate civil servants in the absence of locally qualified personnel. To delay, for selfish reasons, the grant of independence to a country which was otherwise politically and economically ready for it, would increase the risks to British economic interests. The maintenance of goodwill was therefore an important factor.

However, if the economic arguments were not decisive, the CO believed political and military factors both militated against a premature withdrawal. Beyond those territories – Nigeria, a West Indian Federation, a Central African Federation and possibly Singapore if it joined the Federation of Malaya – scheduled for independence over the next ten years, there were no others which could be surrendered. Obligations in multiracial settings (Kenya, Mauritius, Fiji), the danger of creating power vacuums which other powers would fill, reservations about repudiating trusteeship agreements, and concern not to allow South Africa opportunities for expansion, were all put forward as reasons. Considerations of British prestige were central to the CO argument. Withdrawal of influence from East Africa

> would bring to a shabby conclusion an important and hopeful experiment in race relations, with repercussions locally on the Central African Federation and a decline in United Kingdom prestige much more significant and enduring than the self-congratulatory applause of the anti-colonial, anti-Western world.[42]

Similar arguments were advanced for the smaller colonial territories. In the Falkland Islands withdrawal would be 'discreditable and severely damaging to prestige', in St Helena it would be 'degrading', in the Seychelles it would be 'an abdication of moral authority', in Mauritius it would lead to 'a violent upheaval', Fiji would 'lapse into chaos', the Solomon Islands would 'slide into anarchy', and the Gilbert and Ellice Islands would 'relapse into savagery'.

The CO was given a second opportunity to state its case. In October 1957 Sir Frederick Hoyer Millar, Permanent Secretary at the FO, expressed concern at what he described as the 'international poverty' of Britain, and the impact this was having on foreign policy. He argued there was no accepted understanding of essential interests, of commitments which might be cut down or abandoned, and of how scarce resources should be deployed for the remaining commitments.[43] Hoyer Millar called for a wide-ranging investigation but made no mention of the colonial profit and loss account. Macmillan gave reluctant consent to this fresh inquiry. Rather than another set of voluminous papers the prime minister wanted 'pithy notes'. A working party was set up from the FO, CO, CRO, Treasury, MoD, and the Chiefs of Staff Committee. At the outset some permanent secretaries appeared ignorant of the CO profit and loss inquiries. Brook chaired a meeting in December 1957 at which Sir Roger Makins of the Treasury remarked how no one knew if Hong Kong was an asset or liability. Sir John Macpherson from the CO produced a section of the profit and loss papers to provide answers. Notable at the same meeting were the comments of Sir Gilbert Laithwaite from the CRO:

> What we had to keep in mind was that we depended for our influence and authority in the world on the continued existence of the Commonwealth. In the military sphere we had to consider such matters as whether excessive weakness of our forces in the Far East and South East Asia would not drive Australia and New Zealand into the arms of the Americans. We also had to consider what would happen if Commonwealth countries left the sterling area. Ours was the only truly successful Empire in history and we must somehow ensure that we were strong enough to maintain it.[44]

Macpherson expressed 'hearty agreement with the general CRO theme, in its application to the colonies'. He noted with mischievous delight how envious the other permanent secretaries were because for this new inquiry about commitments, the CO had already gathered so much information about its own responsibilities. In its submission, the CO suggested Britain had 'decisive economic, strategic and political interests in the maintenance and successful achievement of its present colonial policy'. It explained again that 'the grant of independence did not of itself substantially affect British economic interests'. Britain, however, had an overall economic interest in strengthening ties between colonial territories and the Sterling Area, especially as commodity prices were falling and the colonies, hitherto responsible for a rise in sterling assets of £650 million over the previous six years, now had a deficit on current account of £100 million, of which about £40 million was with the non-Sterling Area. The CO rejected a regional approach to colonial policy. Policy had to be maintained 'as a whole'. If Britain abandoned its obligations in one part of the world, 'this would have a shattering effect on confidence elsewhere and would undermine the policy even in areas where it is important, from the point of view of British interests, that it should be maintained'.[45]

An inter-departmental report was ready by June 1958. It confirmed that none of the existing commitments could be reduced for economy's sake. On the contrary, it recommended more money for the FO and CRO to assist technical development, military assistance and cultural relations. On the colonies, it suggested not enough was being done for poorer territories. More development finance was needed. Far from scaling down Commonwealth and colonial commitments, the main conclusion was that these should be afforded greater priority. If an expenditure axe had to fall anywhere it should be on domestic spending in Britain. Subsidies to agriculture and the nationalised industries might be reduced. While the recommendations for increased expenditure were not to the liking of the Treasury, the CO found the report 'most satisfactory'.[46]

The policy surveys did not end in 1958. Another inter-departmental future policy study was ready in February 1960, preceded by reports on Africa by an Africa Committee of officials in June 1959 and the Commonwealth by the CRO in July 1959.[47] All three looked ahead to the period 1960–70. But from the colonial viewpoint, these later reports were produced in a climate rather different from that prevailing at the time of the 1957 profit and loss inquiry and the 1958 survey of commitments. Macmillan's 'wind of change' speech to both houses of the South African Parliament at Cape Town on 3 February 1960 was viewed in Whitehall as a major statement of government policy towards the rising tide of African national consciousness. Presiding in London as Secretary of State for the colonies between October 1959 and October 1961 was Iain Macleod, who later offered his own assessment of how policy changed during his two years in office:

> The change of policy that I introduced in October 1959 was, on the surface, merely a change of timing. In reality, of course, it was a true change of policy, but I telescoped events rather than created new ones.[48]

Ronald Hyam has singled out 3 March 1959 as the 'fateful date which signalled the moral end of the British empire in Africa'.[49] On that day 20 Africans were shot dead during demonstrations following the arrest of Dr Hastings Banda, president of the Nyasaland Congress party, and 11 Mau Mau detainees at the Hola Camp in Kenya died as a result of beatings inflicted to force them to work. According to Macleod's later reflection, there was only one way Britain could rid itself of the stigma and embarrassment caused by the Hola killings, 'and that meant inexorably a move towards African independence'.[50] Further impetus was provided by foreign example as both France and Belgium moved rapidly to liquidate their African Empires. But there was another factor influencing policy. It was explained by officials on the Africa Committee in their 1959 report on Africa over the next ten years:

> If Western governments appear to be reluctant to concede independence to their dependent territories, they may alienate African opinion and turn it towards the Soviet Union; if on the other hand they move too fast they run the risk of leaving large areas of Africa ripe for Communist exploitation.[51]

That the risks of going too slow were probably greater than the risks of going too fast, was a long established doctrine in colonial policy. Lord Soulbury, chairman of a commission on constitutional reform in Ceylon, was one of the first to express it when he observed in 1945 that in the long term, 'giving too much and too soon will prove to be wiser than giving too little or too late'.[52] Macleod said much the same in 1964 when he observed that an attempt by Britain to hold the African colonies by force would have led to bloodshed. According to Macleod, the African territories in the early 1960s were not ready for independence, just as India had not been ready in 1947. In India's case the decision of the Attlee Labour government had been 'the only realistic one'. The same applied in Africa: 'Of course there were risks in moving quickly. But the risks of moving slowly were far greater.'[53] Already applied in Ghana and Nigeria, the further application of this principle in Africa may be illustrated by the case of Tanganyika.

Following a conference with East African Governors at Chequers in January 1959, Lennox-Boyd reported a number of conclusions about East African policy to the Colonial Policy Committee in April of the same year.[54] Three courses of action were examined. First, plans might be made for a rapid withdrawal by 1965 at the latest. This would mean the loss of vital defence interests, violence in Kenya, the creation of a vacuum seriously prejudicial to Britain's position further south in Central Africa, and a hand over to governments incapable of standing on own their feet economically and lacking skilled manpower to manage their countries effectively. The second course was to make clear, as has already been made clear for Kenya,[55] that Britain had no intention of relinquishing responsibility in the near future, and would use force to deal with resistance. This would please diehard opinion but it would isolate Britain from world opinion. When ultimately Britain did withdraw it would leave behind bitterness if not active hostility. The third course, and the one recommended, was a 'middle-road' policy of gradualness. Constitutional progress would be by stages, meeting the legitimate aspirations of Africans while allowing adequate time for the countries to prepare for self-government, and, crucially, drawing out the period during which Britain retained control over 'vital matters'.

The timetable envisaged it would be ten years before Tanganyika and Uganda would be ready for internal self-government. Tanganyika was seen as the key as decisions there would determine the pace for Uganda and the rest of East Africa. A balancing act was required, responding to the nationalist demand for an immediate majority of elected ministers in the executive in such a way that Julius Nyerere, the leader of the

Tanganyika African National Union (TANU), would resist the temptation to launch a nationwide campaign. To achieve this the CO recommended parity on the executive (seven officials, seven unofficials, some of the latter nominated) for the lifetime of the Legislative Council, 1961–65, moving thereafter to an unofficial majority (seven to five) for the period to 1969. The government should resist African pressure for greater concessions. A similar scenario was envisaged for Uganda. It was deemed premature to recommend the same development for Kenya.

In May 1959, only five months after the Chequers conference, Sir Richard Turnbull, Tanganyika's Governor, recommended an accelerated timetable, moving to an unofficial majority as early as 1960. His reasoning was that Tanganyika could not remain immune from the upsurge of nationalism elsewhere in east-central Africa, in the Belgian Congo, Nyasaland and Ruanda-Urundi. Turnbull painted a frightening picture of the consequences if Britain refused concessions in Tanganyika. He predicted two insurrections, the first in 1960 or 1961. More serious would be the second which he expected in 1970. It would be 'a combination of Mau Mau and the Maji-Maji rebellion, with the modern techniques of guerilla warfare and fifth column activities'. Britain would not have security forces to deal with such an uprising and Nyerere, identified as a moderate whom Turnbull wanted to build up in order to tame the 'wild men' of TANU, would probably be replaced by an extremist.[56]

Turnbull's recommendations shocked officials at the CO. Initially they were not sure how to respond. Gorell Barnes confessed himself 'extremely unhappy' and worried about a 'slippery slope'. Under Lennox-Boyd, the CO prevaricated, although there were indications that Turnbull's arguments had been recognised before Macleod took over in October 1959. Macpherson, who had served as Governor (1948–54) and Governor-General (1954–55) in Nigeria, observed of Tanganyika in June 1959:

It is of course, much easier for us in London to say 'apply the brakes and have a show-down' than it is on the spot. We can write a minute or draft a telegram and then leave the Office and go to our safe home surroundings. If we are woken in the night it will only be to consider the terms of a further telegram to the Governor. I recall that a stage was reached during the 1953 Nigerian Conference when Mr. Oliver Lyttelton ... decided to break off negotiations because the Nigerian delegates were being very difficult. He said to me, 'Jock you can go back and govern with troops'. I replied, 'That is a very agreeable prospect – for six months or a year. Then what? You can't govern indefinitely with the aid of machine guns. The time will come to resume negotiations, and these will almost certainly have to be with the same characters'. ... The situation in Tanganyika is unique in my experience, in that the Governor has no one, except his officials, opposing the head-long rush to 'Uhuru'. The Europeans and Asians are buying 'protection' by jumping on the TANU bandwagon and the Chiefs have capitulated. In no other Colonial territory that I know of (even all-African territories) has such a situation occurred. ... [A]nd the overseas civil servants, as a whole, feel that the skids are on, and are thinking about 'golden bowlers'.[57]

Macpherson, like Turnbull, was not in favour of what he called 'any quick easy surrender'. The officials' report in 1960 on Africa over the next ten years still envisaged 1970 as the date when Tanganyika and Uganda would achieve internal self-government only, while for Kenya the aim of a 'viable, non-racial State' was unlikely to be achieved by 1970. Yet in July 1960 Macpherson was reflecting in the case of Tanganyika how 'startling' the pace of change had been over the previous six months.[58] Independence he thought was now likely in 1962. It came in December 1961. Uganda's independence followed in October 1962, and Kenya's in December 1963.

During the Conservative governments of Macmillan and Sir Alec Douglas-Home between 1957 and 1964, 18 territories of the British Empire achieved independence. All but eight were African and only two (British Somalia and South Cameroons) took their independence outside the Commonwealth. But as the Union Jack came down, Whitehall was not about to raise the white flag over what remained of the empire. In one key area policy seemed conspicuous by its absence. When the Central African Federation dissolved in 1963 and Nyasaland and Northern Rhodesia proceeded to separate independence as Malawi and Zambia in July and October 1964 respectively, Whitehall's approach to the problem of Southern Rhodesia was, as Macmillan put it in March 1963, to defer a decision 'for as long as possible'.[59] This was another way of saying there was no policy and that Britain was hoping something would turn up.

Elsewhere the watchwords were still controlled or guided development. Aden was an example. In 1958 the CO received sceptically the views of Sir William Luce, Aden's governor, that on account of the strength of Arab nationalism and the danger of Russian expansionism it would be unwise to delay self-government beyond 1967. He was told by the CO, 'if once we get into a state of mind that we shall be out in ten years, then we are in fact likely to be out in 2 or 3'.[60] Julian Amery, Parliamentary Under-Secretary of State (1958–60) at the CO regarded Aden as a strategically important military base which should not be surrendered.[61] The Chiefs of Staff thought likewise. About 8000 British troops were stationed in the base when Aden became the headquarters of Middle East Command in 1961. In 1963 Aden colony was redesignated 'Aden state' and entered the Federation of South Arabia. This misbegotten marriage between Arab nationalism in Aden (thought at the time to be moderate and malleable) and feudal princely rule in southern Arabia was seen as means of securing defence facilities for as long as possible, and keeping hostile powers (Egypt and Yemen) at bay. It collapsed in 1967 when Britain withdrew and handed over, for the first and only time in the history of British decolonisation, to a Marxist government.

Further obstacles to independence in some of the remaining dependent territories seemed all too apparent. Largely to appease the Americans who wanted defence facilities, a new colony, the British Indian Ocean Territory, was actually created in 1965. For a number of other territories – Gibraltar, the Falkland Islands and Hong Kong – independence was impossible because of disputes with third countries over sovereignty. Owing to the dispute with Guatemala, British Honduras seemed destined to remain in the same category. In British Guiana before independence in 1966, Britain faced not only the intractable problem of racial tension between the populations of Indian and African origin but also American resistance to any idea of independence under Marxist leadership. Some territories appeared not to want independence. Anxious about the growing influence of Fiji's population of Indian origin, the Fijians were reassured in 1960 that Britain had 'no intention of forcing the constitutional pace'.[62] In the Caribbean especially, attempts to devise alternatives to independence by means of integration or association with another country were subject to critical and often hostile scrutiny at the United Nations. According to one CO official in June 1962, in the very small territories 'colonial status and all that goes with it is now surely a horrible embarrassment to all concerned'.[63] This would have mortified Poynton, the last Permanent Secretary (1959–66) at the CO, who refused to succumb to 'the anti-Colonial "guilt complex" '. Although it was losing both staff and functions by the early 1960s, Poynton was determined that the CO should have a 'dignified funeral'. In 1964 he reminded the Secretary of State that Britain still had 26 dependent territories, 'some of which may want to continue indefinitely to be dependent'.

> We can take pride in our past achievements and the fact that we have been able to bring a great number of territories to independence. I do not think it is a matter of pride to say that we are getting rid of places

merely for the sake of getting rid of them as if there were more joy in heaven over the Imperialist that repents of his imperialism than over 99 just anti-Colonialists.[64]

But the numbers were dwindling. In 1960, when Commonwealth membership stood at 11, a group of Commonwealth as well as British officials forecast that by 1970 there would be a minimum of 17 and a maximum of 24 new members.[65] That this was an underestimate was recognised by British officials in the Chadwick Report of 1962 which forecast 18–24 members by 1965, and 30–35 by 1970.[66] Membership in 1970 stood at 31. Earlier arguments about restricting membership were revisited in the Chadwick Report, but rejected for the same reasons.

Equally, the notion that Whitehall remained in control of political change in the colonies, or that it was possible to keep change within bounds, had worn thin by the end of the 1950s. Efforts by the CO and colonial authorities in South-East Asia to delay the entry of the Borneo territories into a Malaysian federation earned a prime ministerial rebuke in March 1962. Reacting to a telegram from Sir William Goode, the Governor of North Borneo, who wanted Malaysia 'put off' until the Borneo peoples were ready, Macmillan told Brook:

I am rather shocked by [this] and the attitude it reveals. Does he realise (a) our weakness in Singapore, and (b) our urgent need to hand over the security problem there? The whole mood is based on a false assessment of our power. If this is the Colonial Office point of view, we shall fail.[67]

This was an admission that policy-making in the sense of control had slipped from Britain's hands. As Jeffries had long since realised, control in this sense had always rested on rather fragile foundations. Once political change was on the agenda in a colonial territory, officials in London spent less time initiating policy and rather more reacting to events, or reflecting upon them.

Notes

1. Keeping change within bounds is the title of an article by David Goldsworthy, 'Keeping change within bounds: aspects of colonial policy during the Churchill and Eden governments, 1951–1957', *Journal of Imperial and Commonwealth History*, 18 (1990), 81–108.
2. Sir Charles Jeffries, *The Colonial Office* (London: 1956), pp. 141–2, 200, 202.
3. NA, CAB 129/72, C(54)393, 15 December 1954.

4. Jeffries *The Colonial Office*, p. 115.
5. NA, CAB 129/52, C(52)196, 17 June 1952.
6. NA, CO 537/6696, no. 12, Lyttelton to Churchill, 7 November 1951.
7. NA, CO 1031/1741, no. 3/9, letter, 23 June 1956.
8. NA, FO 371/90114, no. 87, Trafford Smith to Allen, 12 December 1951.
9. Philip Murphy, *Alan Lennox-Boyd, a biography* (London: 1999), p. 104.
10. NA, CO 936/217, nos 1 and 4/5, Strang to Lloyd and Lloyd's reply, 21 June and 9 September 1952.
11. NA, FO 371/118677, no. 26, Pink to Stirling, 24 July 1956.
12. NA, CO 554/371.
13. NA, FO 371/95757, no. 25, minute, 23 December 1951.
14. NA, FO 371/96911, no. 338, Morris to Allen, 25 October 1952.
15. NA, DEFE 7/415, no. 40, minute, 27 November 1954.
16. David Goldsworthy, (ed.), *The Conservative Government and the End of Empire 1951–1957* (London: 1994) part 2, documents 226–42.
17. NA, CO 554/807, minute, 16 August 1956.
18. NA, DO 35/6178, no. 17A, letter to Laithwaite, 21 July 1956.
19. In BDEEP *Central Africa* (London: 2005), part I, p. xxxi. Also, P. Murphy, *Party Politics and Decolonization: The Conservative Party and British Colonial Policy in Tropical Africa, 1951–1964* (Oxford: 1995), pp. 19–23.
20. NA, FO 371/169706, no. 244, Warner to Gilchrist, 13 August 1963.
21. NA, PREM 11/2617, minute to Eden, 26 August 1955.
22. Arden-Clarke was the first governor to submit a report, NA, CO 554/1162, no. 2, 16 July 1954.
23. NA, CO 1015/1009, minute by J.C. Morgan, 26 November 1956.
24. The need to secure more Ceylons and fewer Burmas was first stated in a paper circulated at the London conference of African governors in November 1947. NA, CO 847/36/4, no. 18, para. 19 of paper, 'The colonies and international organisations'.
25. NA, CAB 129/71, C(54)307, 11 October 1954.
26. NA, PREM 11/1726F, brief, 1 December 1954.
27. NA, CAB 128/27/2, CC 83(54), 7 December 1954; CAB 128/29, CM 44(55)5, 1 December 1955.
28. NA, CO 1032/98, minute by Poynton, 14 December 1955.
29. NA, CO 554/1533, no. 7, March 1957.
30. NA, CO 554/1181 All the CO could recommend was that Azikiwe be given a 'talking to' at meeting with the Secretary of State. NA, CO 554/1156, no. 20, meeting of officials, 4 October 1955, and CO 554/1109, no. 54A, Lennox-Boyd meeting with Azikwe, 10 November 1955.
31. NA, CO 537/7181, no. 5, letter to Cohen, 12 May 1951.
32. NA, CO 554/254, minute, 9 February 1953.
33. NA, CO 1032/55, minute, 16 December 1955.
34. NA, CO 554/805, minute, 23 September 1954.
35. NA, CAB 129/95, C(58)213, 20 October 1958.
36. NA, CAB 130/153, GEN 624/10, report by officials, 'The position of the UK in world affairs', 9 June 1958.
37. NA, CO 1025/76, no. 49C, minute, 5 July 1956.
38. S.R. Ashton and David Killingray, eds, *The West Indies* (London: 1999).
39. NA, CAB 128/36/1, CC 17(62)4, 27 February 1962.

40. NA, CAB 134/1315, PR(56)3, 1 June 1956.
41. NA, CAB 134/1556, CPC(57)30, memo, 'Future constitutional development in the colonies', 6 September 1957.
42. NA, CAB 134/1551, CPC(57)27, memo, 'Future constitutional development in the colonies', May 1957.
43. NA, CO 1032/166, letter to Brook, 9 October 1957.
44. Ibid., minute by Macpherson on meeting with permanent secretaries, 9 December 1957.
45. Ibid., draft CO future policy paper, January 1958.
46. NA, CO 1032/167; for the CO response, see ibid, minute by I Watt, 11 June 1967.
47. The report on the Commonwealth is at NA, CAB 134/1935, no. 15, 30 July 1959; the future policy study is at CAB 129/100, C(60)35, 24 February 1960; the report on Africa in the next ten years is at FO 371/137972, no. 24, June 1959.
48. R. Shepherd, *Iain Macleod* (London: 1994), p. 168.
49. Ronald Hyam and Wm. Roger Louis, (eds), *The Conservative Government and the End of Empire 1957–1964* (London: 2000), p. xlv.
50. Shepherd, *Macleod*, pp. 159–61.
51. Reference in NA, FO 371/137972 as in note 47.
52. NA, CO 54/986/6/3, no. 174, letter to Hall, 5 October 1945.
53. 'The trouble in Africa', *Spectator*, 31 January 1964, reproduced in A.N. Porter and A.J. Stockwell (eds), *British Imperial Policy and Decolonisation* vol. 2 *1951–1964* (London: 1989), 570–1.
54. NA, CAB 134/1558, CPC(59)2, 10 April 1959.
55. Lennox-Boyd told the House of Commons on 22 April 1959 that four conditions had to be fulfilled before Britain could relax control in Kenya. A sufficient understanding of parliamentary institutions, racial tolerance, a secure economic future, and a competent and experienced civil service. *H of C Debs*, vol. 604, cols 564–6.
56. NA, CO 822/1450, no. 246, letter to Sir F Crawford (governor of Uganda), 9 July 1959. During the Maji-Maji rebellion in German East Africa, 1905–1906, about 200,000–300,000 Africans died.
57. NA, CO 822/1449, minute, 15 June 1959.
58. NA, CO 822/2299, minute, 22 July 1960.
59. NA, CAB 128/37, CC 20(63)2, 28 March 1963.
60. NA, CO 1015/1911, nos 4–6 and 20, letters from Luce to Gorell Barnes, 27–28 March 1958 and Gorell Barnes's reply, 14 April 1958.
61. NA, CO 1015/1910, no. 23, minute to Gorell Barnes, 8 December 1958.
62. NA, CO 1036/612, no. 58, minute by Poynton, 12 July 1960.
63. NA, CO 936/733, minute by O.H. Morris, 27 June 1962.
64. NA, CO 866/146, no. 7, minute, 19 June 1964.
65. NA, CAB 133/200, C(60)122, 23 July 1960.
66. NA, CO 1032/226, no. 169, 24 April 1962.
67. NA, PREM 11/3867, minute to Brook, 21 June 1962.

3

'Government by Blackmail': The Origins of the Central African Federation Reconsidered

Philip Murphy

> 49 reasons all in a line.
> All of them good ones.
> All of them lies.
> Crosby, Stills & Nash 1969

In 1987, Ronald Hyam published what is still justifiably considered the standard account of the origins of the Federation of Rhodesia and Nyasaland, better known as the Central African Federation (CAF).[1] From 1953 to 1963, the CAF brought together Northern and Southern Rhodesia and Nyasaland in a particularly tempestuous and unhappy marriage. Although far from the earliest attempt to explain its genesis, Hyam's article was the first to be based on the British government's own papers.[2] It is reproduced, virtually unaltered, in the recent study by Hyam and Peter Henshaw of Anglo-South African relations.[3] The piece, in both its original and later forms, represents a clear and accurate account of the various stages in the emergence of the federal scheme. This chapter attempts neither to dispute nor indeed to rehearse the basic narrative it presents. Rather, it seeks to explore and question Hyam's conclusion that the British government's decision to establish the CAF was,

> as nearly monocausal as any historical explanation can ever be. The motive was to erect a counterpoise to the expansion of South Africa, especially by checking Afrikaner immigration ... .The Central African Federation was a geopolitical construct designed to place the first line of defence against South African expansion on the Limpopo not

the Zambezi, and to prevent an anticipated settlers' revolt linking itself up with the Union.[4]

To begin with, two quite distinct causal factors are described in this statement: first, the aim of checking South African expansionism; second, the desire to avert a settler revolt. It might be argued – with good reason as we shall see – that they were closely linked in the minds of British policy-makers. Yet the relative weight we give to each of these two factors will largely determine whether we classify the construction of the CAF as an example of retreat or revival on the part of British imperialism. If we privilege the first, as Hyam implicitly does, then the Federation certainly appears, in the words of Lord Blake, 'an aberration of history – a curious deviation from the inevitable course of events, a backward eddy in the river of time'.[5] It would, after all, be a rare case of Britain seeking to protect its geopolitical interests and impose its notions of good government in the face of the supposedly irresistible force of colonial nationalism; of action rather than reaction, revival rather than retreat.

By contrast, the notion that British policy was influenced by the threat of a settler revolt places the emergence of the CAF in a very different light. In 'The Imperialism of Decolonization', Wm Roger Louis and Ronald Robinson attribute federation to the fact that, in order to maintain the dollar-earning capacity of the Rhodesias, 'the agitation of European miners and tobacco farmers against colonial control had to be appeased'.[6] In his general survey of British decolonisation, John Darwin also sets the origins of the CAF in the context of an assertive 'Rhodesian nationalism'.[7] Indeed, as early as June 1956, the Governor of Northern Rhodesia, Sir Arthur Benson, privately described the emergence of federation in terms of a ruthless drive by the Southern Rhodesian government to achieve amalgamation with Northern Rhodesia (an objective, he maintained, federal leaders were continuing to pursue by stealth).[8] Viewed in this light, the CAF appears far less of an aberration in the history of post-war British decolonisation. Rather, it conforms to the broadly 'reactive' character of British policy elsewhere in the colonial empire, with short-term control being purchased by ever more extensive constitutional concessions to the forces of nationalism. Here, however, the nationalists were white.

This chapter will attempt to do three things. First, it will argue that settler pressure for closer association in Central Africa played a greater role in shaping British policy than Hyam appears prepared to concede. It will suggest that, however sincerely individual policy-makers believed in it, the notion of an Afrikaner threat to the region provided a convenient pretext for surrendering to settler demands. As such, its role as a causal factor in the creation of federation is more ambivalent than Hyam suggests. Second, the piece will demonstrate that once the British government had publicly endorsed the principle of federation, it proved difficult to resist settler pressure for the weakening of key features of the scheme designed to protect the interests of the African community. Third, while the chapter will largely endorse another of Hyam's findings – that economic arguments were peripheral to the government's decision to pursue federation – it will seek to examine these arguments in greater depth, not least in order to discover why the British government was so insistent on including Nyasaland in the federation.

Pressure for the amalgamation of the Rhodesias from the settler communities of the two territories had been mounting since 1930 when the Labour Secretary of State for the Colonies, Lord Passfield, had explicitly reiterated the doctrine of the paramouncy of native interests – first articulated in the 'Devonshire Declaration' of 1923 – in the context of Northern Rhodesia. In 1937, the British government appointed the Bledisloe Commission to explore the options for closer association between the Rhodesias and Nyasaland, with due regard 'to the special responsibility of His Majesty's Government in the United Kingdom for the interests of the Native inhabitants'.[9] The majority report of the commission, which appeared in March 1939, recognised the desirability of ever-closer co-operation between the Central African territories and recommended that the British government accept in principle the aim of ultimate 'political unity'.[10] Yet it ruled against immediate amalgamation, principally on the grounds of the wide divergence in the 'native policy' of Southern Rhodesia and the northern territories. The commissioners also dismissed federation as impractical, given the difficulties of bringing together three territories at very different stages of constitutional development. These conclusions were broadly endorsed in 1941 by Lord Hailey who had been invited to undertake a special study of the feasibility of coordinating 'native policy' in Nyasaland and the Rhodesias as part of his general examination of British administration across Africa.[11]

It was, however, recognised by the British government that London had to make some positive gesture in the direction of closer association. The principal reason for this was the strength of the pressure for amalgamation from the European settlers, and the possible dangers of exhausting their patience. In June 1943, an official brief for the Secretary of State for the Colonies, Oliver Stanley, warned that, were there to be a negative announcement on this issue, 'sections of the European population and particularly those on the Copperbelt might decide to take the law into their own hands'.[12] This might, the brief added, draw the South African government into Central African affairs, and increase the threat of Southern Rhodesia's absorption into the Union.

As a limited concession to the settlers' amalgamationist ambitions, London devised plans for the creation of a Central African Council (CAC) to co-ordinate a number of administrative functions across the three British territories of the region. Yet the statement in October 1944 announcing this initiative represented a double blow to Roy Welensky and his fellow unofficial members on the Northern Rhodesian legislative council. On the one hand it explicitly ruled out amalgamation itself as impractical under the current circumstances. At the same time, it contained proposals for constitutional change in Northern Rhodesia which fell far short of representative government on Southern Rhodesian lines. Since the Bledisloe report had rejected federation on the grounds that the three Central African territories were at such different stages of constitutional development, the new constitution did little to bring forward the prospect of significant political unification.

The Southern Rhodesian Prime Minister, Sir Godfrey Huggins, managed to persuade Welensky not to reject the idea of the CAC. Yet there was, from the very beginning, a fundamental difference between the attitude towards the Council on the part of the British government on one side and of Huggins and Welensky on the other. British officials had envisaged the Council as a means of deflecting pressures for amalgamation.[13] By contrast, Huggins and Welensky made it clear that, in so far as they valued the Council, they did so principally as a step towards the achievement of that objective.[14] That the Council's relatively modest ambitions were not outstripped at an even earlier stage by Huggins and Welensky's amalgamationist ambitions probably owed much to the electoral situation in Southern Rhodesia. In the general election of 1946, Huggins's United Party lost its overall majority, and he formed a minority government with the support of the main opposition group, the Liberal Party, which opposed amalgamation. Huggins was therefore forced to curb his public expressions of enthusiasm for amalgamation. He continued, however, to provide discreet support for the cause, most notably through the creation by political allies in March 1948 of the United Central Africa Association (UCAA).[15]

Meanwhile, in Northern Rhodesia, the issue of amalgamation became ever more closely bound up with the desire of settler leaders to exercise greater control over the affairs of their territory. By November 1946, Welensky was threatening to resign from the executive council. His aim, according to one senior British official was 'to make the present constitution unworkable with the idea of obtaining constitutional advance or, better still, amalgamation'.[16] The following month, Welensky carried out his threat of resignation. In November 1947, he challenged the Northern Rhodesian government either to allow amalgamation or grant European representatives more power within the territorial administration.[17]

The ambitions of settler nationalism in Central Africa extended beyond political institutions, and embraced attempts to impose local European control over key elements of the region's economy. In the late 1940s, there were two principal economic targets: the mineral rights of the British South Africa Company (BSA), and the rail system of the region. The Charter Company's claim to sole mineral rights over large areas of Northern Rhodesia had been confirmed by the British government as recently as 1938. As the Second World War drew to a close, however, settler pressure for the nationalisation of those rights increased. Worryingly, for London, the campaign against the company threatened to become bound up with the political demands of settler nationalism. When, in October 1946, the Northern Rhodesian legislative council debated a call for the amalgamation of the Rhodesias, the CO feared that Welensky, who had tabled the motion, might use it 'as a peg upon which to hang an assertion that the only way of escape for Northern Rhodesia from the strangle-hold of the BSA Company was attainment of self-government by amalgamation'.[18] The issue caught the attention of Andrew Cohen, who, as Assistant Under-Secretary in charge of the African Department at the CO from 1947 to 1951, was to be one of the architects of the policy of federation.[19] Cohen warned that the dispute over BSA's rights was 'entirely political' and that a failure to act would increase settler ill will towards the British government.[20] Yet while the CO was keen to resolve the issue, the Treasury refused to provide the funds to buy out the Charter Company's mineral rights.[21] Salvation (at least in the short term) came in the unlikely shape of Welensky himself, who by that stage had ceased his policy of non-co-operation following a constitutional agreement in July 1948 which had given unofficials a greater say in government.[22] In March 1949, he won support for a motion in the Northern Rhodesian legislative council, calling for mineral royalties to be taxed.[23] The British Secretary of State for the Colonies, Arthur Creech Jones, indicated that he was prepared in principle to allow the tax to be imposed. This succeeded in bringing the company to the negotiating table. Talks, which opened in London in July 1949, reached an agreement under which BSA's rights would expire in 1986. Until that time, the Northern Rhodesian government was assigned 20 per cent of the net revenue from them.

Another economic legacy of Charter Company rule was the railway system in Northern and Southern Rhodesia and Bechuanaland. BSA had a controlling interest in the parent company of Rhodesia Railways Limited, which owned the system. In 1943, the Southern Rhodesian government called for Rhodesia Railways to be nationalised and brought under the control of the governments of the three territories in which it operated. In 1947, in the face of British reluctance to act on the matter, Huggins's administration broke the *impasse* by raising a loan of £32 million on the London stock exchange, all but £2 million of which was intended to cover the costs of nationalisation.[24] Northern Rhodesia and Bechuanaland were nominal co-guarantors of the loan, although it was expected that they would probably never have to meet their commitments. Rhodesia Railways became a statutory corporation responsible to the three governments involved. As well being another symbolic mark of the Central African settlers' determination to take command of their own affairs, the deal enhanced the Huggins government's control over the transport system of the region, giving it a further source of leverage in its negotiations with the British government over closer association. The financial commitment which the loan represented, combined with the costs entailed by other ambitious schemes – in particular his government's massive drive to attract new immigrants from Europe – also gave Huggins a strong incentive to seek to gain access to the mineral wealth of Northern Rhodesia.

If the Central African settlers and the British government appeared to be set on something of a collision course, hopes that there might be grounds for compromise appeared from the middle of 1948. Early in June that year, there was a meeting in Lusaka between a delegation from the UCAA and unofficial members of the Northern Rhodesian legislative council. This concluded 'that the only form of closer union which was immediately practicable from the Northern Rhodesian aspect was a federation'.[25] Shortly afterwards, Welensky announced in the legislative council that he would welcome the opportunity to discuss federation during talks over the territory's constitution due to take place in London the following month.[26] At a meeting with Creech Jones and some of his officials on 30 July, Welensky claimed that he 'had come to the conclusion that nothing was to be gained by pressing for amalgamation', and that, instead, he was in favour of some form of federation.[27]

Huggins's return with a working majority at the Southern Rhodesian general election in September 1948 provided a further vital precondition for progress on closer association. Indeed, Huggins immediately followed his victory at the polls with an announcement that he would use his visit to London in October for the Dominions Prime Ministers' conference to press for the 'marriage of the Rhodesias'.[28] At the time, however, Huggins was still talking in terms of unification. Welensky, who had arrived in London in September, had taken the opportunity to obtain final confirmation from Creech Jones and Oliver Stanley that there was no possibility of either of Britain's major parties supporting amalgamation.[29] On that basis, Welensky approached Huggins during his London visit in October and drew from him a firm declaration in favour of federation.

These developments did not go unnoticed by some in London who had previously been cautious about closer association. Writing in May 1948, the day after D.F. Malan's National Party had won the South African general election, Cohen had suggested that federation would have to wait, 'until Africans in Northern Rhodesia and Nyasaland are sufficiently advanced to express a really valuable opinion on the question of closer political union', a stage he felt might 'be a considerable time off'.[30] By October, however, while still recognising the obstacles in the way of federation, he had come to the view that Huggins deserved the British government's support. Cohen suggested that Britain should make a statement to the effect that 'there were strong arguments in favour of federation, provided that certain difficulties could be overcome, and then ask that local representatives should consider these difficulties'.[31] Yet while he justified such a move in terms of the need 'to strengthen Southern Rhodesia's hand in dealing with the Union', the timing of his change of heart suggests that it was due more to the shift in settler politics *within* Central Africa than by the escalation of the Afrikaner threat from without. Creech Jones, by contrast, remained far more cautious about the government appearing to take the initiative in this matter. 'The political stuff is dynamite' he warned, and 'must be handled with great care. We must go slow with such discussions.'[32] This set the pattern for Whitehall's handling of the matter over the next couple of years, with officials – particularly Cohen at the CO and G.H. Baxter, his counterpart at the Commonwealth Relations Office (CRO) – increasingly enthusiastic about federation, and Labour ministers highly concerned about the political repercussions of the project and determined to go as slowly as possible.

Settler leaders were keen, however, to force the pace. On 20 December, Welensky announced that a conference on closer association would be held at the Victoria Falls. This took place on 16–17 February 1949. Each of the three Central African territories was invited to send four representatives. There were, however, no Africans in any of the delegations.

The proposals that emerged from the conference would have given effective power to a house of representatives containing no African members. The seats were to be allocated to each territory according to their population, following an explicitly discriminatory formula under which 100 Africans were to be considered equal to one European. In a chamber expected to consist of 48 seats, this would have given Southern Rhodesia 30 seats, Northern Rhodesia 12 and Nyasaland 6. Only a relatively limited range of powers was to be left with the territorial governments. The scheme also envisaged the vast majority of territorial revenues going to the federal government, with mineral-rich Northern Rhodesia retaining less than 20 per cent of its existing income. Overall, the proposals appeared to stop not far short of Huggins's previous aim of full amalgamation.

The conference was quickly followed by unmistakable signs that Welensky and Huggins were prepared to use every means available to them to get their way. During talks with an official from the CO in late February 1949, Welensky threatened that if London did not support plans for federation,

> he would first of all try to get the unofficial members to boycott the Legislature and force a general election. He would then try to persuade no candidates to stand ... if this tactic did not appear to have any chance of success he would do everything to hold up the machinery of Government and would completely disregard the agreement for working the Northern Rhodesian constitution.[33]

There was also a warning from Hugh Parry, the Chief Secretary of the CAC, that if the government did not accept federation, Southern Rhodesia might not only adopt a policy of non-co-operation towards the CAC but could actively 'apply economic pressure on Northern Rhodesia and Nyasaland primarily by increasing chrome output and reducing the number of railway wagons available for the transport of copper'.[34] Parry stressed that the British government had to make some response to the settlers' federal proposals.

The Chief Secretary of Northern Rhodesia, R. C. S. Stanley, was also keen that the government should respond as quickly as possible. Stanley was candid in describing the current situation in Northern Rhodesia – under which European representatives were constantly threatening to withdraw co-operation – as 'government by blackmail'.[35] He was equally candid that a Central African federation would be 'a "White Man's Country" in the sense that the Africans will never be likely to achieve full political equality in any foreseeable time'. Yet he was adamant that, in the face of Welensky's threats to 'paralyse the government' the British government had to take the initiative if they wished to retain control of the situation. Amongst officials at the CO, there was considerable sympathy for this view.[36] Again, however, ministers were reluctant to commit themselves, even in principle. Hence, when in April, Creech Jones held talks with Huggins and Welensky in the course of his Central African tour, he merely reiterated the government's earlier position that it would not put forward proposals of its own but was prepared to consider new proposals from Central Africa.

Over the next few months, there were strong indications that Huggins and Welensky were unable to agree on the outlines of new constitutional proposals. By the end of the year, however, this divergence of opinion and consequent stalemate led the settler leaders once again to place pressure on the British government to offer some proposals of its own. In November 1949, Welensky tabled a motion in the Northern Rhodesian legislative council, calling on the British government 'to take the lead in creating a Central African Federal State'. The motion was carried just as talks were opening in London between ministers and officials from the Colonial and Commonwealth Relations Offices and the Southern Rhodesian Minister of Justice, T. M. W. Beadle. Beadle pressed the British government for a clarification of its position on closer association.[37] He also gave notice of his government's chosen means of forcing them to offer one. He revealed that 'if there were prospects of federation in a reasonable time, they [the Southern Rhodesian government] would probably agree that the Central African Council should carry on; but if federation seemed a remote prospect, they would have to reconsider whether continuation of the Central African Council was worth while'. The Southern Rhodesian government acted upon this threat in January 1950, placing on the agenda of the CAC a motion calling for its abolition in 12 months' time.

It is against the background of settler pressure on one hand, and of ministerial caution on the other that the supposed threat from Afrikaner immigration into Central Africa is best viewed. This threat was to prove a valuable resource in the efforts of senior officials in London to reach some kind of accommodation with settler leaders. It is probably no coincidence that Welensky played a significant role in encouraging Whitehall to pay attention to the issue. He raised it during his talks with Cohen in London early in August 1949, suggesting that immigration from South Africa to Northern Rhodesia was taking place at an annual rate of 7000. Following this discussion, Cohen wrote to the Governor of

Northern Rhodesia, Sir Gilbert Rennie, requesting further information.[38] In response, Rennie noted that 'Some of us have been worried about this question, which needs a great deal of investigation and consideration.'[39] Yet the information he provided suggested that the figure of 7000 was an exaggeration and that other pieces of information advanced by Welensky to prove the growing influence of the Afrikaners were incorrect.[40] Welensky persisted with his alarmist reports. In November, he warned Cohen that one of his fellow unofficials on the Northern Rhodesian executive council had predicted that, after the next general election in the territory, 'the majority of Members of the House will be Afrikaans'.[41] The following month, Rennie reiterated this warning, adding that it 'would be a calamity, in view of the trend of events in South Africa'.[42] Significantly, however, while he expressed pessimism about Northern Rhodesia's ability to stem this flow from the South, Rennie did not suggest at this stage that the solution lay in closer association.

It is difficult to assess the precise extent to which both Welensky and Huggins highlighted this issue in order to prepare the ground for their federal proposals. Certainly, however, from 1949 onwards, Welensky (whose own mother was Afrikaans) never lost a chance to impress on the British government his fears of the consequences of unrestricted Afrikaner immigration into Northern Rhodesia. Yet he was notably reluctant to support territorial legislation to address the problem.[43] So far as the British government was concerned, it would be wrong to suggest that the issue of South African influence was a mere smoke screen. It was a long-standing concern, which was taken seriously in London and by the governments of Central Africa. What does seem to be the case is that, as the federal cause gained momentum, the geopolitical argument for the scheme appears to have been progressively foregrounded, and the issue of settler pressure sidelined. Both settler politicians and pro-federal British civil servants clearly recognised that the Afrikaner threat was the sort of thing that played well with Labour ministers. It also, crucially, offered a chance of persuading Africans and their sympathisers in Britain that, far from federation being an instrument of European oppression, it was a means of blocking the northwards spread of apartheid.

One can see this process in operation over the course of 1951. Two developments in the early months of that year served to advance the cause of federation: the visit to Central and Southern Africa by Commonwealth Secretary Patrick Gordon Walker from 18 January–3 March, and the conference of officials from Britain and Central Africa which met in London from 5–31 March. Gordon Walker returned from his tour convinced of the reality of the South African threat to the Rhodesias and persuaded of the benefits of federation.[44] Meanwhile, under the chairmanship of G. H. Baxter from the CRO (and the guidance of Cohen), the officials' conference in March produced an outline for federation that in many of its principal features closely approximated the scheme that was ultimately implemented. A number of the recommendations in the report of the officials' conference (the 'Baxter report') were geared to making federation more palatable to the Africans. Matters directly affecting the lives of ordinary Africans were to remain, so far as possible, in the hands of the territorial governments. There would be an African Affairs Board, the members of which would include an African from each of the federal territories. This would be responsible for vetting federal legislation, and it could, if it objected to a bill, refer it to the UK Parliament. There would also be a Minister for African Affairs who would sit in the federal Cabinet and chair the African Affairs Board.

The Baxter report was produced in a form suitable for publication; but it was accompanied by a confidential minute from Baxter and Cohen which was far more explicit in relating closer association to the threat from South Africa. Although the minute was officially intended to be circulated only within the British and the Central African governments, its exposition of the 'Afrikaner danger' was also clearly designed as a means of softening opposition to the federal proposals. Baxter was keen to find 'some means of confidentially bringing this consideration to the notice of discreet and sensible persons among those in this country who are concerned for the welfare of Africans in the northern territories', in the hope of persuading them that the continuation of the current situation posed a far greater threat to African interests than did closer association.[45]

It is difficult not to gain the impression that, for Baxter, the rhetorical utility of the 'Afrikaner danger' was more important than the threat itself. In the spring of 1951, the Northern Rhodesian government proposed restricting its territorial franchise to citizens of the United Kingdom and the colonies (so excluding Afrikaners). Baxter's response to this initiative was one of alarm. He argued that,

> Afrikaner infiltration is a powerful argument for the radical and salutary policy of 'closer association'. The use of this argument would be weakened if, at the critical time, some piecemeal tinkering is going on which could be represented as sufficiently coping with the danger.[46]

Even among some of Baxter's colleagues in the CRO there was a certain amount of scepticism about the reality of the Afrikaner threat and about the uses to which it was put by settler politicians. One commented that 'Sir Godfrey Huggins is not averse from "making our flesh creep" over this possible danger'.[47] Baxter and Cohen's confidential minute clearly made an impression on Gordon Walker, and reinforced the impressions he had gained from his visit to Central and Southern Africa. The Cabinet memorandum he produced for his colleagues in April describing his visit placed a great deal of emphasis on the danger from South Africa. Yet it was also extraordinarily frank in admitting that the policy had to respond to current and potential pressures from the Central African settler communities to preserve white control. He warned that

> In the last resort we do not control these British communities by power. As they grow richer and more numerous they will become potential American colonies – very loyal, but very determined to have their own way. If we are in due course faced by defiance of our will in the Rhodesias or Kenya there will be in effect nothing we can do about it[48]

The following month, Gordon Walker and Secretary of State for the colonies, James Griffiths, submitted a joint Cabinet memorandum inviting their colleagues to endorse the broad terms of the Baxter report.[49] They included as an appendix Baxter and Cohen's confidential minute. The memorandum is as notable for what it *did not* say as for what it did. In contrast to Gordon Walker's April memorandum, it contained no comparable acknowledgement of the force of settler pressure. Rather, it made even greater play of the threat from Afrikaner immigration, portraying federation as a positive means of preserving British values in the region rather than as a negative surrender to settler agitation.

Yet despite the best efforts of the advocates of federation within Whitehall, the Labour government remained highly cautious about endorsing any scheme that was likely to encounter significant African opposition. The proposals of the officials' conference were published as a White Paper in June 1951. But the government went no further than to commend them as a basis for further discussion. Without a firm commitment to federation, it was difficult to make further progress. A conference at the Victoria Falls in September 1951, although it was attended by both Gordon Walker and Griffiths, achieved very little.[50] Enthusiasts for federation in the Colonial and Commonwealth Relations Offices did, however, manage to put down a marker in the form of a joint Cabinet memorandum in the names of Gordon Walker and Griffiths submitted in October 1951, just a fortnight before that month's general election. It recommended that, as soon as possible after the election, the government should announce that it endorsed the conclusions of the Victoria Falls conference, including the proposal to resume the conference in London around the middle of 1952, and that it would favour in principle the federation of the three central African territories.[51]

As has been well documented by Hyam and others, Cohen and Baxter acted with remarkable speed and single-mindedness to exploit the advent of a new, Conservative administration in October 1951.[52] Within two days of the announcement of their appointment on 28 October, officials had arranged for Lord Ismay and Oliver Lyttelton, the new Commonwealth and Colonial Secretaries of State, to be shown the recent joint memorandum by Griffiths and Gordon Walker.[53] By the morning of 31 October, Lyttelton had already indicated to Cohen that he supported the general line taken in the document.[54] A joint memorandum by Ismay and Lyttelton, recommending that the government announce its intention to pursue federation along the lines set out in the Baxter report, was submitted to the Cabinet on 9 November and approved six days later.[55] A statement to this effect was made by Lyttelton in the Commons on 21 November.

Cohen and Baxter had displayed considerable dexterity in 'bouncing' the newly elected Conservative government into an early endorsement of the Baxter proposals. They were less successful, however, in protecting key elements of those proposals from pressure for further concessions to settler leaders. There were two principal reasons for this. The first was the fact that plans for federation would have to be approved by a referendum in Southern Rhodesia before they could be implemented, a safeguard Huggins had promised his white electorate as early as September 1948.[56] The second factor was a growing realisation that African opposition to federation, at least in the two Northern territories, was unlikely to abate. Towards the end of December 1951, Parry had warned London of his own conviction 'that the chance of converting Africans to any effective form of closer association does not any longer exist'.[57] In the light of this and similar warnings, officials for the first time began to contemplate the possibility of forcing federation through in the face of African opposition. This prospect caused little dismay in the minds of Conservative ministers who, unlike their Labour predecessors, were (at least in private) brutally dismissive of the legitimacy of African objections. In February 1952, Ismay complained to Sir John

Kennedy, the Governor of Southern Rhodesia, that the issue of closer association had been dogged by 'the failure of many people of all parties to realise that the average Northern Rhodesian African is of the mental calibre of a British child of ten, and that if we are to do our job of Nanny and Governess properly, we have got to give him better food and better education before we even think of full political emancipation'.[58]

The combination of these factors made it difficult to resist making further concessions to Huggins. With not only the chance of winning African support, but the very legitimacy of African objections effectively discounted, everything now hinged on whether proposals could be sold to Southern Rhodesian voters. Since it was assumed that Africans would reject federation in whatever form it took, it became less important if the proposals appeared to be weighted towards settler demands. Hence, remarkably quickly after the British general election, the shape of the federal proposals began to change in conformity with Huggins's agenda. During talks in London with the heads of the three Central African governments between 22 January and 1 February 1952, the British government agreed to drop the proposal for a minister for African interests. They also agreed to a number of proposals from Huggins regarding the composition and powers of the African Affairs Board, including the provision that the three territorial Secretaries for Native Affairs should be excluded from membership of the Board.[59]

The only significant counterbalance to this tendency to gear concessions towards the European settlers was provided by the opposition in Britain. On 5 March 1952, the House of Commons divided on a Labour motion tabled by James Griffiths, which was critical of the government's handling of the federal negotiations. Although the motion was defeated, it signalled the breakdown of the previous bipartisan approach to Central African policy, and a decisive move by Labour towards supporting African critics of federation. Further concessions to Huggins were likely to alienate Labour still further and remove any chance of re-establishing a consensus.

Yet this domestic counterweight was not sufficient to overcome the intense gravitational pull exerted by the Southern Rhodesian referendum. At the same time, even in the final stages of the federal negotiations, settler leaders were prepared to resort to extreme forms of pressure in order to secure their objectives. In advance of the London constitutional conference of January 1953, Huggins and Welensky threatened a 'Boston Tea Party' if further political concessions were not made to the white minority (the first of many such threats).[60] By the early months of 1953, with the referendum close at hand, officials at the CRO managed to impose an almost complete embargo on any statements by the British government aimed at reassuring Africans and their supporters in London. In March 1953, officials at the CRO expressed concern that a forthcoming Conservative party political broadcast would emphasise the government's commitment to self-government in Britain's African territories. Baxter complained that the CO showed 'a curious inability to realise both what sort of things may cause alarm in Southern Rhodesia and how easily the referendum may be prejudiced'.[61] Doubts were even expressed about the wisdom of remarks by Lyttelton suggesting that the alternative to federation was racial segregation. One of Baxter's colleagues worried that this might be taken by Southern Rhodesian voters to imply that the government intended the federation as a whole to abandon segregation.[62] The 62 per cent vote in favour of federation achieved in the Southern Rhodesian referendum in April 1953 represented something of a victory for Baxter's approach. Yet it had been achieved by surrendering key elements of the federal proposals, and by discounting any hope of converting African opinion.

This chapter has not hitherto considered the role of Nyasaland in plans for federation. Hyam quite rightly suggests – without discussing the issue in detail – that the economic arguments in favour of federation were not decisive in persuading the British government to support the project. Yet why, if not on economic grounds, was it so keen to see Nyasaland included? It was certainly not due to any significant pressure from inside the territory. As late as March 1952, its Governor, Sir Geoffrey Colby, was insisting to London that it should not be included.[63] Nor was there any direct threat of 'Afrikaner infiltration'. Indeed, Colby suggested that Afrikaner influence over Nyasaland was likely to increase rather than decrease as a result of the territory's closer association with the Rhodesias.[64]

Colby later claimed that the prospect of economic development was 'the main justification of the inclusion of Nyasaland in the federation'.[65] Certainly, there was a widespread and long-standing assumption within Whitehall that Nyasaland was bound to benefit economically from moves towards closer association. A CO briefing paper for the Secretary of State in June 1943 noted that 'Nyasaland is small and poor, and would benefit not only from the resources of her neighbours but also from the power to call on technical and other advice and assistance which she herself has been unable to afford in the past.'[66]

Yet as soon as the supposed economic benefits were subjected to any degree of scrutiny, it became clear that they were based on distinctly questionable assumptions. In January 1952, an official in the Economic

Department of the CO, wrote a long internal memorandum, which demolished in turn each of the main economic arguments for federation. Principal among these was that the notion that closer association was in some sense justified by the fact that the three Central African territories had complementary economies. Nyasaland was a major source of migrant labour for Southern Rhodesia, with about 87,000 workers travelling there annually. Yet as the CO memorandum noted, this could just as well be presented as a powerful argument *against* Nyasaland's participation in a federation. A federal government dominated by Southern Rhodesians might well pursue policies 'designed to maintain Nyasaland as an area of labour supply at the expense of building up the local economy to a point where it can keep its population at home'.[67] Even more striking than this intervention from a sceptic, was the weakness of the response from his pro-federal colleagues within the CO. The essential thrust of their reply was that, if there were no strong economic arguments in favour of it 'there are also no economic arguments against federation'.[68] Assistant Under-Secretary, William Gorell Barnes noted, 'I suspect that politics, not economics, will settle the issue in hand.'[69]

The Treasury undoubtedly regarded federation primarily in terms of reducing British financial commitments towards Nyasaland. On the eve of the London conference of January 1953 which was to decide the final shape of the federal constitution, a Treasury official noted that 'the internal finances of Nyasaland are giving rise to concern, and may give rise to the need for an annual grant-in-aid from HMG. It would thus be to our advantage to have Nyasaland associated with neighbours which are stronger financially'.[70] Yet this consideration merely persuaded the Treasury to offer its broad support for the scheme. It did not lead it to take an active role in advocating federation or indeed in pressing for Nyasaland's inclusion in it. This was probably because the precise nature of the savings it envisaged was far from clear. Had Britain's principal objective simply been to reduce costs in Nyasaland, the obvious course would have been to follow one of the recommendations of the Bledisloe Commission and to combine Nyasaland and Northern Rhodesia to form a single colony. The economic consequences of Nyasaland's direct access to the revenues of her far wealthier neighbour would have been fairly clear and predictable. Yet the savings for Britain and benefits for Nyasaland from federation were far less easy to predict, depending as they did on the fine print of any federal scheme.

Treasury officials themselves accepted that Nyasaland would continue to draw on its allocation of Colonial Development and Welfare funds under the current Act and that, so long as it continued to be a British

Protectorate, it had a *prima facie* case for inclusion in subsequent acts.[71] On past form, the demands made on these funds by the Nyasaland government were unlikely to be modest.[72] Unless its constitutional status changed, the only basis on which these demands could reasonably be resisted was if Nyasaland came rapidly to derive significant financial benefits from membership of the CAF. There was certainly some general optimism on this point within Whitehall. In March 1952, Gorell Barnes suggested to Colby that federation might bring 'a considerable windfall for Nyasaland', one that would have a bearing on London's attitude to any claims for additional funds from the Colonial Development and Welfare reserves.[73] Yet only two months later, Gorell Barnes himself asked, 'can anyone who is charged with watching the interests of either Northern Rhodesia or Nyasaland honestly say that they think federation will be to their advantage until they know what is going to happen about the collection and allocation of income tax ... or export duties ... ?'[74]

The CO had already been warned by, H. T. Bourdillon, the civil servant most closely associated with the fiscal aspects of the federal negotiations, that, as currently envisaged, this process of allocation might actually work to Nyasaland's disadvantage. Under the proposals outlined in the Baxter report, the federal government was to receive all customs revenues from the federal territories. Since Nyasaland's population was made up almost entirely of Africans who did not pay income tax, a far higher percentage of the territory's total revenues came from customs duties than did that of either of the Rhodesias. Hence, Bourdillon warned in February 1952, as the poorest of the three territories, 'Nyasaland, so far from giving up the least, gives up the most (in proportion to its total financial resources)'.[75] Following the establishment at the constitutional conference in April 1952 of a fiscal commission to consider this issue, Bourdillon warned that it would be difficult for British ministers and officials to press for a more generous settlement for Nyasaland without leaving themselves open to the accusation both that 'their main interest in federation is to rid themselves of financial liabilities', and that they wished to impede the development of Southern Rhodesia 'in order to subsidise Nyasaland'.[76]

The position only started to become clear in October 1952 when the fiscal commission issued its report. It recommended that the federal government should take 60 per cent of the revenues raised from customs and excise duties and income tax in the three territories, and give 17 per cent each to Northern and Southern Rhodesia and 6 per cent to Nyasaland.[77] In terms of the extremely small contribution Nyasaland would be likely to be able to make to federal revenues, this was regarded as a generous proposal by the CO, and one that represented a genuine redistribution of funds in Nyasaland's favour. Furthermore, it came at a time when the price of two of Nyasaland's principal exports – tea and tobacco – were suffering a serious decline. Yet by this stage, Gorell Barnes had lost some of his optimism about Nyasaland's 'windfall'. He noted that, although the proposals of the fiscal commission would enable the Nyasaland government to carry out its existing development plans (something it would not otherwise be able to do), 'I do not think that they are likely to make possible much increase in the pace of development or, therefore, that the ordinary African is likely to be conscious of much improvement resulting from federation.'[78]

In terms of the economic benefits of federation to Nyasaland, much also depended upon the spending patterns of the federal government. The allocation of responsibilities between the federal and territorial governments, which was agreed at the London conference in January 1953, had already suggested that Nyasaland was not likely to be a major beneficiary. In particular, the federal government's responsibility for European but not African primary and secondary education across the CAF, and for non-African agriculture in the Rhodesias (two areas which together constituted nearly a third of Federal expenditure by 1955), strongly suggested that Southern Rhodesia was likely to benefit disproportionately.[79] Two decisions taken after the CAF was established – to site the federal capital in Salisbury and to fund the Kariba rather than the Kafue hydroelectric project – exacerbated the concentration of federal government resources on Southern Rhodesia.

It was expected in the Treasury that, in practice, the federal government would guarantee *all* the loans raised by the territorial governments.[80] Hence, federal spending priorities were also likely to have an impact on Nyasaland's ability to raise loans for its own purposes; and so it proved. In January 1956, in one of his final communications to London as Governor of Nyasaland, Colby complained bitterly of the immense difficulties he had had in persuading the federal government to direct development money towards his territory. He claimed that under the federal system, revenue from the northern territories had been 'devoted to bolstering a bankrupt and under-taxed Southern Rhodesia and the major part of the Federal Government's share of loan funds raised since federation has been spent or earmarked in Southern Rhodesia'.[81] He flatly refuted the claim by federal ministers that the high level of government borrowing necessitated by the Kariba scheme would not affect development spending.

In short, in the spring of 1952, when Whitehall finally barred the Nyasaland government from withdrawal from the federal negotiations, it was still unclear precisely what benefits Nyasaland would gain from membership or what savings the British government would make. As late as January 1953, the only specific saving identified by the Treasury in the White Paper that emerged from that month's constitutional conference was the cost of the Nyasaland armed forces, responsibility for which would pass to the federal government. As one Treasury official noted, 'Unlike the Caribbean Federation proposals, finance is not the rock on which this scheme may founder.'[82]

If the assumption that Nyasaland would benefit from inclusion in the CAF was weak and untested, it may have been sufficiently widespread and longstanding to have influenced government policy. Yet there also seems to have been political calculation at work. Robert Holland suggests that Nyasaland's inclusion may have partly been the result of an attempt by London at 'equilibrating African and European power' (in a demographic if not a political sense).[83] Perhaps it would be more accurate to say that Britain needed to include Nyasaland *in order to make federation look like federation.* Any form of association purely between the two Rhodesias would have appeared too much like the settlers' longstanding ambition of amalgamation – or at the very least an obvious first step towards it. This would have been unacceptable to liberal opinion in Britain, and would have forfeited from the start any chance of winning African consent. Cohen virtually acknowledged this point as early as October 1948. He noted that 'Nyasaland would have to come into the federation in order to justify its setting up'.[84] Gorell Barnes made a similar, although *ex post facto* justification of the inclusion of the territory 1956 when discussing whether there were any circumstances in which Nyasaland might be allowed to secede from the CAF.[85]

It appears clear, then, that the British government's decision to establish the CAF was essentially an attempt to regain the initiative in Central Africa in the face of a strain of settler nationalism that had emerged invigorated from the Second World War. In Southern Rhodesia, a fresh spirit of confidence on the part of the settlers had breathed new life into the long-standing ambition of amalgamation with Northern Rhodesia. It did so too in Northern Rhodesia, where the cause was intimately connected with the struggle by the territory's settler community to wrest control of its affairs from the CO and block any chance of African self-government. British officials faced repeated threats from Welensky and his colleagues that they would disrupt the government of the territory if either closer association or settler self-government on Southern Rhodesian lines were not conceded. This pressure from the settlers of the Rhodesias superimposed itself in the minds of British officials on a long-term concern about South African expansionism. Any loss of control in Central Africa on the part of the British government threatened to draw South Africa into the affairs of the region, with the possible consequence that Southern and perhaps also Northern Rhodesia might be absorbed into the Union.

Settler pressure for amalgamation and the corresponding threat of losing control were the essential context within which decisions about the federation were made. British officials in Whitehall and in the two Rhodesias were keen to be able to ease that pressure by offering the prospect of more limited forms of closer association. Yet their room for manoeuvre was constrained by the determination of Labour ministers that the British government should not appear to be relinquishing its special responsibilities towards the Africans of the northern territories. Squeezed between the ambitions of the settlers and the concerns of ministers, British officials came increasingly to stress the Afrikaner threat. It provided a means of justifying a surrender to settler pressure in terms of a positive assertion of British values, one that served the long-term interests of the Africans of the region. Certainly, as Hyam suggests, ministers did not easily bend to settler pressure. Certainly too, the geopolitical arguments appear to have been crucial in easing their concerns over closer association. Yet it was the settlers themselves who kept the issue of closer association alive and whose threats of disruption lent urgency in the minds of British officials to the search for an acceptable compromise. Once they had managed to establish themselves as Britain's chosen 'collaborators' in the federal project, settler leaders were (at least initially) as successful as, for example, the CPP in the Gold Coast or TANU in Tanganyika in extracting further concessions as the price for their continued co-operation.

Alongside the geopolitical rationale for federation there was also a widespread assumption in Whitehall that it would bring economic benefits to the territories concerned and ease demands on the British exchequer. It may well be that this assumption played a part in persuading the British government to insist on the inclusion of Nyasaland. It is important to note, however, that this insistence had taken root within Whitehall before any *specific* savings or benefits had become clear. The Treasury, although it offered its broad support for federation, played very little part in driving the scheme forward. It seems likely that, alongside this 'weak' assumption about the economic benefits of federation, the inclusion of Nyasaland was also considered necessary in order to give the federal project the appearance of being something other than a simple capitulation to the amalgamationist ambitions of the Rhodesians.

Viewed as a product of essentially local political pressures, the genesis of the CAF conforms more closely than Hyam's conclusion might suggest to other imperial 'endgames'. This perspective also enables the Federation to be seen as part of a longer term attempt on the part of the British government to deal with the specific problems posed by the European settlers of Central Africa. Federation offered to provide an accommodation with the settlers in terms of their ambitions both for the amalgamation of the Rhodesias and for greater control over the government of Northern Rhodesian. It also offered the chance of reconstructing Southern Rhodesian politics in ways more likely to make some ultimate surrender of sovereignty by the British government acceptable to international opinion. In practice, however, this accommodation was temporary and superficial. Once Huggins had been installed as Prime Minister of the CAF, his amalgamationist ambitions were channelled towards the objective of increasing the powers of the federal government and of obtaining full dominion status for the CAF. The shock created in London by the Nyasaland emergency of 1959, effectively dispelled any hopes for the achievement of dominion status under white control. Thereafter, as Welensky struggled desperately to hold the CAF together, the government of Southern Rhodesia increasingly looked to the preservation of white power within its own boarders. The collapse of the CAF at the end of 1963 left Britain facing the demands of the Southern Rhodesian settlers for full independence in an international climate that increasingly regarded white-minority rule as anathema. Southern Rhodesia's illegal declaration of independence in November 1965 finally confronted Britain with the full extent of its impotence in the face of an armed and determined settler state. Opinions may differ as to the extent to which the perceived danger of South African influence in Central Africa shaped the actions of British policy-makers in the 20 years after the end of the Second World War. What cannot be in doubt, however, is that, in practice, their problems derived largely from the ambitions of their 'own' settlers rather than those of the Union.

Notes

1. Ronald Hyam, 'The geopolitical origins of the Central African Federation: Britain, Rhodesia and South Africa, 1948–1953', *Historical Journal*, 30, 1 (1987), 145–72.
2. For earlier accounts, see, for example, Prosser Gifford, 'Misconceived dominion: the creation and disintegration of Federation in British Central Africa', in Prosser Gifford and Wm. Roger Louis (eds), *The Transfer of Power in Africa, 1940–1960* (Yale, CT: 1982), pp. 387–416. Before the opening of the British state

papers, Richard Wood had used the papers of Sir Roy Welensky to produce his own detailed account of the federal negotiations. See J.R.T. Wood, *The Welensky Papers: A History of the Federation of Rhodesia and Nyasaland* (Durban, 1983).

3. Ronald Hyam and Peter Henshaw, *The Lion and the Springbok: Britain and South Africa since the Boer War* (Cambridge: 2003), pp. 198–229.
4. This passage appears in Hyam, p. 169 and in Hyam and Henshaw, pp. 224–5.
5. Wood, *The Welensky Papers*, p. 15.
6. Wm. Roger Louis and Ronald Robinson, 'The imperialism of decolonization', *Journal of Imperial and Commonwealth History*, 22, 3 (1994), 470.
7. John Darwin, *Britain and Decolonisation: The Retreat from Empire in the Post-War World* (London: 1988), pp. 194–9.
8. National Archives, Kew (hereafter NA), CO 1015/1129, Benson to Lennox-Boyd, 6 June 1956.
9. Cited in NA, CO 967/184, 'Historical Note on the Question of Closer Union of the Central African Territories', undated, February 1951.
10. *Rhodesia-Nyasaland Royal Commission: Report*, Cmd. 5949 (March 1939), paras pp. 471–7.
11. *Note on the Bearing of Native Policy on the Proposed Amalgamation of the Rhodesias and Nyasaland* (London: 1941).
12. NA, DO 35/1390, 'Future policy in Central Africa', Colonial Office memorandum for Oliver Stanley, June 1943.
13. NA, DO 35/1161, minute by Cohen, 28 February 1945.
14. NA, DO 35/1161, R208/24, 'Report of the Inaugural Meeting of the Central African Council held at Government House, Salisbury on the 24, 25 and 26 April 1945'.
15. Wood, *The Welensky Papers*, p. 114.
16. NA, CO 537/1516, Cartmel-Robinson to Cohen, 11 November 1946.
17. Wood, *The Welensky Papers*, p. 109.
18. NA, CO 537/2118, minute by Watson, 23 October 1946.
19. For an account of Cohen's broader significance in the field of African policy-making see Ronald Robinson, 'Andrew Cohen and the transfer of power in Tropical Africa, 1940–1951', in W. H. Morris-Jones and Georges Fischer (eds), *Decolonisation and After: The British and French Experience* (London: 1980), pp. 50–72.
20. NA, CO 537/2119, minute by Cohen, 7 May 1946.
21. NA, CO 537/2119, minute by Creech Jones, 5 February 1946.
22. Wood, *The Welensky Papers*, p. 121.
23. Wood, *The Welensky Papers*, p. 147.
24. *The Times*, 25 June 1947.
25. *Northern News*, 10 June 1948.
26. NA, CO 537/3608, Rennie to Creech Jones, 18 June 1948.
27. NA, CO 537/3608, 'Record of a Meeting held in the Colonial Office on 30 July, 1948'.
28. Wood, *The Welensky Papers*, p. 124.
29. Sir Roy Welensky, *Welensky's 4000 Days: The Life and Death of the Federation of Rhodesia and Nyasaland* (London: 1964), pp. 22–5.
30. NA, CO 537/3647, minute by Cohen, 29 May 1948.
31. NA, CO 537/3608, minute by Cohen, 12 October 1948.

32. NA, CO 537/3608, minute by Creech Jones, 21 October 1948.
33. NA, CO 537/3647, minute by Vile, 7 March 1949.
34. NA, CO 537/4687, 'Central African Federation: Report by Mr Vile on talks before and during the third S.A.A.T.C. Meeting', 26 February 1949.
35. NA, CO 537/4687, Stanley to Vile, 26 February 1949.
36. NA, CO 537/4687, minute by Cohen, 7 March 1949; minute by Lambert, 8 March 1949.
37. NA, PREM 8/1307, 'Note of a meeting held in the Commonwealth Relations Office on Tuesday 29 November, 1949'.
38. NA, CO 537/4691, Cohen to Rennie, 4 August 1949.
39. NA, CO 537/4691, Rennie to Cohen, 27 August 1949.
40. NA, CO 537/4691, Rennie to Cohen, 27 August 1949, enclosure 1.
41. NA, CO 537/4691, Welensky to Cohen, 20 November 1949.
42. NA, CO 537/4691, Rennie to Cohen, 3 December 1949.
43. NA, DO 35/3433, note on 'Control of Afrikaner Immigration into NR' forwarded by Sedgewick to Baring 13 November 1950.
44. NA, CAB 129/45, CP(51)109, 'Visit by the Secretary of State for Commonwealth Relations to the Union of South Africa, Southern Rhodesia and the three High Commission Territories of Basutoland, the Bechuanaland Protectorate and Swaziland', Cabinet memorandum by Gordon Walker, 16 April 1951, reproduced in Ronald Hyam (ed.), *The Labour Government and the End of Empire 1945–1951* (London: 1992), part III, 433; Hyam, 'Geopolitical origins', pp. 153–6.
45. NA, DO 35/3594, minute by Baxter, 4 April 1951.
46. NA, DO 35/3433, minute by Baxter, 5 April 1951.
47. NA, DO 121/137, Garner to Baxter, 17 April 1951.
48. NA, CAB 129/45, CP(51)109, 'Visit by the Secretary of State for Commonwealth Relations to the Union of South Africa, Southern Rhodesia and the three High Commission Territories of Basutoland, the Bechuanaland Protectorate and Swaziland', Cabinet memorandum by Gordon Walker, 16 April 1951, reproduced in Hyam, *The Labour Government*, part III, p. 433; Hyam, 'Geopolitical Origins', pp. 153–6.
49. 'Closer Association in Central Africa', joint Cabinet memorandum by Griffiths and Gordon Walker. *Annex*: confidential minute by G. H. Baxter and A. B. Cohen to the secretaries of state, 31 March 1951, with appendix on immigration policy, 3 May 1951, reproduced in Hyam, *The Labour Government*, part III, p. 435.
50. Hyam, 'Geopolitical Origins', p. 160.
51. NA, CAB 129/4, CP(51)265, 'Closer Association in Central Africa': joint Cabinet memorandum by Mr Griffiths and Mr Gordon Walker on the Victoria Falls Conference, 12 October 1951, reproduced in Hyam, *The Labour Government*, part III, p. 444.
52. Philip Murphy, *Party Politics and Decolonization: The Conservative Party and British Colonial Policy in Tropical Africa 1951–1964* (Oxford: 1995), pp. 51–2.
53. NA, DO 35/3600, minute by Baxter, 30 October 1951.
54. NA, CO 1015/59, minute by Cohen, 31 October 1951.
55. NA, CAB 129/489, C(51)11, 'Closer association in Central Africa', joint memorandum by Lord Ismay and Mr Lyttelton, 9 November 1951, reproduced

along with Appendix II in David Goldsworthy (ed.), *The Conservative Government and the End of Empire 1951–1957* (London: 1994), part II, p. 302.
56. Wood, *The Welensky Papers*, p. 124.
57. NA, CO 1015/65, Parry to Lambert, 29 December 1951.
58. NA, DO 121/146, Ismay to Kennedy, 9 February 1952.
59. Wood, *The Welensky Papers*, pp. 236–7.
60. NA, DO 121/195, minute by Baxter, 16 December 1952.
61. NA, DO 35/6808, minute by Baxter, 3 March 1953.
62. NA, DO 35/6808, minute by Jasper, 9 March 1953.
63. NA, CO 1015/65, Colby to Lyttelton, 19 March 1952.
64. NA, CO 1015/65, 'Central African Federation', 19 March 1952.
65. NA, CO 1015/1002, Colby to Lennox-Boyd, 24 January 1956.
66. NA, DO 35/1390, 'Future policy in Central Africa', CO memorandum for Oliver Stanley, June 1943.
67. NA, CO 1015/65, minute by Selwyn, 22 January 1952.
68. NA, CO 1015/65, minute by Emanuel, 25 January 1952.
69. NA, CO 1015/65, minute by Gorell-Barnes, 30 January 1952.
70. NA, T 220/253, minute by Charles, 20 December 1952.
71. NA, T 220/253, minute by Charles, 28 January 1953.
72. NA, CO 1015/655 'Sir Geoffrey Colby's request for further financial assistance from H.M.G.'.
73. NA, CO 1015/88, Gorell Barnes to Colby, 10 March 1952.
74. NA, CO 1015/88, minute by Gorell Barnes, 16 April 1952.
75. NA, CO 1015/88, minute by Bourdillon, 19 February 1952.
76. NA, CO 1015/88, minute by Bourdillon, 16 June 1952.
77. Wood, *The Welensky Papers*, p. 308.
78. NA, CO 1015/655, minute by Gorell Barnes, 7 October 1952.
79. Arthur Hazlewood, 'The economics of federation and dissolution in Central Africa', in Arthur Hazlewood (ed.), *African Integration and Disintegration* (Oxford: 1967), p. 207.
80. This was because, with so much of their revenues surrendered to the federal government, the credit of the territorial governments was likely to suffer in the eyes of investors (NA, T 220/253, minute by Charles, 28 January 1953).
81. NA, CO 1015/1002, Colby to Lennox-Boyd, 24 January 1956.
82. NA, T 220/253, 'Central African Federation Conference – Proposed White Paper': minute by Charles, 28 January 1953.
83. R. F. Holland, *European Decolonization 1918–1981: An Introductory Survey* (Basingstoke, 1985), p. 140.
84. NA, CO 537/3608, minute by Cohen, 12 October 1948.
85. NA, CO 1015/913, minute by Gorell Barnes, 28 November 1956.

4
African Prospects: Mining the Empire for Britain in the 1950s

Sarah Stockwell

Few historians dispute the economic importance of empire to Britain in the immediate aftermath of the Second World War. 'In Africa', Stafford Cripps declared, 'is to be found a great potential for new strength and vigour in the Western European economy'.[1] In line with this vision, British personnel descended on British colonies, in what was famously described as a 'second colonial occupation', to oversee ambitious development projects designed to step up production of exports for supply to Britain and for sale to the dollar area.[2] Colonial dollar-earnings were pooled in London, and the colonies' imports from the dollar area tightly restricted by controls first introduced at the outbreak of the war, helping the post-war Labour government to ease Britain through the difficulties of the post-war dollar gap.

The evidence for the 1950s is, however, more equivocal. In certain respects the 1950s appear a key decade in the economic decolonisation of the British Empire. After the Korean War the fall in world commodity prices, the failure of high-profile development projects to deliver the anticipated benefits, the development of synthetic substitutes, and the expansion of British agriculture combined to reduce both the perceived and real value to Britain and the Sterling Area of colonial agricultural exports, in turn making it less worthwhile to retain controls which flew in the face of American desire for a post-war multilateral trading system and for full sterling convertibility. As a result, from 1953 the British government began pursuing a policy of economic liberalisation, culminating in the restoration of sterling convertibility in 1958.[3] As some historians see it, the empire had become at best an irrelevance to modern British economic needs. Thus Feinstein argues that empire had ceased to matter to the British economy, and that 1950s Britain was able to enjoy an economic 'golden age' even while losing the empire.[4] Others have gone further, interpreting the empire as an obstacle to Britain's economic development and consequently a factor in long-term British decline. According to such accounts the empire imposed unmanageable burdens on British resources, lulled British manufacturers accustomed to the 'easy' markets of the empire–Commonwealth into undue complacency and prevented full British participation in European economic integration. The growth of colonial sterling balances, as a result in part of British control over the external trade of the colonies, some have argued, also threatened to destabilise the British economy.[5]

Much of this is indisputable; however, the association between empire and decline now looks more doubtful, especially as a result of Catherine Schenk's analysis of the Sterling Area and the sterling balances in the 1950s.[6] Moreover, when one shifts from calculating the real costs and benefits of empire in this period to excavating contemporary *perceptions* of the value of empire to Britain, it is apparent that there was greater continuity between the 1940s and the 1950s than might at first appear. Recent scholarship shows that however much by the mid-1950s ministers and officials no longer regarded colonial economies as of the same significance as in the critical post-war years, they none the less still attached importance to Britain's economic relationship with the empire–Commonwealth. For example, although British business and government were frequently divided over policy issues in the decolonisation era,[7] officials and ministers naturally hoped for the preservation of established commercial networks, including those with former British colonies as they became independent.[8] Above all, British governments wished to maintain established financial relations through the vehicle of the Sterling Area.[9] Moreover, historians of Europe and the Commonwealth argue that, even at the time of the first British application for membership of the European Economic Community (EEC), the British government did not regard the preservation of Commonwealth trade and the development of British commerce in Europe as mutually exclusive.[10] Moving further into the 1960s, Jim Tomlinson has recently argued that the reinvigoration of commercial ties with the Commonwealth was a central plank in the economic policy of Harold Wilson's Labour government.[11]

This chapter aims to contribute to this literature on the place of empire in 1950s British economic planning. It examines a neglected aspect of British development activity in the empire: colonial mining. To date historians of development and of decolonisation have focused disproportionately on colonial agriculture.[12] While from around 1953 official interest in colonial agricultural exports appears to have declined from its post-war heights, the 1950s were in contrast *the* era of post-war

British interest in colonial mineral development; an interest which only weakened at the very end of the decade.

Admittedly, interest in specific minerals waxed and waned over the period from 1945 to 1960, and it would be misleading to suggest that colonial mining falls entirely outside the chronology and explanatory framework derived from studies of colonial agriculture. By the mid-1950s there was certainly declining interest attached to the dollar-earnings to be won from the increased exploitation of some colonial mineral exports. For example, it is clear that the intense interest shown by both the Bank of England and the Treasury in increasing Gold Coast gold production in the late 1940s was short-lived, and entirely conditional upon the value of gold in the short-term for international sale and to swell British reserves.[13] Equally the development of colonial mining could be subject to many of the same disappointments as other more notorious agricultural development projects, with mineral exploitation stalled by ongoing shortages of necessary plant and materials,[14] as well as on occasion generating inter-Whitehall differences and prevarication.[15] Some commodities were in particular demand for rearmament purposes during the Korean War, but from 1953 were no longer regarded with such significance. Moreover, the market for some minerals in the 1950s as for other commodities also proved volatile, subject in no small degree to fluctuating American demand, leading some British officials to bemoan the ill effects of sudden changes in American stockpiling requirements on the market price of colonial mineral exports.[16]

Nevertheless mining was in general subject to quite different dynamics, not least as a result of the fixed location of mineral assets and the heavy capital investment in plant and machinery. Whereas the development of industries in new locations and of synthetic alternatives potentially reduced the importance of some traditional colonial agricultural supplies to Britain, there were no available substitutes for minerals. The onset of the Cold War, by restricting access to some mineral deposits, only served to increase the importance of discovering new mineral resources under Western control. Most importantly for the argument to be presented in this chapter, scientific discoveries, especially within the field of atomic energy, created demand for hitherto unexploited minerals.

The period from 1945 to 1960, and particularly the 1950s, consequently saw something of a mineral rush within the British Empire, and especially, in line with the re-centring of the British Empire on Africa in this period, in British Africa. African mineral discoveries in the 1950s included new copper deposits in the Cape and Transvaal, and a new diamond 'pipe' in the Northern Cape. These years also saw the expansion of gold mining in the Transvaal, of copper mining in Northern Rhodesia, and of diamond mining in Sierra Leone, as well as the development of plans for the exploitation of Ghanaian bauxite.[17] None the less for a variety of reasons the results of prospecting in the 1950s were limited. But this chapter is not concerned with outcomes: instead the focus is on the way government and Whitehall *perceived* the importance of the empire to Britain as a potential source of mineral resources.

The first section of this chapter illustrates the nature of this 'mineral rush'. The second section argues that British authorities were anxious to keep colonial mining as primarily the preserve of British commercial interests despite the Anglo-American 'special relationship' being re-formed in this period. Finally, the chapter considers the degree to which interest in colonial mineral resources in the 1950s informed discussions of colonial political change, and outlines the measures taken to protect the British stake in colonial mining industries in this period.

I

Perhaps the best illustration of the interest in mineral prospecting in the empire in the 1950s is the increase in scientific personnel on the ground. Spearheading the British government's drive to discover new mineral resources was a small army of British geologists, geophysicists and geochemists. Between 1947 and 1956 the number employed on colonial geological surveys rose from 58 to 212 (the numbers fell slightly thereafter as a result of the independence of the Gold Coast and Malaya). The success of the surveys varied from colony to colony (in Malaya, for example, surveying was obstructed by the emergency), but by 1957 the colonial surveys had absorbed some £2.5 million of colonial development and welfare money, resulting in extensive mapping and some discoveries of new mineral deposits.[18] Back in Britain, a variety of organisations were formed to oversee and co-ordinate the development of colonial mineral resources. From the late 1940s these included the directorate of the colonial geological surveys, headed by a director who also served as geological advisor to the Secretary of State;[19] an Advisory Committee on Overseas Geological and Mineral Resources;[20] the Metals and Minerals Panel of the Colonial Primary Products Committee; and a newly established Commonwealth Committee on Mineral Resources and Geology.[21]

In the 1940s official interest in colonial minerals resulted primarily from the drive to increase exploitation of all colonial resources either to generate dollar-earnings or to enable Britain to meet its own requirements from within the Sterling Area (this, for example, was the purpose behind the creation of the Metals and Minerals Panel). By the 1950s, however, it increasingly cohered around the pressing need to secure supplies for Britain of strategic resources for defence purposes. In 1951 a new Defence Advisory Committee on Commonwealth Minerals was formed to assume the task of Commonwealth liaison over minerals required for defence purposes. It included geological and scientific representatives from all the independent Commonwealth countries as well as representatives for the colonies, and was initially chaired by the Australian member.[22] In addition a separate, purely British, body, the Strategic Minerals Committee, had already been established specifically to investigate and exploit minerals deemed of strategic significance. It first met in November 1947 and continued to meet regularly until December 1954 when it was dissolved, its functions to be assumed by a new committee, the 'Raw Materials Research and Development Committee', which in turn continued to meet for the duration of the 1950s.[23] Reporting to the Atomic Energy Authority at Harwell, both the Defence Advisory Committee and the Strategic Minerals Committee were of broad geographical remit (extending to foreign countries as well as the British Isles, the dependent empire and the Commonwealth). Their discussions none the less testify to the considerable interest in the resources of the empire.

Above all in the 1950s interest was attached to the discovery and development within the British Empire of new supplies of uranium and thorium (regarded as a possible cheaper alternative to uranium).[24] This was not entirely new: as early as 1944, and only six years after the discovery of uranium fission, the British government had taken steps to control the production and export of all known and future deposits of uranium and thorium throughout the colonies and dominions.[25] However, the launch of Britain's nuclear programme in the 1940s and later the Conservative Government's more fulsome commitment to the development of nuclear weaponry,[26] as well as the efforts of the US Atomic Energy Commission to stimulate production, fuelled more demand for uranium.[27] Told that the 'security of the free world may depend on such a simple thing as people keeping their eyes open', North American prospectors raced to discover new sources of uranium in what amounted to a latter-day gold rush.[28] For their part, in a scramble to secure new uranium supplies, British and American governments produced their own paper partition of the non-Soviet world, agreeing responsibility for prospecting in different world regions with a view to joint control and division of all uranium under the auspices of a Combined Development Trust (from 1948 the Combined Development Agency). Britain was allocated responsibility for the exploration of the Commonwealth and colonial empire, as well as some 'third' countries.[29]

By the early 1950s the Agency had reached agreements for the long-term purchase of South African, Canadian and Australian supplies; in addition Britain on behalf of the Agency was purchasing uranium from Portugal (where the mines were partly British-owned), and, most importantly, from the Belgian Congo, where Britain had an option on half of deposits following a wartime agreement with the *Union Minière du Haut Katanga*. However, in Britain there was also considerable interest in discovering new colonial deposits, which could reduce existing dependency on supplies from 'difficult' currency areas.[30] Hence in March 1949 colonial governments were informed that it was 'of the utmost importance' that any workable deposits of thorium, and especially of uranium, within the British Commonwealth 'should be located and worked as soon as possible'. In this task colonial governments were encouraged to consider the creation of public corporations, as well as to 'enlist the active and energetic interest of mining houses and private prospectors in the search'. For its part the British government promised to help supply colonial geological surveys with the necessary equipment, pledged the services of the UK Atomic Energy Section of the British Geological Survey for assaying ores where local services were not available, and announced terms on which the Ministry of Supply offered to purchase all uranium ores over the next ten years at fixed price.[31] Terms were subsequently revised to further encourage prospecting and development.[32]

Official interest in sourcing uranium from the colonial empire increased rather than declined in the early 1950s and was maintained throughout most of the decade. With the contract with the Belgian Congo due to expire in the mid-1950s and growing fears that the Congo reserves were becoming rapidly exhausted, it was held at the start of the decade that the search for new sources should 'for both currency and political reasons ... be concentrated on the Colonial Empire'.[33] In May 1950 the Strategic Minerals Committee recommended a five-year plan for the systematic investigation of colonial uranium resources,[34] and in the following months arrangements were undertaken for the Ministry of Supply to sponsor a car-borne geiger survey of Sierra Leone and the Gold Coast, and for a representative from the British Geological Survey and Museum to visit Sierra Leone, the Gold Coast, Nigeria, South Africa, Southern and Northern Rhodesia, Tanganyika, Kenya, Uganda, as well as French West Africa.[35] By the mid-1950s the currency argument may have lost some of its urgency, but the search for uranium was spurred on by anticipation that world demand would increase as more countries commenced their own atomic energy projects.[36] In addition, by this time it was becoming increasingly apparent that Britain was unlikely for the foreseeable future to achieve any surplus, and consequently 'a maximum effort' was still deemed desirable in seeking out sources of uranium in the colonial empire in particular.[37] From 1952 the government also decided that in view of difficulties in bearing its share of the costs of the Combined Development Agency, British prospecting should henceforth be restricted to the empire and Commonwealth.[38]

At this stage no significant uranium deposits had been located in colonial Africa, although Malayan and Nigerian supplies were largely meeting British requirements for thorium.[39] Perhaps encouraged by the discovery of uranium in Niger and Gabon sufficient to meet French domestic needs,[40] British authorities none the less remained convinced that there were uranium deposits to be found in British colonies, although interest by then had become almost exclusively focused on east, central and southern Africa, where it was believed the geology (especially in the Rhodesian copperbelt) seemed most likely to yield deposits. Hence in 1956 a quarter of a million pounds was approved for primary prospecting in these regions; offices were also established in Southern Rhodesia, Tanganyika and Swaziland to be staffed by British geologists as well as technical staff from Harwell.[41]

In return for a variety of forms of assistance and inducement to the discovery of uranium ores in east and central Africa (including the offer of a £25,000 reward),[42] the UK Atomic Energy Authority (AEA) sought to ensure that it would obtain options on any deposits to be discovered. It found a useful ally in the federal government of the Central African Federation, which not only secured control of radioactive minerals from the governments of the constituent territories in the federation, but agreed to use export control (intended to prevent supplies being sold to the Eastern bloc countries and for overriding exchange control reasons) to ensure that until around 1970 any future uranium exports would be sold to the AEA. Similar guarantees were subsequently reached in relation to the East African colonies, Swaziland and British Guiana in 1957, although colonial officials in London objected that in the United Nations trust territory of Tanganyika no preference should be given to British interests and, more generally, that the colonies should not be bound into an arrangement which might prevent them from obtaining a market price.[43]

The AEA's activities represented the last significant interest in the 1950s. By the end of the decade calculations of British and world uranium requirements were being revised, with the result that British authorities no longer prioritised uranium among minerals required for British needs. As a result in 1960 the Central African, East African, British Guianan and Swaziland governments were informed that the AEA was withdrawing from the agreements only recently offered to purchase all uranium exports. In the circumstances it was perhaps fortunate that despite extensive investigations no significant uranium reserves had yet been discovered in the colonial empire (nor indeed in the British Isles), although significant deposits were located in Namibia in 1966.[44]

For a short period the British authorities switched their emphasis towards another mineral, beryl, a silicate of aluminium and beryllium.[45] The existing principal supplies of this mineral were located primarily in South America and India. But Southern Rhodesia, which had begun producing beryllium in 1950, had by 1955 become the world's fourth most important supplier. The British authorities feared nevertheless that this source, mined by the Selection Trust, was in the future likely to yield diminishing returns, and although smaller supplies were also being produced in Uganda, South West Africa, Northern Rhodesia as well as Australia, there was a perceived need for further sources.[46] The new emphasis upon beryl supplies meant that interest in prospecting in the Commonwealth and the colonial empire, and in Africa in particular, was sustained until the end of the decade, but by 1960 revised requirements of beryllium had also led to the closure of some of the AEA offices in Africa and the confinement of interest to the Rhodesias and Uganda.[47]

II

Although the British and colonial governments hoped eventually to secure the interest and collaboration of private enterprise, these prospecting activities were essentially state-led; a reflection of official interest in securing strategic mineral supplies and also the particular difficulties of enlisting private enterprise in the search for minerals for atomic energy programmes which tended by their nature to receive limited publicity.[48] It was anyway difficult to attract sufficient British private investment for prospecting perhaps because of the initial capital outlay required with no guarantee of return and also because of what were frequently regarded as punitive colonial taxation arrangements.[49] Even as it was increasingly acknowledged that the development of colonial mining would continue to depend upon private enterprise, a variety of often conflicting colonial and British government concerns could conspire to circumscribe the offer of local concessionary taxation rates to private enterprise.[50]

The lack of interest frequently exhibited by British investors potentially left the field wide open to American concerns.[51] Indeed mineral prospecting in the 1940s and 1950s was anyway to a considerable extent Anglo-American. British authorities worked in consultation with their American as well as Commonwealth counterparts, and there was a considerable degree of information sharing. Under Article V of the Economic Co-operation Agreement the British government (as well as other European governments) was obliged in return for Marshall Aid to assist the American government in sourcing raw materials once Britain's own needs had been met.[52] As a result the British government by 1949 had used Marshall Aid funds to stimulate production of certain strategic raw materials and had assisted US authorities in their negotiations with the producers of Gold Coast manganese, and South African and colonial exporters of industrial diamonds.[53] The US agencies, disappointed nevertheless that more new projects had not been undertaken, also sent its own team to Africa to investigate further possible opportunities for the development of new mineral industries which visited ten British African territories.[54]

Access to raw materials for application in atomic energy programmes was also one area of notable co-operation between Britain and the United States during what was otherwise a period of diminished collaboration over atomic energy after the US Atomic Energy ('MacMahon') Act passed in 1946 restricted the sharing of information. Indeed the British government was able to negotiate some relaxation of this restriction in part by conceding greater American access to uranium ores from the empire, especially from South Africa, as well as to an increased share from the Belgian Congo,[55] in a period in which until the discovery of new domestic sources the United States remained dependent on external uranium supplies.[56]

However, whether in relation specifically to strategic minerals or to minerals more generally, there was a clearly articulated concern from different quarters of government to ensure that Britain retained some independence in relation to mining. Hence anxiety was expressed at the growing preponderance of North American capital in areas of colonial mining which had traditionally been largely the preserve of British companies. For example, in 1957 Sir Frank Lee, Permanent Secretary at the Board of Trade, writing to his counterpart at the Treasury, Sir Roger Makins, explained that the Board was 'worried about the tendency ... for the control of non-ferrous metals mining in the sterling area Commonwealth and the "underdeveloped countries" to reside less and less in the hands of our own firms and increasingly in those of

American, Canadian, or locally-controlled firms'. He went on to explain that the experience of the Korean War in particular had demonstrated the importance of ensuring in any emergency that either British or what he deemed 'UK-minded firms' controlled a large proportion of British metal supplies.[57]

Comments of this kind pointed to a tension in British policy towards American investment in the colonial empire. In 1950 the British government, unable to satisfy the capital requirements of British colonies, welcomed selective American investment in the empire,[58] so long as it did not impact adversely on the empire-Sterling Area's balance of payments by incurring a liability for the remission of profits and dividends in dollars. This line was reiterated in the early 1950s.[59] In the next few years there were instances where the provision of American investment certainly assisted Britain in extricating itself from difficult situations when it proved unable to supply development capital itself. Thus the interest of an American consortium in developing a hydro-electric dam on the Volta River in the Gold Coast to process aluminium usefully coincided with both declining British interest in sourcing aluminium from the country and a reduced Treasury ability to foot the bill.[60] Yet behind public statements there was a distinct ambivalence towards American investment and prospecting activity. On the one hand officials lamented the difficulties of attracting American capital to the empire.[61] On the other, the Colonial Office accepted only rather reluctantly that they had in official policy statements to respond to interest from the United States in order to 'preserve a co-operative and forward-looking reputation', as well as to assuage concerns emanating from the colonies of those who worried that they were being prevented from benefiting from useful foreign investment capital.[62] As Lee acknowledged, since Britain lacked the resources to develop the entire empire–Commonwealth alone, it had of necessity to accept 'outside' help, but it was crucial that this unfortunate truth did not detract from the 'importance of doing as much as we can ourselves'.[63]

Lee's line of reasoning echoed sentiments which had been expressed by Conservative ministers from the early 1950s, and which were in turn informed by the lobbying activities of British firms and mining associations which argued that they were subject to much greater rates of domestic taxation than American businesses and were consequently disadvantaged even in British colonies (since under double taxation arrangements, companies offset tax paid locally as a credit against home taxation rates).[64] For instance, in December 1951 the new Conservative minister of state at the Colonial Office, Alan Lennox-Boyd, complaining to the Chancellor about British taxation levels, observed that American companies were 'in a more advantageous position than British even when they are operating in our own colonies',[65] and colonial officials noted how recent large-scale mining developments in Nigeria and Jamaica had depended upon foreign investment.[66] Simultaneously other interested departments of government began expressing similar sentiments,[67] while the chair of the AEA feared that in prospecting too the Americans were ahead of the game, with some 500 geologists engaged in government service worldwide to detect for new strategic minerals.[68]

To some degree this desire to uphold British interests reflected a concern with prestige. Some British personnel were anxious that Britain should not be seen to be a second player in the development of new mineral and geological industries. In a paper submitted to the Strategic Minerals Committee, the chief geologist to Britain's atomic energy associations advised that this was the 'primary objective' in relation to a particular research programme, fearing for the country's reputation at a forthcoming scientific meeting at Entebbe when unfavourable comparisons could easily be drawn between the state of British science and that of the Belgians, French and South Africans.[69] More concretely, maintaining British participation in colonial mining was of political significance as Britain sought to demonstrate continued commitment to colonies which were finding it easier to attract foreign, especially American, investment for significant mineral development projects.[70]

The growing assumption of American control in what had hitherto been largely British spheres of activity was also feared likely to have a number of damaging economic consequences. The Board of Trade, for instance, worried that the erosion of British participation in colonial mining could undermine the international reputation of the London Metal Exchange, important because this contributed to British invisible earnings and helped ensure the 'general attractiveness of sterling for strangers'.[71] Concern with metal markets did not always point to British control of the mining industry concerned – but instead to the more indirect advantages which resulted from the location of any industry in a British territory. Hence in 1951 there was some anxiety that the short-term withdrawal of the United States from purchasing Malayan tin as a result of a dispute over pricing might, if it led the Americans to buy from other sources, lead to eventual American domination of the international tin trade and to the closure of the London Tin Market.[72] More generally perhaps British officials were also finding unattractive a world in which Britain no longer had the same leverage over the way in which the markets were organised; if only because of the innate suspicion

British officials seemed to harbour concerning the Americans' ability to handle issues with appropriate sensitivity and political acuity. This was the case, for example, in London's manoeuvring to prevent greater American involvement in the Gold Coast African-won diamond industry lest this undermine a central-selling organisation, the Diamond Corporation, which for a variety of reasons including strategic ones the British government wished to protect.[73]

For the sake of 'our industrial future', the Board of Trade was also keen to protect Britain's position in the development of new industries especially in engineering that depended upon continued access to reliable mineral supplies. Recent developments underlined the potential commercial dangers for Britain if the country were no longer able to shape world metal markets: for example in an ongoing nickel shortage in the mid-1950s British exporters found themselves disadvantaged in comparison to American competitors by Britain's inability to influence the International Nickel Company. Equally, the exercise of some control over overseas mining was also regarded as of commercial importance in other ways: in order to maintain and develop Britain's export trade in mining equipment and stores.[74] Following a visit to South Africa, one leading British geologist reported on talks with various industry, government and scientific personnel, noting that many of those whom he had met 'were concerned and even perturbed' at the hold which American 'vested interests' had obtained in the supply of plant and equipment to the uranium industry. 'It is quite apparent', he informed the Strategic Minerals Committee, 'that we must do better if we are to compete'.[75]

Much of the interest in colonial mining in the 1950s derived, as we have seen, not just from the industry's perceived importance to the British economy, but from its significance from a defence perspective. In this respect too, although the British authorities worked in liaison with their American counterparts in seeking out and developing new resources of strategic minerals, they were none the less keen to retain some independence of action. In 1952, for example, it was agreed that an effort should be made to interest British companies in the development of Nigerian pyrochlore deposits as a source of uranium before official contact be made with the American authorities about its prospects. Simultaneously the AEA was to be informed that persuading a British mining house to undertake the development work was the 'only chance' of retaining this source of uranium 'within our own hands', with fears that if the American government were convinced that British enterprise were not up to the task the Americans would 'apply irresistible pressure to be allowed to exploit the deposit themselves ...'.[76] Similarly, in 1952, the Strategic Minerals Committee recorded its preference that arrangements be made by the Ministry of Supply for the purchase of uranium from Northern Rhodesia in such a way that it could protect the colony's production of the mineral as 'a source of uranium under our own control'.[77]

Behind this concern lay the fact that Britain had agreed to share all uranium found outside the United Kingdom or the colonies with the Americans. For Britain it was therefore especially valuable to find domestic or colonial sources both to boost domestic supplies and with which to bargain with the United States.[78] Moreover, the British government had already had its fingers burned with the Americans assuming the lead role in negotiations with the Australian and South African governments over uranium – despite the fact that under the terms of the agreement with the United States Britain had been allocated responsibility for the detection of new supplies in the Commonwealth.[79] Tensions over uranium supplies were all the worse for American reluctance to see the location of supplies on British soil primarily as a result of concerns about security in Britain.[80]

III

The possession of the colonial empire was, then, crucial to British plans for sourcing strategic minerals for industrial, defence and energy purposes. The African colonies especially were clearly regarded by British scientific and governmental authorities as a field in which they could undertake exploratory work in much the same way as they were doing in the British Isles so long as the permission of the necessary authorities had been obtained – and for the 1950s this for the most part meant liaison with administrations still largely comprised of British officials. This did not mean complete unanimity among British agencies in approaches to colonial mining. At the very least there was tension between the Colonial Office, colonial administrations and other British interests (with one senior colonial official deeming the Defence Advisory Committee shortly before its first meeting 'a lot of nonsense').[81] The proprietorial stance that the AEA appeared to adopt in relation to colonial radioactive minerals and the 'wholly unacceptable' views its top brass sometimes exhibited proved especially irksome to a Colonial Office concerned also to protect the economic interests of the colonies.[82] Nevertheless the colonial governments and the Colonial Office shared a vested interest in the successful identification of new mineral resources that could be exploited commercially and in the maintenance of existing industries in order to assist the economic development of the territories concerned. Because the Colonial Office was also responsible for engaging technical and scientific personnel to the relevant branches of the Colonial Service and (since there was little or no academic training in geology in colonial universities) geologists were generally recruited to colonial government positions from British or other Commonwealth universities, scientific personnel in the colonies were also either British or under the general supervision of the British government.[83]

In view of the relative freedom which the colonial empire offered to investigate and source supplies from within the Sterling Area and the opportunity to access resources under effective British control, it is perplexing that there was relatively little comment in the deliberations and correspondence of the various committees investigating colonial mineral resources on the likelihood of colonial political change. Indeed only very rarely was any comment made other than by Colonial Office personnel. The observation made in 1954 by Britain's chief geologist in relation to a proposal to establish a local office of the AEA on the Rhodesian copperbelt, that Northern Rhodesia was not only a promising source of uranium, but that 'local conditions are more stable in the C[entral] A[frican] F[ederation] than in most colonial territories', is consequently one rare example of political reflection.[84]

The apparent absence of political observation may have reflected the increasing focus on the mineral resources of the east and central African territories, where the Colonial Office's own estimates of when the transfers of power would take place remained highly conservative. Hence when questioned by the AEA about the prospects for the political stability of Tanganyika and Uganda up to around 1970, the Colonial Office was 'able to reassure them sufficiently on this point'.[85] Notwithstanding the Colonial Office's own complacency, some significance must also be attached to the fact that the Colonial Office was only represented on some of the relevant committees. But it can also be suggested that the lack of consideration given by those outside the specialist departments to the momentum for change in the dependent empire reflects more than the lack of 'joined up' government or the Colonial Office's own very conservative projected timetables for further transfers of power. Indeed as historians turn to investigating the cultural and social impact of end of empire in British society, it becomes apparent that the persistence of an 'imperial culture' into the 1950s reflected contemporaries' ignorance of colonial and international realities, and the distinction which was surely drawn between the empire already lost in India and other empires in Africa and elsewhere.[86] As Darwin and others have commented, the Commonwealth model also served to massage hopes of sustained British influence after the end of empire and of 'post-imperial' co-operation;[87] the establishment of machinery to facilitate liaison over mineral resources issues between independent Commonwealth countries which included representatives of the colonies providing a pertinent example.

It was only at the very end of the 1950s that this complacency was shaken. By 1960 the Advisory Committee on Overseas Geological and Mineral Resources confronted the disappointing news that the British 'directorate' was finding it hard to persuade newly independent former colonies to accept the continued use of its services especially now that it was competing with other governments offering similar facilities on 'generous terms'. The creation in 1961 of the new Department of Technical Co-operation – which assumed responsibility from the Colonial Office for the Directorate of the Colonial (now Overseas) Geological Survey – represented one way in which the United Kingdom hoped to address this and other similar problems.[88]

If there was strikingly little discussion of the impact of future political change on British mineral interests in the colonial empire, there was certainly no question that concerns about colonial mining and access to colonial mineral resources might in any way inform the process of constitutional change in the empire in general. In this respect the findings presented here bear out conclusions others have also reached.[89] It is hardly surprising that this was the case. Realistically there was little that the British government could do to manipulate the transfers of power to protect access to colonial resources without jeopardising the more important policy aims of building good relationships with their post-colonial successors and of addressing international criticisms of British colonial policy.

But while the British government was generally unwilling or unable to intervene in the course of political devolution of individual colonies, it did initiate measures to assist mining interests in British colonies in the 1950s in coping if not with constitutional change then at least with the shifting economic relationships which were equally part and parcel of the whole 'decolonisation' process. These initiatives need to be seen within the context of the great interest in the 1950s in discovering new colonial mineral resources.

The first such initiative addressed the particular risks which mining companies faced of appropriation and nationalisation. It was informed by the Iranian government's nationalisation of the Anglo-Iranian Oil Company in 1951, but also followed discussion of the pros and cons of nationalisation in the Gold Coast. In what was the most significant innovation in colonial mining policy since the Fabian-inspired memorandum of 1946, the Secretary of State for the Colonies Oliver Lyttelton recommended in 1952 that where major new concessions were under negotiation colonial governments consider either public or private equity participation in the enterprise in order to effect a 'community of interest' between mining firms and colonial governments and people.[90] For the most part the proposal was well-received by colonial governments, although in some territories where mineral rights were not vested in the state, and government was consequently not the principal party in negotiations, there were only limited opportunities for acting on Lyttelton's suggestion.[91]

In the 1950s economic nationalism was less of a problem in the colonial empire, where nationalists were not only often relatively conservative at least in relation to economic issues but also focused on attaining political freedoms. Arguably more problematic at least in the 1950s was the displacement of British capital by other foreign concerns, especially American; a risk which arose not only from post-war British economic weakness, but also from the growing Anglo-American partnership in British Africa and from the gradual dismantling of controls which had hitherto circumscribed American economic penetration of the colonies.[92] As we have seen officials from a variety of government departments as well as from different business associations had since the early 1950s expressed anxiety about just this threat to British mining interests. As a result a series of minor alterations were made to British regulations governing the taxation of mining companies operating overseas and, most importantly, a major innovation in the British taxation code was introduced in 1957. The introduction for taxation purposes of 'overseas trade corporations' (whose undistributed profits would be exempt from British taxation, and whose management and control could be exercised from the United Kingdom but whose other activities would take place overseas) represented a major change in the fiscal context in which British companies in the colonial empire and elsewhere overseas operated.[93] It was intended among other purposes to assist colonial governments struggling to attract investment capital, but it was above all an attempt to improve the British position in colonial mining. In this respect it also constituted an acknowledgement that the British system of taxation had been sufficiently punitive as to disadvantage British interests overseas in comparison to both locally registered and foreign businesses. A significant change to British taxation, the new scheme was introduced in the face of ongoing Treasury concerns about its effects on Britain's balance of payments and underscores the importance attached to continued access to colonial resources and to British mining interests at this time.[94]

IV

Hence in many respects the 1950s were if not exactly a time of imperial revival at least one of some continuity. Although it is hard to resist the conclusion that in absolute terms the empire was of diminishing economic importance to Britain, there was no 'retreat' in British interest in the resources the empire had to offer – even if this interest, which had once extended to a wide range of colonial commodities, now coalesced more exclusively around deposits of strategic minerals. Indeed, as the Cold War developed and Britain embraced the nuclear age, the mineral resources of the colonial empire assumed a new importance in the mind of British officialdom. This study consequently provides one example of how empire remained central to British economic and strategic planning in the 1950s. It demonstrates how the colonies were deemed crucial to Britain's bid to become a nuclear power, even as ironically it was nuclear capability rather than empire that came increasingly to denote 'superpower' status. Furthermore British governmental and scientific agencies in looking to the colonial empire to support Britain's atomic defence programme showed little acknowledgement that the empire was on any rapid path to dissolution. Indeed the history of the colonial geological surveys provides one illustration of continued and even enhanced integration of empire and metropole: between 1947 and 1956 the scientists recruited to meet the expanding needs of the colonial surveys accounted each year for between one quarter and one half of all British geology graduates.[95]

But the writing was on the wall for those willing to read it. Among other difficulties for British planners was the fact that British business often proved reluctant to be co-opted into new schemes for mineral development. Evidence discussed elsewhere in this volume suggests that especially in the more 'politically advanced' West African colonies the rapid transition to African self-government had shaken the confidence of some mining concerns,[96] and, even where constitutional change was more limited, investors all too often fought shy of uncertain returns and what were perceived as punitive taxation regimes. British governments and business also found themselves snared by the wider geopolitical and economic shifts of the 'decolonisation' period. In the sourcing of uranium and the development of nuclear weaponry Britain was forced to work at best in partnership with the United States and by the end of the 1950s Britain had abandoned its ambition for the establishment of an independent nuclear deterrent. Moreover, the transition to multilateralism and the relaxation of controls which occurred during this period eased the path of American economic penetration of the colonial empire. British officials acknowledged that by reason of both political and financial reality they had little choice but to accept this development, yet it sparked anxiety on account of the economic and strategic imperatives discussed earlier – and, in a bid to improve the competitiveness of British business in comparison to other foreign firms, it provoked reform of the fiscal environment in which British firms overseas operated.

Ultimately, hopes invested in colonial resources belied reality: for all their activities, British geologists failed to discover significant new deposits of minerals for application in atomic energy programmes. Even so, ten years later Africa was the principal source of many of the world's most important minerals; Britain in 1970 remained almost entirely dependent upon Africa for supplies of copper, chromium, manganese, bauxite and plutonium. Namibian uranium mined by Rio Tinto Zinc constituted the third most important British source of uranium.[97]

By 1960 British and American interest in the particular minerals which had excited so much activity was waning. Yet throughout the 1950s the colonial empire especially in Africa had once again been the focus of intense hopes and planning. This was surely the very last attempt to develop what Joseph Chamberlain had famously described during the late nineteenth-century European 'scramble' for Africa as the 'great estate'.

Notes

1. Cripps to the African Governors' Conference, 12 November 1947, CO 852/989/3, reproduced in A.N. Porter and A.J. Stockwell, (eds), *British Imperial Policy and Decolonization 1938–1964*, 2 vols (Basingstoke: 1987), vol. 1, p. 280.
2. D.A. Low and A. Smith (eds), *History of East Africa*, 3 vols (Oxford: 1976), vol. 3, introduction.
3. See, especially, A. Hinds, *Britain's Sterling Colonial Policy and Decolonization, 1939–1958* (Westport, CT: 2001); and G. Krozewski, *Money and the End of Empire: British Economic Policy and the Colonies, 1947–1953* (Basingstoke: 2001).
4. C. Feinstein, 'The end of empire and the golden age', in P. Clarke and C. Trebilcock (eds), *Understanding Decline: Perceptions and Realities of Britain's Economic Performance. Essays in Honour of Barry Supple* (Cambridge: 1997), pp. 212–33.

5. See, for example, A. Schonfield, *British Economic Policy Since the War* (London: 1958). For a review of other literature on this theme, see J. Tomlinson, 'The decline of the empire and the economic "Decline" of Britain', *20th Century British History*, 14 (2003), 201–21.
6. C. Schenk, *Britain and the Sterling Area from Devaluation to Convertibility in the 1950s* (London: 1994).
7. N.J. White, 'The business and the politics of decolonization: the British experience in the twentieth century', *Economic History Review* LIII (2000), pp. 544–64.
8. S.E. Stockwell, 'Trade, empire, and the fiscal context of imperial business during decolonization', *Economic History Review* LVII, no. 1 (2004), 142–60; S.E. Stockwell, *The Business of Decolonization: British Business Strategies in the Gold Coast* (Oxford: 2000), pp. 217–22; N. White, 'The survival, revival and decline of British economic influence in Malaysia, 1957–1970', *20th Century British History*, 14 (2003), 222–42.
9. See, for example, R. Hyam and R. Louis (eds), *the Conservative Government and the End of Empire 1957–1964* (British Documents on the End of Empire, Series A. Volume 4, London, 2000), 2 parts, part 1, p. lxii and document 304; S.E. Stockwell, 'Instilling the "Sterling Tradition": decolonization and the creation of a Central Bank in Ghana', *Journal of Imperial and Commonwealth History*, 26 (1998), 100–19; S. Smith, ' "A vulnerable point in the Sterling Area": Kuwait in the 1950s', *Contemporary British History*, 17 (2003), 25–42.
10. See, for example, A. May, 'Commonwealth or Europe? Macmillan's dilemma, 1961–63' in A. May (ed.), *Britain, the Commonwealth and Europe: The Commonwealth and Britain's Applications to join the European Communities*, (Basingstoke: 2001), pp. 82–110.
11. Tomlinson, 'Decline of the empire'.
12. This is the case, for example, with D.J. Morgan, *The Official History of Colonial Development*, 5 vols (London: 1980). The publication of L.J. Butler's forthcoming book on copper mining in central Africa should begin to redress this imbalance.
13. Stockwell, *Business*, pp. 197–203.
14. See, for example, N[ational] A[rchives], Kew, London], CO 852/939/3, minute by A. A. Morris, 26 November 1947, on the slow progress of the Minerals and Metals Panel.
15. Stockwell, *Business*, chap. 7.
16. NA, CO 537/7078, no. 4, 'US Strategic Stockpiling', paper by M. McDougall, 8 August 1951.
17. G. Lanning with M. Mueller, *Africa Undermined: A History of the Mining Companies and the Underdevelopment of Africa* (London: 1979), p. 87.
18. NA, CO 1001/3, no 38, 'Progress Report for the Ten Years 1947–1956', paras. 11–52, para 86; CO 1001/4, no. 20, 'Progress Report 1959–1960'. The surveys fulfilled other functions in addition to prospecting.
19. Initially based in the Imperial Institute, the directorate came under the more immediate control of the CO when in April 1949 the CO assumed responsibility for the Mineral Resources Department of the Institute: *ibid.*
20. It comprised representatives from the CO, industry, the Geological Survey, and academia. See NA, CO 1001/1–4 for the papers of this committee.

21. To meet every three years to facilitate co-operation between Commonwealth countries.
22. NA, CO 537/7056, minutes of the first meeting of the DAC, 22 August 1951.
23. See NA, AB [records of the Atomic Energy Authority] 16/1587, minutes of first meeting of SMC, 24 November 1947.
24. On thorium, see M. Gowing, *Independence and Deterrence: Britain and Atomic Energy 1945–1952*, 2 vols (London, 1974), vol. 1, p. 357.
25. See NA, CAB 126/117 (for colonies) and CAB 126/99 (for dominions).
26. L. Freedman, *Britain and Nuclear Weapons* (London: 1980), pp. 2–4. For adoption of a nuclear strategy, see I. Clark and N. Wheeler, *The British Origins of Nuclear Strategy 1945–1955* (Oxford: 1989).
27. N. Moss, *The Politics of Uranium* (London: 1981), pp. 30–2.
28. Gordon Dean, former chairman of the US Atomic Energy Commission, 'Report on the Atom' quoted in Moss, *Politics*, 27.
29. A. Pierre, *Nuclear Politics: The British Experience with an Independent Strategic Force 1939–1970* (London: 1972), p. 128. Gowing, *Independence*, vol. 1, pp. 358–88.
30. NA, D[ominions] O[ffice] 35/8304, draft note on uranium supplies (c.1960); CO 1026/263, circular telegram to colonial governments, 1 March 1949.
31. NA, CO 1026/263, circular telegram to colonial governments, 1 March 1949.
32. NA, AB 16/1285, paper attached to SMC 36, 'Draft revision of the terms offered for uranium ores and concentrates', n.d. [1951].
33. NA, AB 16/1918, Paper SMC 23, 'Uranium Supply and Demand', circulated 8 Feburary 1950.
34. NA, AB 16/569, 'A proposal for the investigation of certain low grade uranium deposits in the colonies', submitted by SMC, 15 May 1950, to the AEA.
35. See NA, AB 16/1285, 'Some notes on an African tour 1951', C.F. Davidson.
36. NA, AB 16/1494, minutes of 3rd meeting RMR&DC, 21 April 1955.
37. NA, AB 16/1410, notes of a meeting between representatives of UK AEA and British Geological Survey, 2 May 1955.
38. Gowing, *Independence*, p. 391.
39. NA, CO 927/585, no. 52, draft reply to parliamentary question tabled by Hector Hughes (1956).
40. Moss, *Politics*, p. 29.
41. NA, AB 16/1494, 8th meeting RMR&DC, 15 May 1956, item 7; NA, AB 16/1410, notes of meeting between representatives of UK AEA and British Geological Survey, 2 May 1955; NA, AB 12/372, RMR&DC paper 50 (1957).
42. NA, CO 927/585, paper E 33, 1 June 1956.
43. NA, CO 927/585, L.E.T. Storar, UK High Commission, Salisbury, to Mark Annan, 4 Aug. 1956; minute by H.A. Harding, CO, 11 February 1956; minute by J.M. Kisch, 16 May 1950, about a meeting with representatives of UK AEA.
44. NA, DO 35/8304, no. 69 telegram to govts. of Kenya, Uganda, Tanganyika, and British Guiana, 13 March 1960, and at no. 62, to govts of N. Rhodesia and Nyasaland, 10 March 1960; AB 16/2489 correspondence relating to withdrawal of offer to CAF. For Namibia, see Moss, *Politics*, p. 29.
45. NA, AB6/2119, E.J.S. Clarke to J.M. Fletcher, Atomic Energy Research Establishment, 14 October 1958.
46. In 1955 Brazil produced 1820 long tons, Argentina 1250, India 1000, S. Rhodesia 963, Mozambique 960 and the USA an estimated 580: NA, AB 12/372, RMR&DC paper 47, 'Some additional notes on the occurrence of

Beryllium and Bismuth'; see also AB 12/372, RMR&DC paper 65, note by Beryl working party, October 1957.

47. NA, AB 12/412, RMR & DC, paper 50, July 1958; DO 35/8304, no. 19.
48. Cited as a problem in NA, CO 1036/263, circular telegram 1 March 1949.
49. See, for example, NA, AB 16/1002, annual report, SMC, 1952.
50. Including fear of local political opposition and the risk of encouraging companies to accelerate production leading to rapid exhaustion of mineral deposits.
51. Hence, for example, the official encouragement initially given to an American prospector interested in ores in Swaziland and Bechuanaland. NA, DO 35/4471, correspondence 1952–55, and DO 35/8303, minute by G. Cumber, 15 Feburary 1956.
52. In addition Article IV provided for the establishment of a 'special account' into which the British government was required to pay the sterling equivalent of a special grant made by the United States to Britain, of which 5 percent was to be available to the US government for its own expenditure in the United Kingdom and the colonies.
53. NA, CO 537/5153, no. 39, 'US Stockpiling and the colonies', n.d. but *c*.Febuary/March 1949.
54. NA, CO 537/5153, no. 51, Geoffrey Wilson, Cabinet Office, to Sir G Clauson, 16 June 1949; no. 54, minutes by Clauson, Gorsuch, Wallace and Cohen 17–18 June 1949; and no. 71, copy of telegram Sir O. Franks to the FO, 16 August 1949.
55. It was only from 1954 that significant changes began to be made to the MacMahon Act. J. Baylis, *Anglo-American Defence Relations 1939–1984*, 2nd edn (New York: 1984), 30–5, 42–3; Pierre, *Nuclear Politics*, pp. 128–33.
56. J. Simpson, *The Independent Nuclear State: The United States, Britain, and the Military Atom*, 2nd edn (London: 1986), p. 86.
57. NA, B[oard of] T[rade] 213/73, no. 25, Sir F. Lee to Sir R Makins, 21 January 1957.
58. NA, CO 852/1347/2, statement, 28 June 1950.
59. See NA, CO 852/1347, no. 79A, circular savingram to colonial governments, 19 May 1950; CO 852/1418, no. 58, circular savingram to colonial governments, 15 August 1953.
60. See Stockwell, *Business*, pp. 215–17.
61. See NA, CO 537/7358, no. 38, M.T. Flett to E. Melville, 30 June 1952, and CO 537/7844, no. 155, A. Emmanuel to E. Melville, 12 June 1952, reproduced in D. Goldsworthy (ed.), *The Conservative Government and the End of Empire 1951–1957* (British Documents on the End of Empire, Series A, Volume 3, London, 1994), part 3, documents 402 and 404.
62. NA, CO 537/7844, minute by Mr Wood, 15 July 1952.
63. NA, BT 213/73, no. 25, Lee to Makins, 21 January 1957.
64. For example the British Overseas Mining Association, the Gold Coast Chamber of Mines, and the West Africa Committee, all of which complained about the effects of what they regarded as a punitive British taxation system: Stockwell, 'Fiscal Context'.
65. NA, CO 537/7762, no. 15A, A. Lennox-Boyd to R. A. Butler, 3 December 1951.
66. NA, CO 537/7762, no. 14, minute by Harding addressed to Bourdillon, 2 November 1951.
67. NA, CO 537/7762, no. 17, Lord Swinton to Butler, 1 January 1952.

68. NA, EG [Dept. of Energy] 1/38, no. E63, Lord Cherwell to O. Lyttelton, 25 July 1952.
69. NA, AB 16/1279, 'British research in geochronology', paper by C.F. Davidson, 28 April 1954.
70. See for example, NA, T[reasury] 236/4366, no. 29, 'Note on certain aspects of the UK and US policies for the taxation of overseas profits as they affect industrial development in the British Caribbean Territories', 6 October 1955, paper produced by the Jamaican government and circulated by the CO to the interdepartmental working party on the taxation of overseas profits.
71. NA, BT 213/73, no. 25, Lee to Makins, 21 January 1957. The 'Exchange' was referred to as 'Market'.
72. NA, CO 537/7064, minute by H.M. Harding, 27 September 1951, and nos 382 and 384 telegrams to the governments of Singapore and the Federation of Malaya.
73. NA, CO 537/6635, no. 14A, CO to Gold Coast govt., 2 February 1950.
74. NA, BT 213/73, no. 25, Lee to Makins, 21 Janurary 1957.
75. NA, AB 16/1279, 'Report on a visit to South Africa, Dr Dennis Taylor, 24–31 January 1954.
76. NA, AB 16/1279, 'Note of a meeting to discuss the development of pyrochlore deposits', 22 August. 1952.
77. NA, AB 16/1279, minutes of the 27th meeting of the SMC, 8 September 1952, section IV.
78. NA, EG 1/38, no. 63, Cherwell to Lyttelton, 25 July 1952.
79. Gowing, *Independence*, vol. 1, pp. 374–88. Gowing attributes this in part to ignorance on the part of the Australian and South African governments as to the existence of the Anglo-American agreement, and also to the inclination of the Australians by this stage to deal with the United States in matters of defence rather than the United Kingdom. Ironically Britain took more of a lead in negotiations with a 'third' country, Portugal.
80. Pierre, *Nuclear Politics*, pp. 130–1.
81. NA, CO 537/7056, minute by C. Eastwood, July 1951.
82. NA, CO 927/585, L.E.T. Storar, UK High Commission, Salisbury, to Mark Annan, 4 August 1956; minute by H.A. Harding, CO, 11 February 1956; minute by J.M. Kisch, 16 May 1950, about a meeting with representatives of the UK AEA.
83. See NA, CO 537/7564, minute by E.S. Willbourn, 14 December 1951.
84. NA, AB 12/214, 'Proposal that the AEA should establish a Raw Materials (Exploration) Office in the Rhodesian Copperbelt' C.F. Davidson, 10 December 1954.
85. NA, CO 927/585, minute of a meeting 11 May 1956 with representatives of the AEA by J.M. Kisch, 16 May 1956.
86. See. for example, J. Mackenzie, 'The persistence of empire in metropolitan culture', in S. Ward (ed.), *British Culture and the End of Empire* (Manchester: 1991), pp. 21–36.
87. J. Darwin, 'Decolonization and the end of empire', in R. Winks (ed.), *The Oxford History of the British Empire*, vol. 5, *Historiography* (Oxford: 1999), p. 547.
88. NA, CO 1001/1, minutes of the Advisory Committee 12 November 1960; CO 1001/4, no. 37, note on the Department of Technical Co-operation, 11 April 1961.

89. See for example, H. Brasted, C. Bridge and J. Kent, 'Cold War, informal empire and the transfer of power: some "Paradoxes of British Decolonisation Resolved"?', in M. Dockrill (ed.), *Europe Within the Global System 1938–1960* (Bochum: 1995), pp. 11–30.

90. Stockwell, *Business*, pp. 213–14.

91. This was the case, for example, in the Gold Coast where mineral rights were vested in the stools and in Northern Rhodesia where mineral rights were owned by the British South Africa Company: see correspondence on NA, CO 537/7726.

92. On American under-pinning of post-war British imperial power, see W.R. Louis and R. Robinson, 'The imperialism of decolonization', *Journal of Imperial And Commonwealth History*, 22 (1994), 462–511.

93. The scheme excluded exports and invisible income from shipping and financial services.

94. See Stockwell, 'Fiscal Context'. The scheme was abolished in 1965; the introduction of a new corporation tax had anyway changed the context in which it had operated.

95. NA, CO 1001/3, 'Progress Report for Ten Years 1947–1956', para. 88.

96. See Stockwell, *Business*, chaps. 4 and 6, and White's chapter in this book, esp. pp. 105–106.

97. Lanning with Mueller, *Africa Undermined*, tables 5 and 9, 100–1, 112–13; 286; table 33, 398.

5
Decolonisation in the 1950s: The Version According to British Business

Nicholas J. White

As a market for British manufactures and as a means of propping up the exchange value of sterling, the empire–Commonwealth was highly prized by Conservative governments throughout the 1950s. Indeed, in June 1952, the Minister of Housing and Local Government, Harold Macmillan, advocated intensified imperial economic integration to halt the 'slide into a shoddy and slushy Socialism'.[1] With his accession to the premiership following the Suez fiasco of 1956, Macmillan was apparently eager to liberate Britain from the colonial shackle and embrace the multilateral global economy as swiftly as possible.[2] Yet, there remains a danger of exaggerating the degree to which Tory governments 'disengaged' from colonial and Commonwealth responsibilities in the later 1950s. Even after 1959 and the 'wind of change', Macmillan's dreams of maintaining British global sway in a streamlined, multiracial Commonwealth did not dissipate.[3] Indicative of the significance still attached to post-colonial economic linkages was a growing concern about the supplanting of overtaxed British firms in the colonies by US business interests. Hence, the Finance Act of 1957 gave birth to Overseas Trade Corporations, exempted from UK income tax on undistributed profits.[4]

This official sensitivity towards the plight of late-imperial business might support John MacKenzie's assertion that 'capitalism' was the empire's *'raison d'être'*. The personnel that 'made it work' were neither politicians nor bureaucrats but '[c]apitalists ... whether in the metropolis or scattered around the empire'.[5] How, then, did these alleged lynchpins of colonialism regard the state of the macro-imperial enterprise in the 1950s? To what extent did British businesses embrace the official rhetoric of imperial revival?

The case for revival

A glance at the statistics for UK overseas trade and investment would appear to support the case for imperial consolidation: in 1955–59, 45 per cent of British imports were still derived from the empire–Commonwealth, while some 51 per cent of British exports were destined for current and former dependencies. The corresponding figures for 20 years earlier were 39.5 and 49 per cent respectively. In the five years before the Second World War, roughly half of British capital exports went to the empire–Commonwealth; in 1950–54, this figure had leapt to 65 per cent, and still stood at 60 per cent at the beginning of the 1960s.[6] Commonwealth preferential tariffs were certainly much cherished by the UK's electrical engineering industry. The Chairman of English Electric, George Nelson, told sharcholders in 1957 that: 'We as a company have derived great benefit from Commonwealth orders.' Moreover, Nelson was 'thinking in wider terms' about 'the great economic resources developed and still to be developed in the Commonwealth' which could well 'provide an economic trading entity comparable with ... the USA, Europe and in the future, Soviet Russia and China.'[7]

Empire–Commonwealth consumption was also expanding given HMG's ongoing enthusiasm for colonial development. Despite Labour's brief flirtation with the colonial state as the chief agent of economic growth, by the end of the 1940s modernisation overseas came to be viewed as a partnership between public and private capital. The crusade to earn and save dollars, and the limited public resources available in the colonies, made British private enterprises central to integrated Sterling Area development. In November 1951, the new Tory Colonial Secretary of State, Oliver Lyttelton, confirmed that the Colonial Development Corporation (CDC) would confine itself to providing pump-priming, start-up capital.[8] Indeed, given Britain's ongoing balance of payments problems, the Conservatives continued Labour's policy of developing colonial resources 'on the cheap'. Moreover, ministers who were potentially far more sympathetic towards British overseas companies now supervised policy. Lyttelton was an imperial businessman by profession. Through his pre-war employment with the British Metal Corporation, and his wartime role as Minister of Production, the old Etonian had close links to the leaders of the post-war imperial mining fraternity.[9]

Meanwhile, Lyttelton's successor in 1954, Alan Lennox-Boyd, had previously chaired the Parliamentary Committee of the protectionist Empire Industries Association and was linked through marriage to the Anglo-Irish brewing giant, Guinness.[10]

The stress on private-sector-led development was certainly embraced by the directors of British Guiana's sugar, shipping and shop-keeping conglomerate, Booker McConnell, and particularly by Jock Campbell, Booker's chairman after 1952. There was a massive expansion of 'social services' – community centres, large-scale housing development and hospital facilities – on the Booker plantations during the 1950s. This social investment was underpinned by the near doubling of Booker's sugar production in British Guiana in the decade after 1950. Meanwhile, in 1954, Booker began a programme of factory improvement and consolidation to further boost productivity – a level of re-investment running at £3.5 million in 1957.[11] In central Africa, the copper-mining magnate, Ronald Prain, also sought to identify with the Colonial Office (CO)'s commitment to economic development through the provision of £3 million in loans from the Rhodesian Selection Trust (RST) to both Northern Rhodesia and Nyasaland. This was not an entirely altruistic move, since this 'aid' was 'tied' to the rural areas from where the Zambian copper-belt derived its principal labour supply. Moreover, such largesse was reflective of RST's own good fortune. Seven years after the inauguration of the Central African Federation (CAF) in 1953, copper output had increased by 50 per cent.[12]

Outside of formal empire, in the British-protected Persian Gulf, there were also burgeoning opportunities for British mineral extractors. For the Anglo-Iranian Oil Company (AIOC) the opening up of the Kuwait fields more than compensated the losses at Abadan, following the Iranian nationalisation of May 1951. AIOC held a 50 per cent share in the Kuwait Oil Company, which secured its place in the Emirate through a profit sharing agreement with Sheikh Abdullah six months later. Over the following decade, annual oil production expanded three-fold. The multiplier effects of vastly inflated oil wealth also benefited the 'big five' British construction companies in Kuwait. An ambitious five-year development plan after 1952 envisaged expenditure of over £90 million, and the 'big five' picked up many of these projects on a highly lucrative 'cost plus 15 per cent' basis.[13]

Another ascendant primary commodity, increasingly exploited by British conglomerates in the 1950s, was Southeast Asian timber. Wallace Brothers, and its associated firm, the Bombay Burmah Trading Corporation (BBTC), responded to nationalisation of the teak forests in

Burma by relocating into the jungles of North Borneo. By 1960, Wallace/BBTC found that Borneo hardwoods exceeded the volume of logs shipped from Rangoon and Bangkok before the Pacific War. This followed the liberalisation of the old Chartered Company concessions after 1952, a low-tax regime on the part of the new colonial government in Jesselton, the introduction of mechanised extraction techniques and the exponential growth of the demand for timber in Japan.[14] On top of the expansion of rubber, oil palm and cocoa on British-owned plantations, the logging companies contributed to a noteworthy export boom in late 1950s Sabah. Indeed, Governor Turnbull confessed in 1959 that the colony was 'being crowded out with so many propositions [from British companies] that the administration is finding it impossible to accom-modate them all'.[15] British trading companies based in Hong Kong, notably Jardine Matheson, would also reap rewards from North Borneo's prosperity because they marketed the colony's timber in Japan. A share issue on the Hong Kong Stock Exchange by Jardines was oversubscribed by 56 times in 1961, reflecting the huge growth of the firm during the 1950s. Indeed, stable colonial administration, free exchange markets, the evacuation of Shanghai entrepreneurship and capital (as well as overseas Chinese equivalents from Southeast Asia), and the colony's growing role as Communist Beijing's 'window on the West', allowed Hong Kong to re-invent itself as an international financial and manu-facturing centre in the course of the 1950s. At the pinnacle of Hong Kong's buoyant economy was the Hongkong and Shanghai Banking Corporation (HSBC), which was fast emerging as one of the world's largest financial institutions through the purchase of the Mercantile Bank of India and the British Bank of the Middle East at the end of the decade.[16]

It was not merely in East Asia that colonial economic development proved a boon for the growth of the British overseas banks. In Ghana, between 1952 and 1962, the branches of the Bank of British West Africa (BBWA) and Barclays Bank (Dominion, Colonial and Overseas) increased from 15 to 54 and 12 to 60 respectively.[17] Moreover, the Barclays Overseas Development Corporation (BODC), formed in 1946, proved itself a far more successful agent of modernisation than the colonial state. There was a remarkable expansion in Barclays's lending in Africa and the West Indies during the 1950s: by 1958, BODC had lent and invested over £18 million. BBWA chose not to set up a development sub-sidiary, but instead entered the field of medium- and long-term finance directly – focusing its largesse on Ghanaian and Nigerian government projects.[18]

British firms were also contributing to the consolidation of the Sterling Area through strategies of pan-Commonwealth investment. Booker arrived in central Africa as early as 1939 with the takeover of the retailing and distribution business of Curtis Campbell. In the early 1950s, the shops in Northern Rhodesia thrived thanks to the copper boom, and in 1954 a new department store in Ndola was acquired.[19] Indeed, a number of British investment groups were attracted to 'settler' Africa in the 1950s. The Hong-Kong centred, Dodwell & Co., began importing office equipment and also moved into retail stores. Wallaces and its great rival in Burma, Steel Brothers, made trading and other investments in East Africa from the 1950s. The India specialists, James Finlay & Co., diversified into East African import, manufacturing and distribution businesses after 1951.[20] Likewise, the premiere Malayan agency house, Guthrie & Co., purchased an agricultural and building equipment supply firm in Southern Rhodesia in 1951. With the opening of an Australian office in 1953, Guthries increasingly portrayed itself as a pan-Commonwealth enterprise.[21]

In Africa, however, new opportunities at the end of formal empire for the trading companies did not confine themselves to settler-dominated colonies and dominions. During the late-1940s, British firms had withdrawn from 'general trading' and the produce trade in West Africa, following the formation of state-run marketing boards, as well as the Gold Coast disturbances. Nevertheless, new profitable business arose in specialist trading, as economic growth conjured up an increasingly sophisticated middle-class African consumer. Here was a phenomenon most notable in motor distribution. By the late 1950s, the Unilever subsidiary, the United Africa Company (UAC), was the largest importer and part-assembler of motor vehicles in Nigeria.[22] As the UAC example suggests, a symbiosis was developing between the investment needs of British multinational enterprises (MNEs), on the one hand, and the economic nationalism of decolonising regimes, on the other, in the creation of import-substitution industrialisation (ISI). The exemplar was the planning of Unilever's soap production in Ghana throughout the 1950s, which finally came to fruition in 1963. As Clarence Smith has claimed: 'The tariff protection and import controls promised by African nationalists opened up new vistas of safe and profitable industrialization ... [H]owever badly West African countries did after independence at the macro-economic level ... individual British firms often did quite well.'[23] It would prove to be UK MNEs, in partnership with the ubiquitous agency houses, which emerged as the leading investors in mainland Malaya's pioneer industries after 1958.[24] Even for those 'metropolitan'-based firms which did not leap over tariff barriers to engage in local, Commonwealth manufacturing, the 'closed economy' of the post-colonial era was not necessarily an objectionable prospect. The chairman of English Electric was again bullish. In the short-term, the development of secondary industries in Ghana or Malaya might reduce markets for certain goods. But, in the long-term, ISI in the new Commonwealth could stimulate UK exports of both capital and consumer goods:

> With the growth of factories [come] demands for factory machinery ... But the growth of local industries ... also [leads] to the creation of towns, cities and wage-earning populations. From this [stems] a powerful demand for ... consumer goods and shops to sell them[25]

That decolonisation was no threat to British imperial business, indeed that political devolution within the Commonwealth might actually *enhance* development opportunities, would seem to be reflected in the portrayal of late-colonial Africa in UK corporate advertisements during the 1950s. According to Ramamurthy advertisements in the 'establishment' press increasingly presented British MNEs as philanthropic emissaries of 'progress and development', representing the multinationals' subconscious endorsement of 'neo-colonial', 'modernisation theory'.[26]

The case for retreat

However, the self-representations of the imperial MNEs can be read in an alternative light: as Ramamurthy concedes, 'We can see the advertisements as appeals by the Companies to appease shareholders.'[27] Soothing images of post-colonial development partnerships were constructed precisely because the underlying reality was a distinctly disturbed set of British executives as the pace of constitutional change was stepped up in much of Africa, Asia and the Caribbean. Anxieties surrounding the consequences of political change for established British firms are best illustrated in Sarah Stockwell's study of the Gold Coast's transmogrification into Ghana. After the electoral triumph of the Convention People's Party (CPP) in 1951, British enterprises feared nationalisation without compensation and a descent into anarchy. The former vexation, at least, was justified – the CPP came to power with an unashamedly left-wing programme of economic nationalism, including plans for a central bank, ISI, and reforms of cocoa, timber and retailing sectors.[28] As it turned out, Kwame Nkrumah's semi-colonial regime proved far less radical whence in office, and a public assurance against nationalisation was issued by the prime minister as early as March 1954. But, the taming of the CPP was hardly absolute. Significant departures in export, shipping and banking sectors set alarm bells ringing, not just at the less-than-progressive directorate of the Ashanti Goldfields Corporation (AGC), but within UK boardrooms connected with West Africa generally. British firms lost representation on the Cocoa Marketing Board, and a new Cocoa Purchasing Company was formed with close CPP associations. Full Ghanaian independence in 1957 coincided with the establishment of the Black Star shipping line, a partnership of the Accra government and the Israeli Zim Line. Moreover, although Ghana remained within the Sterling Area, with its currency pegged to the pound, the establishment of a national bank (after 1953) and a central bank (after 1956) raised 'questions about the future direction and stability of monetary policy'.[29] The beginnings of African self-government in Ghana also led to a significant loss of political status for British business interests, notably the termination of special representation in the Legislative Council. The campaign on the part of the leading interests in their respective sectors – AGC in mining and UAC in trading – for continued political representation in the first half of the 1950s clearly illustrates a 'widespread antipathy' towards constitutional change amongst British business interests.[30]

A similar pattern of business alienation from the politics of decolonisation eventuated in Britain's largest West African territory, Nigeria. Like the Gold Coast, British businesses had protested at their loss of representation in legislative bodies. These anxieties were further compounded by the rise of African-led regional governments after 1954. In both eastern and western regions, the regimes of Azikiwe and Awolowo respectively, pursued statist economic policies designed to undercut the power of foreign investors and promote indigenous entrepreneurship. Meanwhile, the rise of regional state capitalism was accompanied by a growth in peculation and heightened regional competition/ethnic tension.[31]

Across the Atlantic in British Guiana, the People's Progressive Party (PPP) of Cheddi Jagan included nationalisation of the sugar industry as a long-term goal in its manifesto. In the short-term, however, strikes by PPP-affiliated unions after 1953 were exploited as a political weapon. The declaration of an Emergency and the suspension of the constitution in October of that year, in the aftermath of Jagan's election victory in April, did little to soothe the fears of Jock Campbell. The Booker

chairman castigated PPP leaders 'whose highest aim seems to be to overthrow and destroy all that is ... good and all that is British in British
Guiana'. This outburst was all the more significant given Sir Jock's avowed
sympathies with Caribbean nationalism and his later decision to 'out'
himself as a supporter of the British Labour Party.[32] Booker executives were
equally alarmed by developments in Zambia. During 1956 there were a
series of strikes in the mines, and trade boycotts organised by the African
National Congress.[33] Indeed, in Central Africa we need to be careful of
assuming that another so-called 'progressive capitalist', Ronald Prain, was
in sympathy with political developments. As Larry Butler points out, Prain
was attracted to the CAF for political as well as economic reasons, as a
'third way' between South African-style apartheid and majority rule on the
Ghanaian model. As late as 1956, the head of RST, described the 'law-and-
order outlook as unpropitious', given his fears of rapid population growth
outpacing the employment opportunities available. As Cooper comments,
Prain 'could not see alternatives to a dualistic society and a dual wage
structure' but, at the same time, 'could not get away from a sense of peril'.
It was only after the 1959 Nyasaland Emergency, and the Belgian scuttle
from the Congo soon after, that Sir Ronald began to envisage a limited
future for white paternalism in central Africa.[34]

In general, British mine-owners and mine-managers were hardly
enamoured with the course of decolonisation politics. The decision of
the British South Africa Company (BSAC) to recruit Lord Salisbury to its
board, following his resignation from the Macmillan Cabinet in March
1957 over policy in Cyprus, demonstrates where the 'die hard' sympathies of that conglomerate lay.[35] BSAC also enjoyed interlocking direc-
torships with Tanganyika Concessions Ltd (or 'Tanks'), another mining
group which emerged as a major ally of the Welensky government in
Salisbury. In turn, Tanks held a significant share in the Union Minière
du Haut Katanga, which proved itself 'utterly opposed' to black majority
rule in the Belgian Congo, and came to support the campaigns of the
white settlers of Katanga province for fusion with the CAF (after 1958),
and for separate Katangan independence (after 1960).[36] In East Africa
too, City interests were not convinced by official strategies for bolstering
British influence in post-Mau Mau Kenya. Despite support from CO
ministers, the leading settler politician and expatriate entrepreneur in
Kenya, Michael Blundell, faced great difficulty in raising British business
finance for his multiracial New Kenya Group at the end of 1959.
Meanwhile, the tea giant, Brooke Bond, regarded the Lancaster House
conference of 1960 – which opened up the possibility of majority rule in
Kenya – as a 'disaster'.[37]

Fears of overly rapid decolonisation were not confined to Africa and the Caribbean, but can be detected in the plural societies of maritime Southeast Asia as well. Representatives of Liverpool's dynasty of Liberal shipping magnates in the Ocean Steam Ship Company had severe doubts about the Federation of Malaya's future. The retiring senior partner, Sir John Hobhouse, prophesied a 'dark age and an authoritarian future' with the rapid spread of 'communism and communalism' after independence in 1957.[38] As a means of tying the stagnant economies of Sarawak and Brunei to vibrant Sabah, British investment groups had welcomed the prospect of a Federation of British Borneo after 1958. However, the political liberalisation which was likely to accompany this economic streamlining of the Borneo territories was regarded with grave suspicion: 'Only the maintenance of the traditional British-inspired goodwill (with a large measure of control) can preserve racial harmony and avoid serious communal problems for the future. If they want us out they will invite anarchy.' For Britain's most significant pan-Malaysian firm, the Borneo Company Ltd (BCL), the 'largely illiterate' Dayaks of Sarawak were considered particularly susceptible to the lure of 'the left', a situation made even more dangerous by an irredentist Indonesia, which had nationalised Dutch assets during 1957–58 in the context of the Irian Jaya dispute.[39]

Phobias about the PPP in British Guiana or the CPP in the Gold Coast point to another business disaffection with a key tenet of Labour's progressive package for the post-war empire, which was not substantially overturned by the Conservatives after 1951. This was the encouragement given to the development of 'moderate' and 'responsible' trade unions, which frequently metamorphosed into vessels of anti-colonial protest. As Cooper discovered in late colonial Africa, agribusinesses and shipping lines in Kenya, as well as mining corporations in Ghana, shared a resentment of official initiatives to promote labour organisations, particularly when the prospect of 'stabilisation' would be underscored by wage increases and pension benefits.[40] A penchant for pre-war paternalism, rather than post-war collective bargaining, was replicated amongst the rubber barons of Malaya. CO mandarins were flabbergasted to discover in the spring of 1951 that the planters were still not co-operating with the officially sanctioned non-communist unions.[41] With the progressive influence of Dunlop Plantations, joint consultative machinery in the rubber industry was accepted in principle by 1954. Yet, even then, Dunlop executives regarded the 'Asian socialism' espoused by the moderate unionists as 'half-way to communism'.[42]

The Malayan paradigm also emphasises that working in the late colonial empire was an increasingly dangerous occupation for expatriate managers 'in the field' – during the Emergency of 1948–60, 97 European planters and 16 European mining engineers lost their lives. Even after the arrival of the no-nonsense Sir Gerald Templer in February 1952 (and notwithstanding the General's appointment as director of operations and high commissioner by Churchill and Lyttelton), there remained considerable concern about inadequate security provision on the remote estates and mines.[43] In Cyprus, meanwhile, the benefits of increased military spending and the expansion of mineral exports were nullified by the violent struggle between 1955 and 1959 for *enosis* (union with Greece). The Limassol manager of Barclays was assassinated in 1955, and the deposits of the British overseas banks in Cyprus stagnated.[44]

This sense of exposure as colonial rule unravelled was exacerbated by the contemporaneous experiences of British firms in ex-colonies. The expropriation which accompanied Burma's independence and exit from the Commonwealth has already been mentioned. The Buddhist Socialist regime in Rangoon did choose to abide by Sterling Area rules. But this proved of little solace for timber and mineral extractors, since governments in London were repeatedly restrained from seizing Burma's sterling reserves as retaliation against nationalisation (without adequate compensation), given the more pressing need to maintain the Bank of England's status as an international banker acting in the interests of its clients.[45] Even where membership of the multiracial Commonwealth was secured, there proved to be no guarantees against deteriorating operating conditions. In independent India, taxes soared: in 1948–49, the agency house, Andrew Yule, its managed companies, employees and shareholders paid one-sixtieth of the total revenue of the Government of India in income tax. Commissions, new activities and the number of companies an agent could manage were regulated and nationalisation of coal and insurance ensued. Moreover, the 1950s ushered in what Lord Inchcape described as the 40-year 'period of Indian restrictive economic policies patterned on the Soviet policy'.[46]

Nor did the demise of British investments in pre-war 'spheres of influence' induce confidence amongst British investors. Mainland China provided an ominous precedent of how British business interests could be forced into retreat once populist xenophobia and far-left ideologies combined. In November 1949, as the communist party took power in most of China's major cities, one Foreign Office mandarin characterised

Mao Zedong as 'a patriot' sharing 'many of the prejudices of the late-lamented Empress Dowager'. In their dealings with Jardines or Butterfield & Swire, Mao and his senior cadres were likely to return to an '18th century frame of mind', exacerbated by 'more modern conceptions of spy-mania and the People's Court'. 'Foreign devils' would be shown that they were no longer 'allowed to boss anybody about' through various humiliations and losses of face. In so doing, the party would 'gain face' with the 'common man of China'.[47] This proved a prophetic assessment. After 1951, communist officials began to take a tougher line towards overseas commercial and financial interests: a favourite device was to force firms to run up massive liabilities, which could eventually exceed the value of assets. In this process of 'slow-motion nationalisation', the Chinese government avoided paying compensation for its *de facto* sequestrations.[48] The dilemma faced by Britain in China, and other parts of the post-war developing world, was recognised by a former British *chargé-d'affaires*: British firms had built up vast business empires in colonial and 'semi-colonial' territories, but these countries had not established corresponding investments in metropolitan Britain which could be 'frozen' or used as leverage in any expropriation dispute. China's only substantial assets in British territory belonged to the Bank of China in Hong Kong. But, given Hong Kong's dependence on the mainland for food supplies, any seizure of these assets might result in catastrophic retaliation.[49]

Moreover, the negative experiences in China made Hong Kong appear much less of a safe, colonial bastion for trade and industry in Pacific Asia. Dodwells considered the colony's future 'fraught with uncertainty' in October 1954 – worries that had not eased a decade later.[50] And, when forceful attempts at imperial revival were undertaken, British firms were not necessarily the beneficiaries. Following the abortive Anglo-French invasion of Egypt in October and November 1956, the Nasser regime – which had already nationalised the Anglo-French Suez Canal Company – sequestered all remaining British assets.[51] Western oil companies did return to Iran after the restoration of the Shah's authority in August 1953. However, the new oil consortium agreement ensured that AIOC (now restyled British Petroleum) lost its monopoly and held just 40 per cent of the shares of the marketing group.[52] Kuwait did not necessarily prove a safe haven for British oil companies either. Declining British political influence in the Emirate was reflected in Sheikh Abdullah's 1958 decision to award an offshore concession to a Japanese firm – a departure which was recognised by British officials as a Kuwaiti display of Asian solidarity and anti-Western Arab nationalism. In addition,

Kuwait's elite was increasingly resentful of the 'greed and sharp practice' of the 'big five' construction companies. From April 1953, the Ruler issued instructions that two-year contracts held by the British firms were not to be renewed and that subsequent contracts would be open to non-British companies. Moreover, in the development of new port facilities, the 'big five' were deliberately excluded.[53]

On top of socio-political turbulence and economic nationalism, the future profitability of British investment in the late colonial empire looked increasingly unfortuitous given the hazards arising from over-dependence on primary commodity production.[54] In Northern Rhodesia, high prices for copper were a double-edged sword for British mining conglomerates, since they encouraged the use of alternative materials, such as aluminium. This substitution dilemma increasingly bedevilled the tin miners of Malaya and Nigeria as well as the 'tin can' became a misnomer after 1957.[55] The commodity trades of many British colonies also went into decline thanks to the development of synthetic products. The most striking example was Malayan natural rubber where the quadrupling of prices during the Korean War boom proved the industry's high noon as synthetic production in the United States was massively expanded, and, by 1955, the UK's Board of Trade was encouraging the development of a domestic synthetic capacity.[56] By then, the jute mills in Calcutta had lost their global pre-eminence in packing materials and carpet backing to synthetic (as well as paper) products, and British managing agents, such as Finlays, completely disinvested from the Indian mills.[57] Similarly, empire–Commonwealth palm-oil producers had to come to terms with increasingly competitive substitutes in the production of washing powders, shampoos and toilet soaps.[58]

Nor was the attractiveness of colonial investment enhanced by the economic policies of increasingly autonomous and assertive late colonial governments. In Malaya, the tin and rubber barons resented the growing intrusion of the state into economic life as part of the struggle for 'hearts and minds'.[59] The CDC may have been reined in by the time the Conservatives returned to office in 1951, but it was still regarded with scepticism in expatriate business circles. Hence, BCL was dissuaded from entering into partnership with the CDC in rubber, coconut and oil palm plantations in North Borneo because of the development corporation's 'hopelessly extravagant' working policy.[60] Ronald Prain enjoyed close relations with the leading settler politicians in the CAF but loans from the mining companies to finance the construction of the Kariba dam, as well as railways and coalfields, were extracted by 'strong arm tactics'.[61] We should not assume that the development of secondary industry by late colonial/early national governments was something welcomed by British MNEs and trading companies either. In Malaya, after 1958, it was not the prospect of huge monopolistic profits, guaranteed by generous state protection and subsidy, that propelled local manufacture. Rather, it was the danger that a competitor – often Japanese or American – would be offered pioneer status and tariff protection, and, hence, a long-established and valuable market (plus distribution business) would be wiped out overnight. In line with Fieldhouse's conclusions for the origins of Unilever's and UAC's manufacturing in decolonising West Africa, Malayan manufacture was 'defensive' and a reaction to state policies. It was taken on reluctantly and was not anticipated, influenced or expected to be particularly profitable by British firms.[62] The unfurling of late colonial branch banking networks can also be interpreted as largely defensive in nature. As Stockwell suspects in Ghana, 'rapid expansion may well have represented the banks' attempts to establish themselves in new areas before the branches of the national bank were opened, hence precipitating an [unwelcome] era of intense competition' between Barclays and BBWA.[63]

Given all these frustrations with late colonial political, economic and social developments, it is no surprise that many of Britain's leading imperial firms engaged in wide-scale geographical diversification during the 1950s. The coalescence of political and economic uncertainty in British Guiana ensured that the policy of Booker executives from 1954, if not earlier, was to 'build up, in the form of profitable interests elsewhere, "hedges" against catastrophe ... should the worst come to the worst'.[64] In 1953, a Booker team descended upon Canada with unequivocal instructions 'to form a bridgehead of new investment, no matter what the investment was, provided it was respectable and provided it had established management'. In late-1954, Booker acquired a firm of automotive accessory, household appliance and sporting goods wholesalers in Alberta – in the next decade, a succession of businesses in western and central Canada was taken over. In 1954 Booker also invested in a carpet wholesaling business in the United Kingdom, and one year later acquired interests in Liverpool-Ireland shipping. After the troubles of 1956 in Northern Rhodesia, Jock Campbell became increasingly disaffected by the white-dominated CAF.[65] But, like Ronald Prain, this did not mean that Sir Jock had much confidence in the future of 'One Man, One Vote' either. Campbell's doubts about the quality of future Black African governance were manifest in Booker's first moves into UK food distribution after 1957. This departure was conditioned by the firm's experience in colonial shop keeping, but expertise in

Rhodesian and Guyanese retailing was now to be employed in the metropolitan market, to lessen Booker's dependence on the colonies. Hence, by 1997, nearly 93 per cent of Booker's operating profit was derived from the United Kingdom; whereas, in 1955–59, 59 per cent had been extracted from the Caribbean and 7 per cent from central Africa, as opposed to just 23 per cent from the United Kingdom.[66] This strategy of geographical diversification was not unique to Booker McConnell. Indeed, British imperial business leaders were highly selective in their partiality for Commonwealth investment – it was the culturally familiar and politically safer 'Old Dominions' side of the ex-colonial club which was increasingly attractive to the colonial investment groups. Hence, almost all the Malayan agency houses and Hong Kong trading companies opened branch trading and other businesses in Canada and Australia in the course of the 1950s; not to consolidate intra-Sterling Area linkages but to escape the uncertainties and aggravations of Asian decolonisation.[67]

Indeed, this preference for the 'White' Commonwealth exposed an alienation from the decolonisation process, most obviously illustrated by the reluctance to localise management, evident both in Africa and Asia.[68] '[D]oubts about the honesty and reliability of African recruits held back' localisation in banks and trading companies on the Gold Coast, and those African dignitaries appointed to local subsidiary company boards 'often fulfilled no more than a token role'.[69] During the Korean War boom, inflation in the Far East forced up the sterling cost of expatriate wages. But, from India Buildings in Liverpool, the senior managers of Ocean remained adamant that they 'must do whatever is necessary to retain … the services of competent and trustworthy Europeans'. '[T]he whole character of our business will change and a large part of our Goodwill will be destroyed' should the British shipping lines come to 'rely on Asian representatives'.[70] That nearly 52 per cent of BODC's loans were directed to 'settler' Africa as late as September 1958 is revealing: lending to Black African entrepreneurs was still taken up with great reluctance by the imperial banks.[71]

The Singapore story

A micro-study of the experience of British firms in the decolonising micro-state of Singapore is extracted here to provide a final reinforcement of the argument that the British business version of the end of empire in the 1950s was a story of retreat and not revival. On the surface, this might seem like a bizarre assertion. The left-wing (albeit anti-communist) Peoples' Action Party (PAP), headed by the outstanding Cambridge-educated lawyer, Lee Kuan Yew, won the elections for internal self-government on the island in May 1959. Yet, the opening of the new Legislative Assembly was accompanied by promises that no restrictions would be placed on the activities of foreign investors.[72] In 1960, the British Chairman of the Singapore Chamber of Commerce (SCC) praised Lee's government for its 'solid and business like approach to Singapore's economy' and looked forward to 'close liaison with Government'.[73] Moreover, seven years later, the Singapore prime minister was anxious to encourage increased UK industrial investment on the island. He expounded to Britain's Commonwealth Secretary, Herbert Bowden, the ways in which Singapore provided the 'perfect haven' from which British entrepreneurs 'could attack the whole Far Eastern market'. Indeed, the island might become a 'safer commercial base for Britain than ... Hong Kong'. Furthermore, Lee reminded Bowden that Singapore was 'a stable country' and 'he had now got the unions firmly under control'.[74]

But this anglophilia was far from what had been expected of Lee's government back in the late 1950s. As early as September 1958, Lee was predicted to defeat the incumbent Chief Minister, Lim Yew Hock. In an interview with the PAP boss, the Tory MP and agency house Chief Executive, Sir John Barlow, was shocked to discover that Lee 'could not imagine anyone investing new money in Singapore and certainly would not do so himself if he had any'. After taking office, the PAP hoped to 'retain what capital there is in Singapore and the accrued profits as far as possible'. Not surprisingly, Sir John recommended that Barlow & Company 'get any spare cash out and consider working on a banking overdraft in Singapore'.[75] Sir Norman Kipping, Director-General of the Federation of British Industries, reported on a visit to the island colony at the beginning of 1959 that imminent self-government was viewed with 'misgivings and apprehension'; allowing the PAP to run internal affairs was described by one European agency house head as 'throwing democracy to a bunch of coolies'. Many of the major trading companies were considering a shift of headquarters to Kuala Lumpur since extreme left-wing policies on Singapore were likely to reduce the island to 'economic insignificance'.[76] Indeed, on the eve of the 1959 elections, most of the agency houses split their locally registered businesses between Singapore and the Federation in a damage limitation exercise.[77]

Moreover, Lee remained a bogeyman not only because of his fiery anticolonial socialism but also for his formidable legal skills. It was widely believed that the PAP leader would have no qualms about reforming

Singapore law to permit remittance controls and nationalisation. British firms already had first-hand experience of Lee in his legal incarnation since he had acted as an adviser and negotiator for PAP-affiliated trade unions.[78] Indeed, the PAP represented precisely the blending of radical trade unionism with left-wing intelligentsia nationalism that expatriate businesses had found so objectionable in British Guiana and the Gold Coast. Additionally, as British manufacturing, trading and banking interests complained to visitors from the CO, the new constitution left British firms dangerously exposed because it would not allow the UK Commission any authority to overturn legislation adverse to British economic interests.[79] Hence, when the PAP's victory was even more overwhelming than the boxwallahs anticipated, HSBC's manager in Singapore reported on a 'general feeling of depression' and much speculation regarding the 'burdens' which were sure to be imposed on the commercial community.[80] As late as October 1959, the BCL board in London sought to reduce trading and investments on the island through selling subsidiaries and 'cutting down establishment'.[81]

Yet, even before the creation of the internally self-governing 'State of Singapore', the taipans were hardly comfortable with constitutional developments. In 1954, in line with campaigns on the Gold Coast and in Nigeria, the SCC protested at the proposal to establish party government and abolish special business membership under the Rendel Constitution. As in West Africa, this lobbying got nowhere. Oliver Lyttelton preferred to see expatriate business represented by elected parliamentarians.[82] Apparently taking the Colonial Secretary's advice, the big commercial houses and exchange banks in Singapore directed M$5000 each to the right-wing Progressive Party – indicative that, as in the Gold Coast or the Federation of Malaya, British firms in Singapore were hardly passive, indifferent bystanders in the decolonisation process.[83] Yet, as in Malaya or Ghana, big business funding could not swing elections. That the Progressives were pushed aside in April 1955 further illustrates the declining influence of expatriate enterprise on political developments. The newly enfranchised working-class Chinese made David Marshall's 'moderate' Labour Front the strongest party in the assembly with ten seats, while the PAP won three seats. The Progressives had just four of their representatives elected.

Immediately following the election, British firms found themselves caught in the crossfire of a struggle between the PAP and the Labour Front for the control of the trade unions – in April 1955, BCL's chief executive in Malaya reported that the PAP was 'out to wreck the Labour Front government' and there was a wave of industrial action in that month, most famously at the Hock Lee Bus Company which ended in triumph for the PAP-associated unions. The situation had become so tense in May that Lennox-Boyd informed Macmillan that arrangements were being made for extra British troops to be made available to support the civil power. The Secretary of State for the Colonies did demonstrate a characteristic sensitivity towards the confidence of the business community by persuading Governor Nicoll to postpone his departure from the island. But this did little to placate the irate boxwallahs. Marshall's negotiations with the transport unions were described by BCL managers as 'nothing short of a complete capitulation to the strikers and to threats from "sympathetic" unions with similar [PAP] affiliations'. That the left-wing Chief Minister had negotiated the settlement 'destroyed whatever confidence anyone might still have had that the government is prepared to take anything like a reasonably firm stand against thuggery and sheer intimidation'. Between June 1955 and February 1956 there was a further general strike called by the Singapore Factory and Shop Workers' Union (SFSWU) in which British industrial enterprises were 'deliberately spotlight[ed]' as 'uncooperative employers' and Governor Black fretted about 'the dangers of racial feeling which may arise from this'.[84]

The white-collar labour leader, Lim Yew Hock, replaced Marshall as Chief Minister in June 1956 and rode the tiger – the SFSWU was ruthlessly suppressed following evidence of its involvement in the october riots. Lim was soon regarded as an 'excellent man' in British business circles, and the support of the boxwallahs was increasingly directed towards his Singapore People's Alliance – not least, because Lim's close links with Tunku Abdul Rahman in Kuala Lumpur held out the best prospect of merger with the right-wing Federation.[85] But, in May 1959, Lim's party won only 4 out of 51 seats compared with 43 seats for the PAP.

The subsequent de-radicalisation of Lee's party also proved cold comfort for British firms – 1961–62 witnessed a further wave of labour unrest inspired by an intense struggle between the radical breakaway Socialist Front and the rump PAP. In the course of 1963, the threat of Lee's government falling was avoided by the round up of alleged communists during 'Operation Coldstore', as well as the creation of Malaysia. But then came Lee's 'moment of anguish' in August 1965 when Singapore was expelled from the expanded Federation. With Indonesian Confrontation still raging, it looked likely that the PAP leader might re-discover his radical roots and realign Singapore with the emerging Jakarta/Beijing axis.[86]

The 1950s Singapore was also littered with economic frustrations for the long-established agency houses. In the following decade, the PAP regime did develop a reputation for economic efficiency. Nevertheless,

British shippers remained exasperated by the slow introduction of port improvements advocated by a commission of enquiry back in 1957: 'Such is the pace of British democracy filtered through oriental susceptibilities', sardonically commented a senior executive in the Ocean group in 1962.[87] Moreover, the island's shift towards ISI in the last year of Lim Yew Hock's political reign was not welcomed by the import–export managers of Singapore – protective tariffs and tax holidays seemed to be encouraging uncompetitive 'backyard secondary industry'. Import substitution also appeared to be tearing mainland and island economies further apart.[88] Imperial economic policy was not necessarily bolstering the position of British business interests in Singapore either. The liberalisation of Sterling Area trade with Japan after 1954 was deprecated by the head of the SCC on the grounds that 'Malayan markets were being thrown into chaos and confusion' and were likely to become subjected to 'dumping and other forms of attack'.[89] The lifting of strategic controls on trade with Communist China in mid-1956, meanwhile, produced a massive increase in imports of cheap consumer goods from the People's Republic, and BCL's plywood factory found its markets 'flooded with cheap imports' from China, as well as Japan.[90] Following the advent of current account convertibility for sterling in 1958, Singapore importers could do substantial business directly with North America. A BCL manager complained in the summer of 1960 that there had not 'been so many Yankee carpet-baggers around since General Lee surrendered at Appomattox'.[91]

The agency houses of Singapore were experiencing a global phenomenon: although the empire–Commonwealth was increasingly important as a market for UK-based industry in the 1950s, British imports were becoming steadily less significant for Sterling Area countries given 'lagging design and quality, slow delivery dates, lack of salesmanship, insufficient investment in research and development, and prices rising about 1 per cent faster than those of competitors'.[92] Moreover, that ultimately the principal threat to British business interests in Singapore emanated from international capitalism, and not international communism as expected, reminds us of the pitfalls of reading the history of decolonisation backwards. From the perception of UK companies during the 1950s, the British imperial system – in both its political and economic guises – was disintegrating and not consolidating.

Notes

1. CAB 129/52, memorandum, 17 June 1952 reproduced in A. Porter and A. Stockwell (eds.), *British Imperial Policy and Decolonization, 1938–64*, 2 vols (Basingstoke, 1989), vol. 1, pp. 154–63.

2. R. Holland, 'The imperial factor in British strategies from Attlee to Macmillan, 1945–63', *Journal of Imperial and Commonwealth History*, 12 (1984), 165–86; P. Cain and A. Hopkins, *British Imperialism, 1688–2000*, 2nd edn (Harlow: 2002), ch. 26; G. Krozewski, *Money and the End of Empire: British International Economic Policy and the Colonies, 1947–58* (London: 2001).

3. J. Darwin, *The End of the British Empire: The Historical Debate* (Oxford: 1991), pp. 48–9.

4. S. Stockwell, 'Trade, empire and the fiscal context of imperial business during decolonization', *Economic History Review*, LVII (2004), 142–60.

5. J. MacKenzie, 'Prejudice behind the pomp and baubles', *Times Higher*, 27 July 2001, 25.

6. M. Barratt Brown, *After Imperialism* (London: 1963), table vi, 111. Figures are by volume.

7. AGM Address March 1957 cited in A. Ramamurthy, *Imperial Persuaders: Images of Africa and Asia in British Advertising* (Manchester: 2003), pp. 203–4.

8. L. Butler, *Industrialization and the British Colonial State: West Africa 1939–51* (London: 1997); F. Bostock, 'The British overseas banks and development finance in Africa after 1945', *Business History*, 33 (1991), 157–76.

9. N. White, *Business, Government, and the End of Empire: Malaya, 1942–57* (Kuala Lumpur: 1996), pp. 37–8, 59 n. 67, 110; S. Stockwell, *The Business of Decolonization: British Business Strategies in the Gold Coast* (Oxford: 2000), p. 210; P. Murphy, *Party Politics and Decolonization: The Conservative Party and British Colonial Policy in Tropical Africa, 1951–64* (Oxford: 1995), pp. 96–7; L. Butler, 'Sir Ronald Prain, the Mining Industry and the Central African Federation', unpublished paper presented to the Imperial History Seminar, Institute of Historical Research, 17 March 2003. I am indebted to Dr. Butler for allowing me to make reference to his unpublished paper. His forthcoming book on colonial mining in Zambia will be a major contribution to the historiography of big business and decolonisation.

10. Murphy, *Party Politics*, p. 97; Murphy, *Alan Lennox-Boyd* (London: 1999).

11. J. Slinn and J. Tanburn, *The Booker Story* (Norwich: 2003), pp. 56, 70–4.

12. Butler, 'Prain', pp. 2, 4, 7.

13. S. Smith, *Kuwait, 1950–1965: Britain, the Al-Sabah and Oil* (Oxford: 2000), pp. 27, 32–3, 50–1, 143; S. Smith, 'The making of a neo-colony? Anglo-Kuwaiti relations in the era of decolonization', *Middle Eastern Studies*, 37 (2001), 162–3.

14. G. Jones, *Merchants to Multinationals: British Trading Companies in the Nineteenth and Twentieth Centuries* (Oxford: 2000), p. 138; A. Pointon, *The Bombay Burmah Trading Corporation Limited, 1863–1963* (Southampton: 1964), chaps 18–19; E. Lee, *The Towkays of Sabah: Chinese Leadership and Indigenous Challenge in the Last Phase of British Rule* (Singapore: 1976), pp. 7, 16, 18–19.

15. N. White, *British Business in Post-Colonial Malaysia, 1957–70: 'Neo-colonialism' or 'disengagement'?* (London: 2004), p. 37; N[ational] A[rchives, Kew, London], CO 1030/1245, letter to H. Morford, chairman, Borneo Company Ltd enclosed in Malcolm, BCL to Martin, CO, 15 February 1960.

16. C. Schenk, *Hong Kong as an International Financial Centre: Emergence and Development, 1945–65* (London: 2001), especially pp. 111–12, 123–4.

17. R. Fry, *Bankers in West Africa: The Story of the Bank of British West Africa Ltd* (London: 1976), p. 197.

18. Bostock, 'Overseas Banks'.
19. Slinn and Tanburn, *Booker*, p. 89.
20. Jones, *Merchants to Multinationals*, pp. 138–9.
21. *Straits Times Directory of Malaya and Singapore 1957* (Singapore: 1957), p. 67.
22. Jones, *Merchants to Multinationals*, p. 143; D. Fieldhouse, *Merchant Capital and Economic Decolonization: The United Africa Company, 1929–1989* (Oxford: 1994), p. 533.
23. W.G. Clarence Smith, 'The organization of "Consent" in British West Africa, 1820s to 1960s', in D. Engels and S. Marks (eds), *Contesting Colonial Hegemony: State and Society in Africa and India* (London: 1994), p. 75.
24. White, *Post-colonial Malaysia*, pp. 165–8.
25. *English Electric and Its People*, August 1958, 14 cited in Ramamurthy, *Imperial Persuaders*, p. 210.
26. Ramamurthy, *Imperial Persuaders*, ch. 6.
27. Ibid., p. 174.
28. Stockwell, *Business of Decolonization*, pp. 95, 107.
29. Ibid., pp. 95–7, 99–102, 103–5.
30. Ibid., 111–12, 123, 126–7; Murphy, *Party Politics*, pp. 107–11.
31. R. Tignor, *Capitalism and Nationalism at the End of Empire: State and Business in Decolonizing Egypt, Nigeria, and Kenya, 1945–63* (Princeton, NJ: 1998), pp. 246–62.
32. Address to AGM 1954 cited in Slinn and Tanburn, *Booker*, p. 62.
33. Ibid., p. 89.
34. Butler, 'Prain', pp. 3, 9–14, 16–17; F. Cooper, *Decolonization and African Society: The Labor Question in French and British Africa* (Cambridge: 1996), pp. 345–7.
35. Murphy, *Party Politics*, p. 92.
36. M. Hughes, 'Fighting for White rule in Africa: The Central African Federation, Katanga, and the Congo crisis, 1958–65', *International History Review*, 25 (2003), 592–615; Murphy, *Party Politics*, 92, 95, 111–17.
37. NA, CO 967/353, Blundell to Lennox-Boyd, 29 August 1959; Tignor, *Capitalism and Nationalism*, pp. 357–8.
38. M. Falkus, *The Blue Funnel Legend: A History of the Ocean Steam Ship Company, 1875–1973* (Basingstoke: 1990), pp. 324–5.
39. I[nchcape] A[rchives, Guildhall Library, London], Ms. 27417, private letter to the Hon. Secretary of the Sarawak Association, c. Aug. 1959; copy of letter from Simpson, Singapore to MacEwen, London, 7 March 1960; Ms. 27182, minutes of OGM, 4 December 1959.
40. Cooper, *African Society*, p. 264.
41. See material in NA, CO 859/185/3.
42. NA, CO 1022/121, minute by Barltrop for MacKintosh, 11 August 1953; White, *Business, Government*, pp. 127–8 n. 57.
43. White, *Post-colonial Malaysia*, p. 101; White, 'Capitalism and counter-insurgency? Business and government in the Malayan Emergency, 1948–57', *Modern Asian Studies*, 32 (1998), 149–77.
44. K. Phylaktis, 'Banking in a British colony: Cyprus, 1879–1959', *Business History*, 30 (1988), 424, 427–8.
45. See NA, OD 39/19, minute by Berkoff, Ministry of Overseas Development (ODM) for Mitchell, ODM, 1 July 1969.
46. S. Jones, *Merchants of the Raj: British Managing Agency Houses in Calcutta Yesterday and Today* (London: 1992), pp. 111, 370.

47. F 17349/1261/10, Minute by Franklin, 23 November 1949 reproduced in S. Ashton, G. Bennett and K. Hamilton (eds), *Britain and China, 1945–50: Documents on British Policy Overseas*, Series I, vol. VIII (London: 2002), p. 407. I am most grateful to Stephen Ashton for furnishing me with this reference.
48. A. Shai, *The Fate of British and French Firms in China, 1949–58: Imperialism Imprisoned* (Basingstoke: 1996), pp. 25–38, 75, 99–101; D. Clayton, *Imperialism Revisited: Political and Economic Relations Between Britain and China, 1950–54* (Basingstoke: 1997), pp. 134–8, 152–6.
49. Humphrey Trevalyan cited in Shai, *British and French Firms*, p. 68.
50. Jones, *Merchants to Multinationals*, p. 149.
51. R. Tignor, 'The Suez crisis of 1956 and Egypt's Foreign private sector', *Journal of Imperial and Commonwealth History*, 20 (1992), 274–97.
52. F. Bostock and G. Jones, 'British business in Iran, 1860s to 1970s', in R. Davenport-Hines and G. Jones (eds), *British Business in Asia since 1860* (Cambridge: 1989), p. 48.
53. Smith, *Kuwait*, 48, 51–2, 54, 109–10; Smith, 'Making of a neo-colony', pp. 164–6.
54. Jones, *Merchants to Multinationals*, p. 117.
55. Butler, 'Prain', p. 5; White, *Business, Government*, pp. 267–8.
56. White, *Business, Government*, pp. 181–95.
57. G. Stewart, *Jute and Empire: the Calcutta Jute Wallahs and the Landscapes of Empire* (Manchester: 1998), p. 139; Jones, *Raj*, p. 118.
58. W. Corlett, *The Economic Development of Detergents* (London: 1958), ch. 4.
59. N. White, 'The frustrations of development: British business and the late-colonial state in Malaya, 1945–57', *Journal of Southeast Asian Studies*, 28 (1997), 103–19.
60. IA, Ms. 27417, note of 29 July 1959.
61. Butler, 'Prain', pp. 5–6.
62. White, *Post-colonial Malaysia*, pp. 178–9; D. Fieldhouse, *Unilever Overseas: The Anatomy of a Multinational, 1895–1965* (London: 1978), pp. 405–17; Fieldhouse, *Merchant Capital*, pp. 391–410.
63. Stockwell, *Business of Decolonization*, p. 162.
64. Slinn and Tanburn, *Booker*, p. 62.
65. Ibid., 89; Murphy, *Party Politics*, p. 106.
66. Slinn and Tanburn, *Booker*, pp. 80, 84, 109–10, 216–17.
67. Jones, *Merchants to Multinationals*, p. 151; N. White, 'The diversification of colonial capitalism: British Agency Houses in Southeast Asia in the 1950s and 1960s', in I. Cook *et al.* (eds), *Dynamic Asia: Business, Trade and Economic Development in Pacific Asia* (Aldershot: 1998).
68. Jones, *Merchants to Multinationals*, pp. 221–5.
69. Stockwell, *Business of Decolonization*, p. 145.
70. O[cean] A[rchives, National Museums Liverpool, Maritime Archives & Library], 4003, 87th Annual Meeting, 25 April 1952, Chairman's Report.
71. Bostock, 'Overseas Banks', pp. 170–1.
72. NA, DO 35/9864, copy of Woodruff, Kuala Lumpur to Reynolds, Board of Trade, 2 July 1959; Tory, Kuala Lumpur to Hunt, Commonwealth Relations Office, 6 January 1960.
73. *SCC Annual Report for 1959* (Singapore, 1960), Chairman's Address, 31 March 1960.
74. NA, FCO 24/294, extract from record of meeting, 3 March 1967.

75. Cambridge University Library, Barlow Papers, 63/855, letter to Tom Barlow, 22 September 1958.
76. Modern Records Centre, University of Warwick, Confederation of British Industry archive, Mss. 200/F/3/D3/6/75, D/5527, report on Singapore, undated.
77. White, *Business, Government*, 248–9; NA, DO 35/9864, copy of Woodruff to Reynolds, 11 June 1959.
78. For example, see Institute of Southeast Asian Studies Library, Singapore, S.Q. Wong papers, SQW/XI/21a, copy of letter from Lee Kuan Yew to Wilson, Singapore Traction Company, 17 October 1958 and IA, Ms. 27429, Donald, Singapore to Malcolm, London, 4 October 1960.
79. NA, CO 1030/876, West to Wallace, 14 February 1959 enclosing 'Note of informal meeting with representatives of the Chambers of Commerce and the British European Association, 6 February 1959'; minute by Wallace for Gidden and Melville, 20 February 1959.
80. HSBC Group Archive, London, Chief Manager's Private File: Singapore (Personal & S/O OUT), January 1957 to December 1960, Cruickshank, Singapore to Stewart, Hong Kong, 8 June 1959.
81. IA, Ms. 21178/26, Board of Directors' Minutes, 21 October 1959.
82. NA, CO 1030/78, savingram from Singapore enclosing 'Memorandum by Combined Chambers of Commerce on Representation of Commercial Interests, 23 March 1954'; 'Note of a Meeting held in the Colonial Secretary's Room on 2 April 1954'.
83. HSBC, Chief Manager's File: Singapore – Private Duplicates, January 1954 to December 1961, Morrison, Singapore to Stacey, Hong Kong, 16 November 1954. On business finance for conservative, counter-nationalist political parties in West Africa and Malaya see Stockwell, *Business of Decolonization*, pp. 191–3; White, *Business, Government*, pp. 143, 147–8.
84. White, *Business, Government*, 228–9; NA, CO 1030/366, memorandums of 18 and 24 May 1955; minute by Johnston for Martin, 29 May 1955; CO 1030/367, letter to Barltrop, 30 September 1955.
85. White, *Business, Government*, 248; IA, Ms. 27259/5, Donald to Malcolm, 28 November 1958; HSBC, Chief Manager's File: Singapore and Malaya: Politics, May 1958–March 1963, Perry-Aldworth, London to Turner, Hong Kong, 5 February 1959; Lydall, Singapore to Turner, 11 February 1959.
86. White, *Post-Colonial Malaysia*, pp. 28–30, 46.
87. OA, 1064, K. St. Johnston to P. Nelson, 9 January 1962.
88. *SCC Annual Report 1958*, Chairman's Address, 20 March 1959; IA, Ms. 27259/5, Donald to Malcolm, 28 November 1958.
89. *SCC Annual Report 1953* (Singapore, 1954), Chairman's Address, 25 September 1954.
90. IA, Ms. 27259/5, Donald to Malcolm, 20 October 1958 enclosing copy of letter to W.C.S. Corry, Malayan Commercial Association of Great Britain, 20 October 1958; BCL, *Annual Report and Accounts 1958*.
91. IA, Ms. 27298, Young, Singapore to Simpson, London, 26 July 1960.
92. D. Fieldhouse, 'The metropolitan economics of empire', in J. Brown and Wm. R. Louis (eds), *The Oxford History of the British Empire*: Vol. 4: *The Twentieth Century* (Oxford: 1999), p. 107; see also C. Schenk, 'Decolonization and European economic integration: The Free Trade Area negotiations, 1956–58', *Journal of Imperial & Commonwealth History*, 24 (1996), 444–63.

6

Things Fall Apart: The Erosion of Local Government, Local Justice and Civil Rights in Ghana, 1955–60

Richard Rathbone

It is easy to understand why the history of Ghana between 1948 and 1957 has been regarded by the generalist literature as a relatively successful transfer of power. With the benefit of hindsight we know that it was, sadly, one of the only successful transfers of power in Africa if success is measured by the relative absence of broken skulls. It is, after all, a story which competes with a depressing collection of messy narratives which range from very bloody examples like Algeria, the Belgian Congo, Kenya and the Portuguese territories to those initially gentler but unsustainable compromises which sooner or later paved the way to bloodshed like Nigeria, Sierra Leone, Tchad or Uganda. Ghana's claim to be exemplary and unusual is sustained by a melange of fact and myth. It is undeniable that Ghana's long period of transition provided her politicians and administrators with an extended period of formal bureaucratic and institutional apprenticeship, the longest such in British Africa, which left the country with an impressive civil service by 1957.[1] Additionally in comparison with virtually everywhere else in Africa, Ghanaians had enjoyed a comparatively robust history of wealth-creation for many years; as a consequence, substantial levels of revenue along with Ghana's creditworthiness meant that the national transport infrastructure, including an international airport[2] and by the late 1950s, a new deep-water-port at Tema, was extensive and functioning.[3] Northerners were, however, to complain with justice that much the best of its road-system and all of its permanent way was to be found in the area to the south of the River Volta.[4] Ghana had experienced, well-trained military[5] and police forces, expanding educational and health services; and this genuinely happy list could go on and on.

But usable myth plays its part in this legend of success. In the extensive literature produced by Ghanaian scholars and journalists over the past half century, there is remarkably little of the bitter language of rancour about colonial rule and its ending which haunts some of the literatures of other African states. Only recently have some younger Ghanaians begun to describe the long-departed colonial regime as 'our colonial masters'; this idiom, with its postmodern, built-in sneer, has almost certainly been appropriated from Nigerian writing where that phrase has a much longer history. Ghana's national mythology demands that the period of the transfer of power be regarded as a particular kind of success. It is hallowed as a time of heroic struggle which ushered in the domination of Kwame Nkrumah and his Convention People's Party (CPP) who together, for an attenuated period, thrust Ghana, small and geopolitically insignificant as she was, into the world's limelight; two generations after independence in 1957, this long-faded prominence is still recalled by the old with pride and by the young as an *age d'or* [6] when Ghana punched above her weight and did so for many years. Ghanaians are nostalgic about this era even if they were, as a large majority of its population were, born long after independence. Perhaps this lack of bitterness owes something to an acknowledgement that the British had played their part as adversaries in accordance with the requirements of the myth of struggle.

Despite the grating disharmonies, this heroic tradition very neatly, if very perversely, dovetailed with the entirely different and necessarily opposed narrative of British officialdom. Just as the Ghanaian struggle narrative required a stern adversary, the British myth of subtlety needed an intractable, near-revolutionary opponent. The run-up to independence was, in this version, a triumph of shrewd statesmanship, of successful, cool management[7] leading to a peaceful transfer to a regime, thrice democratically chosen by a newly enfranchised population, which then tragically chose to squander all of its manifest advantages after independence like an ungrateful, spendthrift child. The infantilizing imagery is not mine; for example Lord Home, Secretary of State at the Commonwealth Relations Office, referred to the imminently independent Ghana as 'this highly unattractive baby ...'[8] and that language pervades the contemporary official discourse. While there were voices in Britain, just as there were voices in Ghana, which did not share this predominantly paternalistic vision, the importance of the British myth for

Westminster and Whitehall policy-makers was underlined by necessity. As some of the documents in Martin Lynn's Nigerian volume in the British Documents on the End of Empire (BDEEP) sequence show, the history of Ghana's transfer of power haunted that of Nigeria's terminal colonial period. The transfer of power in Ghana had quickly become the model for subsequent transfers and the template for the route-maps devised for other aspirant colonies manifestly owed much to the Ghanaian precedent;[9] even if it in reality failed to impress in either general or detailed terms, this transfer of power simply had to be seen to be excellent in moral as well as political terms.

These two sets of actors, Ghanaian and British, unwittingly constructed two accounts of a process which were to provide contemporary detractors with copious ammunition. For critics from the left, the nature of Ghana's separation from British over-rule, negotiation rather than physical conflict, demonstrated the falsity of the Nkrumahist claim that a serious struggle had resulted in a hard-won socialist revolution; by such a radical reckoning between 1945 and 1960 a black bourgeoisie had done little beyond filling recently vacated white-men's shoes.[10] For critics from the right, Ghana was the richly endowed, well-brought-up heir who proved to be incapable of resisting ideological impetuosity,[11] corruption and the attractions of the arrogance of office.[12] Many of the critiques from both left and right agree on an underlying theme of betrayal; closer reading suggests that these betrayals are often the betrayals of the author's expectations[13] rather than that of the hopes of ordinary Ghanaians.

Ghana at independence was however not nearly as well-placed as both Ghanaian and British official orthodoxies suggested. In a long-term perspective, the ending of history's longest secular boom in tropical commodities was the country's most significant weakness. Ghana's cocoa industry (and its gold and other mineral industries about whose histories we know much less) had ensured healthy government revenues from the mid-1940s.[14] These had funded the palpable developments in social, medical and educational provisions as well as infrastructural improvements and expansion while indicating to a wider world the credit-worthiness of this small colonial state. As much of that change became visible *after* the CPP came to office in 1951, Nkrumah's governments became, with considerable justice, identified with visible progress and modernisation; Nkrumah and his party's ambitions to transform Ghana were undoubtedly genuine but hard to achieve. The fall in the world cocoa price, the object of much conspiracy theorising on the left in the 1960s, which lay behind Ghana's accelerating economic decline, came as no surprise to the country's government. As early as June 1954, *before* the country's second general election, Komla Gbedemah, Ghana's Finance Minister, presented an important memorandum to the Cabinet. He wrote:

> I am quite certain that the price will fall. When it does fall, I am equally certain that it will fall heavily. I do not however believe that it will fall much if at all in the crop years 1954–5 and 1955–6. As I see it therefore, we have before us two or three years of immense prosperity to be followed by a very doubtful future. My view is that we should make use of the years of prosperity to safeguard the future as far as we are able ... the experience of the last six years has shown quite clearly that the internal economy turns wholly upon the local price paid for cocoa.[15]

This early awareness of the grim reverses to come helps explain, even it cannot excuse, policies which were frequently seen by commentators to be merely heedless extravagance.

'The Gold Coast Government', the Governor wrote to the Secretary of State for the Colonies,

> has overreached itself during the recent boom years in launching more services than it can afford to maintain and it will shortly be difficult for the Government to find funds for its essential requirements ... ordinary expenditure is three times as high now as six years ago ... Not only is there likely to be little or no money for further development, much less new education or welfare services, but it seems inevitable that there will soon have to be entrenchment ... It is particularly unfortunate, and indeed disquieting, that the change should happen to coincide with the transfer of power.[16]

Arden-Clarke's apparent detachment is partially explicable in terms of his personal lack of interest in economic issues but it is also a crude bit of exculpation; colonial methods of attempting development were deeply implicated in the nurturing of the blinkered, bureaucratic rigidities of Nkrumah's governments and their successors.[17] Although the CPP governments' dash for development and the eventual resolution to achieve growth through increasing state control, industrialisation and import replacement were to achieve little beyond mounting misery, the context and timing of those decisions is at least understandable.

However, as this chapter's title suggests, its concern is not with the economic history of Ghana, a subject which has generated some good scholarship[18] but rather with what Ghana was beginning to look like in the final years of the colonial period and the first years of independence. In economic terms it is fair to say that whilst insiders knew that things would take a decided turn for the worst, the achievements of the post-war years still allowed for a depiction of a relatively wealthy and tolerably well-governed state. It was a picture that suited both Ghanaian and British image-makers.

Air-brushing techniques were deployed in the presentation of Ghana by both British and Ghanaian officials as an exciting new democracy whose institutions were modelled upon those of the United Kingdom and whose citizens were equal before widely respected law. Neither set of actors could really have believed in this convenient fiction but, being equally eager to be rid of one another, both subscribed to it. From the formation of what was in effect the first CPP administration in 1951, the Party had openly sought to control the organs of the state; their gradual, legal but undeniably devious takeover of the local justice system provides a well-documented battery of examples of their intentions and methods.[19] Some of this was to be locally challenged; the emergence of significant, rather than a flabby armchair opposition in late 1954 provided the Party with its first serious adversary, a challenge Nkrumah was to minimise in a letter to Lennox-Boyd as 'the odd spots of bother we have experienced in the past year'.[20] Opposition claims about foul play were received by the colonial regime but were in real terms, brushed under the carpet. The extent to which British officials conduced at such complacency can be judged from Sir Frederick Bourne's[21] appreciation of the situation in late 1955:

> The Gold Coast as a whole presents a most encouraging picture of prosperity and general well-being. My own observations and the conversations I have had with *responsible* persons in the various districts I have visited support the view that the people have little to complain of and much to be thankful for.[22]

There can be little doubt that this positive impression was the product of spin and it had been sold to Bourne by officials and ministers as there was certainly enough significant contemporary evidence to suggest that things were going awry. It was of course *realpolitik* which prompted an increasing amount of pragmatic ignoring by British officials and politicians of malpractice in the Gold Coast. As the political power of the CPP grew, not least through electoral success, British faith in their own *prise* declined and the impression of retreat grew. For example, thinking through the damning conclusions of the Jibowu Commission into corruption by members of the government in the affairs of the Cocoa Purchasing Company, Zoe Terry[23] concluded that '... we are far too committed to Dr. Nkrumah to apply the ultimate sanction of refusing to grant Independence ...'. What now happened in the Gold Coast 'is not, however, something which it is in our power to control ...'. A subsequent minute by Gorrel Barnes[24] agreed with Terry and referred to what was already known '... about corruption and Fascist tendencies in the Gold Coast ...'.[25] Similarly there was some official and governmental belief in the allegations made to senior Colonial Office (CO) officials by the Gold Coast's Trade Commissioner in London, Kodwo Mercer, that Nkrumah and senior ministers had deceived the Governor about the Party's sanctioning of political violence and corruption.[26] Gorrel Barnes wrote that there were grounds for believing that 'if the Gold Coast is given independence next spring, its Government is likely to misuse its powers in order to consolidate its position and turn itself into a dictatorship ... and I fear that it is questionable whether it would be accepted by public opinion generally as an adequate reason for not carrying out the undertaking to fix a date for independence ...'.[27] In the same minute sequence Hilton Poynton agreed that it was '... virtually impossible for us to go back on the promise of independence ...'. Although the history of British Guiana suggests that there might have been an alternative, the British knew that they risked dangerous, costly public disorder if they challenged what felt like the ineluctable turn of events; London was undoubtedly in retreat.

While compromise is a necessary ingredient of all practical politics, CO minutes suggest a weary bowing to the inevitable rather than cynicism. Such a sympathetic reading is, however, more difficult to sustain when examining the relatively under-scrutinised world of rural Ghana, a world in which the vast majority of her newly enfranchised citizens lived.[28] It is striking that British commentary on the state of the Gold Coast in the terminal colonial period is so little concerned with the issues which had for so long dominated the conduct of colonial rule, namely law and local administration. In much of the discussion about the post-war governance of the Gold Coast – and elsewhere in Africa – heavy emphasis had been placed upon the importance of introducing democracy 'from the bottom up'. Although there was some sentimentality about the fate of chiefs if and when democratic local government was introduced, much of that was occasioned by apprehensions about the costs of change. But if reformed local government was so central to CO thinking before the riots of 1948 and in the construction of the Coussey Constitution, it is interesting and not entirely understandable that it so rapidly became marginal. Throughout the 1950s the two major flows of information into Whitehall[29] basically ignored these spheres whilst emphasising national politics, the economy and Ghana's likely international affiliations after independence.

A partial explanation of this lies in the fact that local government had been one of the first areas of government surrendered to African control in 1951. From the formation of Nkrumah's first government, local government was not merely an African-held portfolio but had come to be regarded as an essentially African matter.[30] Although it was never directly expressed as a welcome escape from the sensitive complexities[31] of chieftaincy, one senses the relief amongst British administrators in being able to leave the incomprehensible world of shape-shifting custom to others. Additionally, the unreformed nature of the justice system[32] maintained that system's somewhat atomised nature which, in turn, made critical scrutiny difficult.

By the 1940s local government was a dreadful mess and it continued to be a dreadful mess. Ten years after independence, there was a clear perception that local government finance was a central, besetting problem. Put briefly, the problem was '… the question of how local authorities can obtain sufficient revenues to meet the increasing cost of services without depending largely upon the central government for financial assistance'.[33] The deficits reported in that *Report* were enormous – 'dismal and disappointing' in the words of the Commissioners.

There was nothing new about this. The Secretary of State's *Despatch on the Coussey Report*, ghosted by the Gold Coast government in late August 1949, stressed that: 'The earliest consideration will doubtless be given … to placing the finances of Local Authorities on a satisfactory basis. Much ingenuity will be required to overcome the difficulties in levying rates.'[34]

One searches in vain for evidence of discussion of, let alone planning to overcome those difficulties. Some of the strands of this unresolved dilemma are to be found in an inherently boring but important story. The collection of local taxation was in disarray well before the riots of 1948. It was even more of a mess after the riots when non-payment of rates was, for some, a political act. Following the supersession of Native Authorities and the democratisation of local government at the end of 1951, the mainstay of their revenue was supposed to consist of the basic local tax, a rate, levied on ratepayers. The nominal rolls of ratepayers were however incomplete and inaccurate; they had always been deficient. Shortly after independence Cabinet were told that 'at least 25% of the potential revenue is not being collected'.[35] This was a considerable under-estimate. A scatter of evidence suggests that refusal to pay rates was widespread. Some CPP supporters clearly felt that the electoral victory in 1951 ended their obligation to pay rates.

> N[ative] A[uthoritie]s are relaxing their efforts towards collecting revenue, the present NA members are less prepared than ever to court the unpopularity which goes with the enforcement of taxation … the Minister's attention should be called to the need for the dominant political party propaganda machine to 'soften up' the opposition to direct taxation.[36]

There is no trace of such a campaign of persuasion and the widespread assumption of political approval of non-payment of rates was to persist.[37] This pattern was not confined to CPP supporters; National Liberation Movement (NLM) supporters were later to refuse to pay rates to CPP controlled councils.[38]

Secondly, whilst it was entirely reasonable that the amount of the local rate varied in a country with such stark contrasts of factor endowment, the distinctions were enormous. The rate could be as low as four shillings in some areas and as high as three pounds in others.[39] But over 40 per cent of authorities levied rates of less than 12 shillings *per* male ratepayer. Property rates were introduced in 1956–57 in some areas but the arrears records show that many rate payers were successfully avoiding this much resented local tax. The consequences were constricted revenues[40] which were further shrunk by the fact that in many cases the cost of local tax collection actually exceeded the total amount of revenue collected. And it was acknowledged that the high cost of collection was related to the fact that collectors were largely unsupervised and that the entire process was largely unaudited.

While the range of functions exercised by local councils differed slightly from region to region, most of them retained the extensive responsibilities of the old native authorities. These extremely poorly financed institutions were required to run local police forces, to maintain roads, to provide local educational provisions as well as the local clinics and dispensaries. They supervised markets, public latrines; they licensed letter writers, traditional medical practitioners and animist shrines. In addition they were also required in many cases to undertake major new projects such as piped water supplies. Local government was, despite its inherent dullness, central to the success or otherwise of the vast majority of Ghanaians' pursuit of happiness. Local government may lack the excitement of national politics but it regulated much of the day-to-day life of many Ghanaians.

These councils were obviously extremely poorly adapted to the multiple tasks that were laid upon them. Almost without exception their estimated net expenditures were far in excess of their income. This was apparent from the beginning of the reformed system in 1951. The Chief Commissioner for Ashanti wrote to the Minister of Local Government at the close of 1951 that 'Native Authorities finances [are] deteriorating'.[41] In some cases, especially those of the smaller authorities, the costs of administration[42] appear to have absorbed 30 per cent of income.[43] Taken together, the inherent failure of local government produced at best 'an air of indifference to local government' and at worst 'vigorous protests about the inadequacy of the services and the cost of … administration'.[44] These units of local government were palpably not economically viable and were in most cases barely functioning. And there were a huge number of them; Ghana, with a population of about 6 million at independence in 1957, boasted 252 local and urban councils, 26 district councils and 4 municipal councils. They were, moreover, of strikingly uneven size, an unwelcome inheritance of the sloppy decision in 1951 to retain the old native authority boundaries as the boundaries of the new councils. 31 councils had populations of under 5000 people and smallest governed the lives of less than 1000. 75 councils had populations of less than 10,000.

Most of these councils continued to function only because of sizable grants from government and the Cocoa Marketing Board. In 1955–57, central government gave grants to local authorities of about £700,000 *per annum* for projects such as schools, markets, roads, bridges and so forth.[45] As the Greenwood Report made clear, 'The amount of development financed from councils' own revenues was comparatively insignificant.'[46] Although the figures are both hard to get at and inherently unreliable when available, central government grants paid for considerably more than 50 per cent of the expenditure of local councils.[47] In 1953–54 government grants to local councils in the Ashanti region had provided as much as 16 shillings of every pound of local revenue.[48]

Had government continued to reap the rewards of high commodity prices and then redistributed consequent tax revenue this might not have mattered. But by 1958 the Ministry of Finance made it known that large subventions would not be available in the financial year 1959–60.[49] The growing financial crisis in local government had been exacerbated by central government's decision in 1956 to increase the pay of government employees which came to include employees of local government.[50] The cost of this pay increase amounted to over £440,000 and this sum was found in 1956–58 from a central government subsidy which was not paid in 1959–60. By the time of independence these crucial agencies were increasingly dependent upon fees, tolls, rates and fines and, as we have seen, these were inefficiently collected and produced small sums even in the case of well-run authorities.[51]

While the Greenwood Report succeeded in encouraging reform, most notably in the amalgamation of this scatter of micro-authorities, the financial weakness of local government continued – and continues to this day. While the structural issues[52] have dominated this account of the weakness of this system, the fragility and underperformance of local government was also a function of the complex political situation.

The elbowing aside of the chiefs after 1951 was contested and the squabbles over power and most especially over 'stool income' continued after independence. But the volatility and even the violence of local politics monopolized the energies of elected councillors. This was picked-up by Ghana's most astute journalist, Bankole Timothy, in a series of well-researched articles in 1956.[53]

'Political acrobatics', he wrote, 'were undermining the efficient running of local Councils ... where a Local Council ... is CPP dominated and a town or village in the area has a strong NLM following, projects designed for such a village or town are shelved by the District Council development Committee ... the development of such an under-developed country ... is an important matter which should not be impaired by political juggling or favouritism.'[54]

Timothy's research continued and in a further long article, which makes very grim reading, he listed the appalling poverty of coastal Shama. He noted the paucity of private cars, the lack of drainage and the scarcity of fresh water:

> The one standpipe is often empty and women can wait 6–8 hours before being able to fill their buckets. It is a filthy town. The smell is unbearable. The so-called houses are a mass of rickety-rackety houses, badly ventilated and overcrowded ... horrible conditions under which the children live and grow up. Many of them show signs of malnutrition ... I asked [a senior official of the local council] what amenities the Council had provided ... 'We are now planning', 'Planning since 1952?' ... there was no reply.[55]

Timothy's articles deeply alienated the government and he, a Sierra Leonean, was an early victim of the government's programme of deportation immediately after independence.[56] His general conclusions, in a further article on 28 April 1956, are persuasive: '... party politics is destroying the future of Local Government and impeding progress'. It was the stagnation encouraged by the seemingly endless local wrangles which account, in part, for the routine suspension by central government of local councils and the substitution of, in effect, direct administration in the years both immediately before and after independence. The grounds for such suspensions varied from case to case[57] and there were a lot of such suspensions; but many appear to have been initiated by orchestrated[58] formal complaints directed to the Ministry of Local Government by local CPP members describing themselves as Ratepayers Societies, Youth Associations and Citizens Organisations. Several Cabinet memoranda use the formulaic comment that this or that council 'has forfeited the confidence of the ratepayers'.[59]

These suspensions paved the way for the eventual creation of first Regional and then Political Commissioners. The former, Nkrumah claimed, were to bring 'Government and people closer together' and the latter were to be the 'the Regional Commissioners' political "eyes" in the District ...'.[60] Government frustration, some of it entirely understandable as we have seen, led to a situation by 1960 in which what had been sold as democratised local government was now direct rule by central government. 'The general administration and supervision of *their* Regions ...' was, the Prime Minister wrote, the responsibility of Regional Commissioners whilst Districts were to be administered and supervised by the District Commissioners working under the Regional Commissioners. Both 'should act not only in consultation with the Minister of Local Government but also in accordance with directions issued by him'.[61] He made no mention here of the wishes of local people or of the value of consultation. Two weeks after the Prime Minister had drafted this letter, no less than 26 functions previously reserved to the Minister under the Local Government Ordinance were delegated to Regional Commissioners who thereafter formally as well as informally controlled the working of local councils. Despite this centralising response to the manifest failures of local government, the deteriorating economic situation and the narrow and sometimes foolish understandings of development continued to conspire to deny ordinary Ghanaians serious improvements in their material conditions.

This was a tragedy that had been long in the making and despite being ignored in the British and Ghanaian official accounts, the failure to promote a functioning, let alone a democratic system of local government in the run-up to independence was a serious one. Local councils were not merely the nominated providers of a vast range of social, medical and educational provisions; they were the *only* providers and were failing dismally in that duty. Maxwell Owusu commenting upon the performance of the Swedru Urban Council in the period under review wrote that the Council could not, without substantial grants from central government, 'embark on new development projects or even ... meet other urgent recurrent expenditure such as buying new pans for the removal of night soil or street repairs'.[62] Such substantial grants were a memory by 1961. The impact of all this was felt most heavily by the numerous poor, the improvement of whose welfare was supposedly at the heart of late colonial rule and of the Convention People's Party's project.

The erosion of citizens' rights also tended to be conveniently ignored by the British, who were perhaps distracted by the hectic business of securing a peaceful disengagement. Although the great set pieces of Ghanaian authoritarianism[63] were to await, impatiently one senses, for the freedoms which were to be delivered by independence, the Gold Coast's local legal system was in serious disarray well before March 1957. There is no doubt that the structurally unreformed local court system,[64] the part of the system which impacted most upon ordinary rural Ghanaians, was politicised throughout the 1950s and 1960s. While the old chiefly domination of the local courts produced innumerable abuses, modernisation took the form merely of replacing chiefs with CPP stalwarts; that cannot be claimed to have levelled the playing field. Bias and patronage of one sort was replaced by bias and patronage of another. The politicisation of the lower levels of the justice system provided the backdrop for the deterioration in law and order from 1954 onwards. Although their opinion was certainly biased, the Joint Provincial Council of Colony Chiefs (JPC) dated this deterioration from much earlier. 'The criminal ideas installed [sic] into the minds of the public found crude expression in the disturbances of February, 1948.'[65] Despite the obvious political intention of the JPC's conclusion, the government, in attempting to rebut this idea, unintentionally confirmed it: '... such friction as occurs ... [results] from a conflict of ideas between the traditionally-minded and those who favour wider popular representation ...'[66] The foundation of the NLM provoked a worsening of the situation in which CPP-dominated courts were defied, threatened and even closed by opposition actions. There were 'a large number of cases varying in severity from threatening and minor assaults to small riots, murder and arson and the use of explosives'.[67] The violence was undoubtedly political. The Anglican Bishop of Accra, no friend of the

NLM, commented:

> The people have a right to ask that even though elections must at present ... be won or lost by the votes of the still largely illiterate masses, leaders and organisers should control the activities of their less responsible supporters whose acts of studied abuse and intolerance were deeply shocking to more educated people and to those whose traditional upbringing had endowed them with a natural courtesy and respect for others which are among the most treasured possessions of the Gold Coast. The potential fruits of democracy might all too easily be lost in a dreadful upsurge of mob-rule if hooligans are allowed to give unrestrained expression to their ignorant prejudices. Enthusiasm and party slogans are not enough. If our country is to advance towards true unity and common happiness and prosperity the rights of all men of whatever political party must be safeguarded and honoured.[68]

Although the police attempted to bring many of these cases to court, there are strong memories of intimidated tribunals throwing out cases or imposing absurdly light punishments for serious offences. Stipendiary magistrates were imposed where local court members were fearful of sitting but they too were threatened and on some occasions, prevented from sitting and even chased from court. This is borne out to some extent by the report of the judicial *Enquiry into Allegations of Intimidation, Threatening and Extortion in Ashanti* which reported in December, 1957.[69] This looked at 491 cases which had been ignored by the police or had resulted in no further action and demanded re-investigation of 57 of these.[70] There was undoubtedly a *lacuna* when it came to due process in many parts of pre-independence Ghana and unsurprisingly it was a *lacuna* which invited authoritarian interventions.

Manifest disorder provoked the first of several postponements of scheduled local council elections. In March 1956, government deferred those elections to October 1957.[71] This was again discussed by Cabinet on 7, 21 and 28 August, when elections were again postponed 'until it had been possible to carry out re-registration'.[72] No reasons were given for the delay in registration but local turbulence had made this task difficult. A month after independence the Minister of Local Government had no trouble in persuading his Cabinet colleagues that the tenure of members of Local Councils should be further extended until the last day of February, 1958. There is no evidence beyond gossip which suggests that there were electoral irregularities during the eventual holding of those elections in 1958 although it surprised many when the CPP took twelve of the fourteen councils in Ashanti.[73] Throughout Ghana the CPP emerged again as the dominant force on the vast majority of local councils.

As is well known, the CPP government reacted to opposition and local disorder in an increasingly forceful manner. The banning of the NLM under the Avoidance of Discrimination Act,[74] the deportation of many of the Moslem Association Party's activists and the use of preventive detention constituted the tip of the iceberg. Behind the scenes, the Special Branch of the Police Service was being used in specifically political fashion to counter the campaigns of the United Party under the control of the Cabinet's National Defence Council chaired by the Prime Minister.

This is a deeply sad story made sadder by its earlier presentation as a success story; there is much, much more of it and importantly for ordinary Ghanaians it is a tragedy which has, as yet, no ending. It is an important story not least because of the modern interest in 'failed states' and the international agencies' conditional insistence upon the construction of 'democracy'. I hope that some of the following teases out some conclusions.

The first of these concerns the scholarly literature on the terminal colonial period in Ghana and perhaps elsewhere in Africa. That literature betrays the enthusiasm of mostly younger scholars confronted with a great epic in which the old institutions and attitudes of colonialism were successfully challenged by radical, modernising nationalism. This was an appropriate story for a post-war world, for the second half of the twentieth century. But its focus was inescapably upon, for lack of a better phrase, national politics.[75] National politics were most assuredly exciting and there was never any need to 'sex up' our narratives. It was a story full of larger-than-life protagonists performing, sometimes histrionically, on a big stage.

This 'big picture' was, however, a story which excluded the vast majority of Ghanaians. At the most formal of levels that exclusion is apparent. Although it may well have been the case that these 'exciting times' enthused many Ghanaians, they did not show that enthusiasm in terms of participation in national politics. In all of the three pre-independence elections, participation rates were low. The growing awareness of the nature of electoral politics and the challenge mounted by a real opposition in the 1956 election might have led to the registration and turnout figures exceeding those of the 1954 – or the 1951 – elections. They did not. In the southern third of the country, the most developed part of the country, significantly less than half of those enfranchised bothered to register and very many fewer than half of those who registered bothered to vote.[76] That general picture was repeated in the other three regions with some variation. The number of voters actually declined after the 1954 election. The claims of many contemporary scholars that this was a new era of 'mass politics' and that the CPP was a 'mass party', are clearly challenged by these data.[77]

Most Ghanaians lived through a political experience which was rather different from the important epic being played out between the CPP and British governments. Politics for them consisted of localised struggles between factions which were in some cases allied to political parties and in some cases were not. Politics, as it is everywhere, was about the sorts of concerns nicely caught by Harold Lasswell's title, *Politics; Who Gets What, How and When?*[78] But the institutions which managed the 'what' of Lasswell's question, those flows of resource which ultimately either aided or impeded individuals, were broken-backed affairs about which we know far too little. We know too little about the history of local government for many reasons, the most significant of which is that national politics is about famous people whilst local government is inherently dull. As a consequence very little of the literature we have produced over the near half-century of Ghana's independence has bothered itself with the politics of rural areas.

This is not just nit-picking as it is a gap not only in the historiography but also in the extensive literature on 'failed states' or 'state collapse'; much of that seems to be relatively unconcerned with what is meant by 'the state' just as it is shy about telling us when and indeed how 'failure' commenced. For most Ghanaians then – and now – the 'state' is an immediate, local set of institutions which appropriate and aid, which afflict and heal, which reward and punish and so forth. Without an appropriate command of the histories of localities and their institutions, ideas such as 'the contraction of the state' seem to have little meaning beyond a skewed understanding of what metropolitans might regard as 'the periphery'. Much of the political literature also seems convinced that states, like fish, rot from the head downwards. But in Ghana things began to fall apart in the countryside well before independence; much of the CPP governments' gross heavy-handedness grew out of their inability to reform local government. All they – and most of their successors – have sought to do is a far cry from the radical pretensions of the 1940s and 1950s; their concern is simply to control the countryside not to enrich or empower its denizens.

To shift the focus of the transfer of power narrative in Ghana away from the national and international political struggles which are captured in national archives and then in the BDEEP series, tells a rather different story about that period. In this alternative narrative, the British 'side' is seen in a much more negative light. Looking only at 'high' politics, Britain emerges from the Ghana chapter with some credit. It appears to have acted with a degree of consistency, to have mostly honoured its promises, to have balanced its own interests with those of Africans and to have dealt equitably rather than cruelly with its adversaries. The documentary record is mostly a record of patience and diligence, of sensitivity and percipience in which the inevitable is bowed to without the loss of much dignity or integrity. There appears to have been the application of serious 'due diligence' when it came to the planning of new structures in a new state. But using the microscope rather than the telescope presents us with a different picture.

The colonial state in the Gold Coast until the Second World War was in effect a federation in which the Regional Chief Commissioners acted without much let or hindrance from Accra. This reflected the fact that the core values of colonial administration were crucially bound-up with the provision and management of local government and local justice. The administrative elite, in the estimation of others as well as themselves, were the field administrators whose business this was. While the economic determinants of such a concentration upon rural affairs are apparent to us, most of its practitioners were caught up in an idealised even sentimental vision of 'the country' and 'country-folk'. In an equal and opposite way, colonial administrators regarded towns and townspeople with exasperated toleration at best and hostility at worst. The Elysian view of the countryside and the negative view of towns bore little resemblance to reality as, for example, there were many more disturbances in the countryside than there were in towns in the interwar period.

The challenge to government that erupted in 1948 reversed this polarity in abrupt fashion. Colonial emphasis upon the protection of rural areas from the pollution of urbanity, the provision of ring-fenced 'traditional' forms of justice governed by 'customary' law and the 'naturalness' of 'natural rulers' were rapidly abandoned in favour of an urban vision and an urban focus. This meshed neatly with exasperation with the failure of chieftaincy to deliver 'development' during and immediately after the war along with a Labour government's discomfort with institutions as palpably undemocratic as chieftaincy. While the causes of this change of heart are complex, the results were clear. While constitutional change and the structural implications of these were exhaustively gone over in Whitehall between the publication of the Watson Commission Report and the 1951 elections, there was very little consideration of the fate of local government besides rather general statements about 'democratisation'. There was virtually no discussion of the financing of local government institutions, a matter of considerable importance given that local government was required to be the agency delivering rural improvement.

It was left to the all-African Coussey Committee to plan the reform of local government. And after 1951 it was left to African ministers of local government to preside over what was clearly a mess which worsened throughout the 1950s. Senior British administrative critics of local government policy were regarded by the Governor as rocking a boat whose next port of call had to be independence; there were enough wrangles with African ministers without gratuitously adding to them as local government was, after all, *their* business now. And so far as Westminster and Whitehall were concerned, local government and local justice simply disappear off their radar. The notion of a 'planned' transfer of power which was so close to Andrew Cohen's heart tends to fall apart when the focus falls upon the immediate governance of 85 per cent of Ghana's population.

It is easy to account for this shift from a rural focus. Nationalists were not much concerned with rural areas being in large measure either townsmen or relieved escapees from rural life. It was with nationalists rather than chiefs that the colonial now had to deal and old concerns and old allies were the immediate victims of that process. Ghana's local government structure fell apart in the 1950s and with that collapse the chances of serious agricultural renewal and expansion along with the aspirations of many, many Ghanaians were disappointed.

Notes

1. A view conditionally shared in the Colonial Office. On 20 June 1956 C.G. Eastwood, an Assistant Under-Secretary of State at the CO, agreed with Gordon Hadow's assessment that while '... standards had deteriorated ... this was an inevitable part of the process of self government ... the quality of local recruits is good. ...' National Archives, Kew (NA), DO35/6174, no. 14.
2. Although its main runway has proved to be too short for the biggest and most heavily laden of jet craft.
3. Ghana's railway system has sadly long since ceased to operate.
4. Road and rail building had everything to do with the regionally specific needs of cocoa marketing and mining.
5. And the beginnings of a navy and air force.
6. This was especially marked after the official rehabilitation of Nkrumah and his symbolically important re-interment in the late Rawlings era. Several contemporary political parties claim to be 'Nkrumahist' although their publications appear to be confused about what that might mean.

7. Arden-Clarke's first post-Independence letter (15 March 1957) to his family begins with the self-congratulatory and excessively bullish words: 'Now all the crises have been resolved ...'.

8. NA, DO 35/6178, no. 2, minute, 4 July 1956.

9. Its impact upon the morale, tactics and strategy of nationalists throughout Africa is incalculable; but if from nowhere else as clearly, it emerges strongly from the African newspapers (in many languages) of the 1950s.

10. Amongst those criticisms, those of Frantz Fanon, who had briefly worked in Ghana were the harshest and the most long-lived. See *The Wretched of the Earth* (London: 1959). Less blood-curdling is a remarkable piece of contemporary fiction, Peter Abrahams' *Wreath for Udomo*, (London: 1956), an intriguing *roman a clef*, and an accessible radical critique. Bob Fitch and Mary Oppenheimer's *Ghana; End of an Illusion* (New York: 1966) was written without having worked in Ghana or in any archive and this shows.

11. Most especially the regime's somewhat fruitless flirtation with the eastern bloc which was then perceived sincerely as being threatening.

12. The angry final chapter of Dennis Austin's *Politics in Ghana* (London: 1964) is a bitter, informed reflection which contrasted with much of the Cold Warrior denigration which took its cue from Nkrumah's ostensibly warm relations with Moscow. Henry Bretton's *Rise and Fall of Kwame Nkrumah* (New York, 1966) is certainly the best of that genre.

13. Especially if these had found their way into published form and had been proved to be poor prophesy.

14. Derived as these were almost entirely from import and export duties rather than direct taxation.

15. National Archives of Ghana (NAG), ADM 13/2/17, Cabinet Papers, 8th June 1954.

16. NA, DO35/6178. no. 17a Arden-Clarke to Lennox-Boyd, 14 July 1956. The disquieting coincidence was, of course, to stimulate the conspiracy theories mentioned earlier.

17. This point is argued in more detail in my article 'Some aspects of the prehistory of the Ghanaian economy', in *The Journal of Commonwealth and Comparative Politics*, xxxi, 1 (March 1993), 7–20.

18. See, for example, Andrej Krassowski, *Development and the Debt Trap: Economic Planning and External Borrowing in Ghana* (London: 1974); Tony Killick: *Development Economics in Action: A Study of Economic Policies in Ghana* (London: 1978) and Douglas Rimmer *The Economies of West Africa* (London: 1984).

19. The fourth chapter of my *Nkrumah and the Chiefs: The Politics of Chieftaincy in Ghana, 1951–60*, (Oxford: 2000), pp. 48–59 is still the most detailed account of this complex process.

20. NA, CO 554/806, no. 140, Nkrumah to Lennox-Boyd, 21 November 1955. In the same letter Nkrumah describes the ongoing transfer of power as 'a jump from age old feudalism to twentieth century democracy'.

21. Bourne had been chosen to 'mediate' on the vexed issue of federation in 1955. A member of the Indian Civil Service since 1920, he had been Governor of Central Provinces and Berar for the year before Indian independence and then Governor of East Bengal from 1947 to 1950.

22. NA, CO 554/806, no 167, Bourne to Arden-Clarke, 19 December 1955. The italics are mine.

23. A Temporary Principal at the CO.
24. Assistant Under-Secretary of State, CO.
25. NA, CO 554/807, minutes by Z.Terry, W.L.Gorell Barnes and others on the Report of the Jibowu Commission, 16 August 1956.
26. NA, CO 554/1210, no. 43, R.J.Vile to Gordon Hadow, 5 July 1956.
27. NA, CO 554/807, minute by W.G. Gorrel Barnes on the Jibowu Report, 10 August 1956.
28. There are some important accounts of the decline of local government, the best researched of which are Maxwell Owusu's *The Uses and Abuses of Political Power* (Chicago, IL: 1970) and John Dunn and A.F. Robertson's *Dependence and Opportunity; Political Change in Ahafo* (Cambridge: 1973).
29. To the CO from the Governor and to the CRO from the Advisor on External Affairs to the government of Ghana (Francis Cumming-Bruce). These flows were firstly the link between the CO and the Governor, and secondly that between the CRO and the Advisor on External Affairs.
30. Senior field administrators were clearly offended by the marginalisation of their expertise, a matter which is very apparent in Hugh Beeton's diaries and Colin Russell's memoirs.
31. The British were cowed by the apparent cultural otherness of chieftaincy and other forms of African governance and by the 1940s alarmed about the implications of causing cultural and hence political offence even if much of this was opportunistic political posturing.
32. The structure of local justice remained intact until well after independence even if the makeup of the tribunals had been manipulated to exclude Chiefs and members of opposition parties whilst empanelling local CPP figures.
33. See *Report of the Commission of Enquiry into Electoral and Local Government Reform*, Part 3, Section 5. Accra, 1968.
34. NA, CO 96/8000/1, no. 8, 5 September 1949.
35. NAG, ADM 13/2/40, Cabinet paper by the Minister of Local Government, 13 August 1957.
36. NAG, ADM 13/2/2, Chief Commissioner, Ashanti to Minister of Local Government, 11 December 1951.
37. A long memorandum by the Minister of Local Government which rehearsed many of the problems re-addressed by the Greenwood Commission four years later, includes this comment: 'in a democratic state the amount of money which can be raised in taxes ultimately depends upon the willingness of the people to accept taxation'. Cabinet paper, 28 April 1953, unclassified in NAG when consulted.
38. See, for example, *the Report of the Commission on Local Government*, Accra, August, 1957, para 15[ii], p. 11.
39. Rates were also levied according to gender. Women paid half the rate levied on men. The extensive literature on the success of female entrepreneurs in Ghana has not noticed this relative advantage.
40. Areas in which higher rates and higher revenues applied were, unsurprisingly, cocoa growing areas.
41. NAG, ADM 13/2/2, 11 December 1951.
42. This included the salaries of officers like clerks and treasurers, office expenses and the stipends of councillors.
43. A level of top-slicing which will be familiar to most British academics.

44. NAG, ADM 13/2/40, quotations from part 1 of the first draft of the *Report of the Commission on Local Government* (Chairman, A.F. Greenwood) read by Cabinet on 13 August 1957.
45. Government grants were intended to be used for capital expenditure on development projects and formally could not be used to subsidise recurrent expenditure. In practice it seems unlikely that this rule was frequently breached.
46. *Report of the Commission on Local Government*, para 14, p. 10.
47. G. Kay with S. Hymer, *The Political Economy of Colonialism in Ghana: A Collection of Documents and Statistics, 1900–1960* (Cambridge: 1972) provides little assistance for anyone looking for data concerning any Council other than the municipal authorities of Accra, Cape Coast, Kumasi and Sekondi.
48. This high proportion had been reduced in 1954–55 'to provide larger grants to local authorities in other regions' according to the Prime Minister. NAG, ADM 13/2/21, *Memorandum to the Standing Development Committee by Nkrumah*, Cabinet, 22 March 1955. This was restored in late 1955 for largely political reasons and by 1958 was twice as large, in *per capita* terms, than that paid to any other region.
49. Despite this grants to local government constituted between one-sixth and one-seventh of government's annual expenditure by 1960. According to one of the rare surviving District Council estimates for 1958–59, the Buem-Krachi Authority expected to spend nearly £237,000. Of this sum they expected central government to provide £159,000.
50. In the light of years of price inflation, this was a long overdue concession.
51. Maxwell Owusu's case study of the Swedru Urban Council, a relatively efficient Council, shows this with great clarity. See his *Uses and Abuses of Political Power*, p. 283.
52. For example the number of authorities, their varied sizes, the burdens placed upon them and most importantly the mismatch between declining national and individual incomes and the expectations of development.
53. Beginning with a column in *The Daily Graphic*, of which he was Deputy Editor, of 11 April 1956, entitled 'Too much politics'.
54. *The Daily Graphic*, Accra, 11 April 1956.
55. Ibid. 27 April 1956. It is an account which is curiously like that provided in Ayi Kwei Armah's gloomy novel about Sekondi in the Nkrumah years, *The Beatyful [sic] Ones are Not Yet Born* (London: 1975).The novelist uses decay, filth, excrement as powerful images of corruption, incompetence and disappointment.
56. Timothy's deportation on 1 August 1957 was amongst the first acts of the newly appointed Minister of Information and Broadcasting who assumed office on 31 July 1957. Journalists, Kofi Baako said, 'can write what they think right. It is only when they write what is wrong that the law will deal with them.' *Daily Graphic,* 2 August 1957.
57. Accra Municipal Council was suspended because of 'the unsatisfactory manner in which the ... Council has performed its functions'. NAG, ADM 13/2/37, Cabinet paper, 16 April 1957. A scatter of Trans-Voltaic Councils were suspended because of 'political differences and traditional jealousies. A majority of the people ... support the United Party but this Party does not command a majority on the Council ... the Council has been used on too

many occasions for political purposes ...'. Manya Krobo Council was suspended because of 'repeated petitions and deputations from the Ratepayers' Associations enumerating many irregularities committed by the [pro-United Party] council ... failure to follow contract procedure ... no proper control over accounts ...'. NAG, ADM 13/2/44, Cabinet paper, 14 January 1958.

58. Oral informants suggested that Party Branch committees organised such campaigns.

59. See, for example, NAG, ADM 13/2/44, Cabinet papers on the suspension of Atwima Mponua Council, 28 January 1958.

60. NAG, ADM 13/2/52, Cabinet paper, 9 September 1958.

61. NAG, ADM 13/2/69, Prime Minister's draft letter to Regional Commissioners, Cabinet, 2 February 1960.

62. See *Uses and Abuses of Political Power*, p. 283.

63. At a formal level one must mention the abandonment of *Habeas Corpus*, the Preventive Detention Act, and the use of deportation orders. Eighteen months after independence 43 members of the United Party had been arrested and denied the rights in *Habeas Corpus*. Two MPs had been detained and through subsequent legislation had been stripped of their seats. Twenty-six people were detained without trial. For more on this, see chs 7–11 of *Nkrumah and the Chiefs*.

64. However I am sympathetic about the structural reasons which inhibited real reform. See pp. 55–7 of *Nkrumah and Chiefs*. The binary legal system was a nightmarish mess and its resolution constituted a significant problem. For those reasons and because of concern about the necessity to keep chiefs 'on side', it was a problem which had been systematically evaded by the colonial regime over a long period.

65. NAG, ADM 13/2/4, minutes of the JPC's 16th Annual Session, 11 February 1952.

66. NAG, ADM 13/2/5, Cabinet minutes, 16 February 1952.

67. NAG, ADM 13/2/31, Minister of the Interior's Cabinet memorandum, 14 August 1956.

68. A speech to the Accra Diocesan Synod on 25 August 1956.

69. Under the chairmanship of the judge, Emmanuel Quist.

70. The government had hoped that the enquiry would produce damning evidence about the activities of the opposition but it produced as much evidence of CPP intimidation. In NAG, ADM 13/2/61 the Minister of the Interior complained in a Cabinet paper that 'the practical results of the Quist Commission have not been impressive. ...' (16 June 1959).

71. A move described by Modesto Apaloo, an NLM supporter from south-eastern Ghana, in the Legislative Assembly as 'a danger to democracy'. *Daily Graphic*, Accra, 28 March 1956.

72. NAG, ADM 13/2/33, Cabinet paper, 28 August 1956.

73. Part of the explanation of this huge shift in the regional electoral balance lies in the history of intimidation and perhaps especially in the politically stupid opposition policy of encouraging people to boycott polls.

74. NAG, ADM 13/2/42, Cabinet paper, 5 November 1957. Its original title was the Emergency Powers Bill. For the conspiratorially minded, the date was a nice coincidence.

75. As an historian of Ghana I am of course deeply implicated in what I am about to criticise.
76. While there may have been apprehensions about registration especially if one was a rate defaulter, this does not explain the extraordinarily low turnout of registered voters.
77. The credulity of those scholars who accepted CPP statements about membership figures in excess of one million while the voting figures showed that the Party had not attracted more than 400,000 voters in any election needs no further comment.
78. First published in New York in 1936.

7
'We Cannot Let the North Down': British Policy and Nigeria in the 1950s

Martin Lynn

British colonial officials were aware that the ending of the Second World War would be followed by demands for political change in their West African colonies generally and in Nigeria in particular. How successfully this growing nationalist sentiment was contained, it was recognised, would be one of the major issues to face British policy once peace prevailed. On its success or failure would hang the success or failure of British rule and British interests therafter. The aim in the re-assessment of West African policy that the Colonial Office (CO) undertook from 1943 onwards therefore, was to 'manage' these nationalist demands by channelling them into directions that British officials saw as constructive, thereby blunting any demands for immediate independence that more radical political leaders might articulate. In itself, however, nationalist sentiment was not seen as a necessary threat to British interests; it was something that, if constructively addressed, could be harnessed to British ends. Eventual self-government was recognised as being implicit in this engagement between British policy and local leaders, but it was, at this stage, seen as being many decades in the future.[1]

In the Nigerian case, the implementation of this policy was, in the short term, poorly handled. The so-called 'Richards constitution' that came into effect in 1947 was clearly a case of 'too little too late' as far as much educated opinion in Nigeria was concerned. The newly formed National Council of Nigeria and the Cameroons (NCNC) and its leader, Nnamdi Azikiwe, were allowed the opportunity to build both considerable support in Nigeria and valuable sympathy in the United States.[2] In 1946 indeed, a militant body prepared to use violence, the Zikist movement, had emerged with threats of a revolutionary rising against British

144

rule.[3] In the longer term however, the CO line of pre-emptive reform that had emerged after 1943 was broadly effective. By 1950 a new Governor, Sir John Macpherson, who had arrived in 1948, had, by astute use of the carrot of constitutional revision and the stick of a security crackdown, channelled the nationalist movement into an essentially constitutionalist path that re-established the collaborative mechanisms that his predecessor, Sir Arthur Richards, had undermined.[4]

The constructive management of nationalism remained one of the central policy objectives of the administration in Nigeria. That nationalist parties would continue to grow, and indeed that their growth would be stimulated by the constitutional reforms the CO was pursuing, was recognised as an inevitable and not-unwelcome feature of this management of political change in the territory. For Macpherson, the key was, as he put it, to maintain 'the initiative' in this process, thereby shaping nationalism in ways that suited British interests.[5] The so-called 'Macpherson constitution' of 1951 was the centrepiece of his policy. This was designed to produce a constitution more acceptable to Nigerian opinion than the 1947 one, but it was one which remained within the political limits established in the early 1940s; the Council of Ministers was no Cabinet, the Governor presided and there was no ministerial responsibility. For Macpherson at this stage, the road to self-government was still seen as one that would take several decades; it was at this moment that he stated to a new recruit to the colonial service in Nigeria that he had at least 30 years service ahead of him.[6] This was still to be, as planned in the early 1940s, a move to a very distant self-government.

However it is the argument here that Macpherson's regaining of the initiative in Nigeria in 1948–50 was a relatively short-lived phenomenon. Very rapidly pressures built up in the territory that forced policy-makers, in both London and Lagos, to reassess their approach. Out of this re-evaluation of the policy that had evolved in the early 1940s came a new line which was pursued by British officials during the rest of the 1950s. This new line, marked by an acceptance of imminent self-government and a much stronger emphasis on what was called 'regionalism', and on the Northern region in particular, characterised British policy to Nigeria through to independence in 1960.

Regionalism – the idea that power in Nigeria should be devolved to its constituent parts, though there was much debate as to what those parts were – had, given the size of the territory, long been an acknowledged feature of British policy. Indeed the two separate protectorates of Northern and Southern Nigeria had only been united in 1914, and even thereafter, the North had remained outside the remit of the central

Legislative Council. When Richards' eponymous constitution emerged it broke Southern Nigeria into two while leaving the North intact. Implicit in this was the assumption that the North, with a population of 17 million out of a total 31 million for Nigeria as a whole, would be the dominant part of Nigeria. The 1951 constitution, building on Richards' moves in this direction, introduced formal regionalism into the territory, dividing Nigeria into three regions, East, North and West, each reflecting the predominance of the major ethnic groupings of Igbo, Hausa-Fulani and Yoruba. Crucially, the constitution conceded equal representation to the North, compared to the two southern regions combined, in the central House of Representatives, thereby ensuring a legislative 'veto' in all but name to the former.[7]

To understand the background to this regionalism, it is necessary to stress that Nigeria was, of course, an entirely British creation. Obafemi Awolowo, leader of the Action Group (AG), the Yoruba-based party that emerged in 1950, described the territory as 'a geographical expression' and there is much truth in his observation.[8] The Hausa-Fulani states of Northern Nigeria – Islamic in faith and under the control of a conservative Muslim aristocracy that had come to power in the jihads of the 1800s – had little if anything in common with the segmentary societies of Eastern Nigeria or even for that matter, the Yoruba states of Western Nigeria. These differences had been emphasised by the impact of British rule once Nigeria had been united in 1914. The reluctance of the British to allow Christian missionaries to operate in the Islamic heartland of Northern Nigeria had meant that educational provision in the North had seriously lagged behind that in the more Westernised South.[9] Differential access to the economic and social opportunities that came with British rule reinforced this. Equally, the policy of Indirect Rule, which emphasised ethnic particularities across Nigeria, ensured that the power of the ruling Islamic aristocracy of the North had been, if anything, enhanced through its control of local native authorities.[10]

It would be wrong, however, to argue that this approach by the British represented, at this stage at least, a policy of 'divide and rule'. Certainly the regionalism that characterised the 1951 constitution determined much of the course of constitutional development thereafter. Yet it is difficult, given the size of Nigeria, to identify a sinister agenda in this approach in the 1940s and difficult to see what the British might have done in its place. With the independence of India and Pakistan in 1947, Nigeria was far and away the largest remaining colonial territory; one in four of all British subjects lived in Nigeria. Given the size of Nigeria and given the pre-existing social, educational and political differences between its inhabitants, some form of regional devolution of power made sense in a system of administration that, through the idea of Indirect Rule, was predicated on the utilisation of collaborative networks. Patently, a unitary system of administration based on Lagos for a territory the size of Nigeria would hardly work as power came to be conceded, as assumed in the 1940s policy of the CO, to Nigerian leaders.[11] Further, the demographic structure of Nigeria in the late 1940s did mean that the interests of the 17 million Northerners, and the 12 million Muslims within that number, could hardly be ignored.

Equally, it was not unreasonable for the British to acknowledge Northern leaders' fears in this period. Understandably, Northern leaders, conscious of their region's educational and economic backwardness compared to the South, viewed the upsurge of southern nationalism in the 1940s with alarm. For this they did not need British prompting. Given the relative lack of Western-educated Northerners, nationalist demands for 'Nigerianisation' of the civil service, for example, were seen in the North as demands for 'Southernisation'. In 1953 only 30 or so out of 700 Nigerians holding senior civil service posts were Northerners.[12] The bringing of the North under the Legislative Council's remit in 1947 was seen as a measure that would allow Southern lawyers to challenge the decisions of Northern rulers in the courts. Famously, a Northern representative, Abubakar Tafawa Balewa, spoke in the Legislative Council that Britain's withdrawal would be a time for the settling of scores; the North would resume, he threatened, its interrupted 'conquest to the sea' and he sharply disassociated himself from the NCNC.[13] It was in reaction to the emergence of Southern nationalism indeed, that in 1949 a cultural society in the North, the Jam'iyyar Mutanen Arewa, was transformed into the Northern People's Congress (NPC) as a vehicle to defend Northern interests and to preserve the political, religious and social status quo in the North.[14]

None the less, it is also clear that the decision – or in reality, series of decisions – to adopt a regionalist approach to constitutional change in Nigeria that finally reached fruition in the 'Macpherson constitution', had a serious longer term impact on Nigerian politics. The constitution of 1951 set up three elected regional Houses of Assembly and, by making representation in the central House of Representatives dependent on victory in the regional Houses, encouraged the creation of regional parties to fight regional elections.[15] The post-war hopes of the NCNC to lead a pan-Nigerian movement against the British were finally laid to rest by this, since the introduction of regional elections drove political leaders to look for regional support for building electoral success.

A stress on ethnic identity was the inevitable way of achieving this. In the face of this the NCNC became moribund as a pan-Nigerian party and when it re-emerged in the early 1950s it was as a party of the Igbos of the Eastern region. Similarly in the West, the fear of Igbo domination via the NCNC stimulated the founding of the AG, led by Awolowo as an overtly Yoruba party.[16]

It was precisely these developments that meant that the 1951 constitution, while being an initially successful attempt to reassert British control over the politics of Nigeria, was also simultaneously the moment when things began to change fundamentally in the territory. Developments in the Gold Coast, where Kwame Nkrumah won the elections of early 1951 and was appointed first as Leader of Government Business and then in 1952 as Prime Minister, were critical in stimulating these demands in Nigeria for change.[17] Macpherson's problem derived from his central success, in that the length of time he had spun out the constitution-mongering of 1948–50 meant that the constitution that emerged in 1951 was, given Gold Coast developments, no longer adequate for Nigerian leaders' expectations.

The irony in this was that the reaction of Nigerian leaders to the 1951 constitution was driven by the very regionalism that Macpherson had made so central to it. Given that control of a region's House of Assembly was essential for representation at the centre, the elections of 1951 generated an intense struggle for power at the regional level. This could be seen especially in the West where these years were characterised by a bitter struggle between the two Southern parties for power in the region.[18] In mid-1952 the AG, in an attempt to pre-empt the NCNC by portraying itself as the leader of Nigerian nationalism, presented to Macpherson a lengthy memorandum criticising the new constitution and demanding full ministerial responsibility for the Council of Ministers.[19] It was very clear, less than a year after the constitution had commenced, that its provisions no longer satisfied Nigerian leaders.

The need to revise the constitution was also driven by events in the East, where once again its regionalist assumptions had unexpected consequences. Here NCNC control over its Igbo heartland was by no means guaranteed, given deeper ethnic tensions both among Igbos and between Igbo and Efik. Azikiwe's attempt to assert his control over the NCNC led to its split in early 1953 in the so-called 'sit-tight' crisis and to political stalemate in the region.[20] The CO realised that the only solution to the deadlock in the East was to dissolve the Eastern House and call for elections but this, due to poor drafting of the constitutional instruments, it soon learned was not possible without dissolving all the regional Houses.[21] The answer, it appeared, was to revise the 'Macpherson constitution' but with the danger of opening a Pandora's box in the process.

By early 1953, these pressures were making it clear that the 'Macpherson constitution' was in need of reconsideration, with all that that implied for a policy originally designed to kick the issue of self-government into the long grass. This problem was to become acute on 31 March of that year, when Tony Enahoro, an AG member of the House of Representatives, introduced a motion in the House calling for self-government for Nigeria by 1956, the year the constitution was to be reviewed.[22] The background to this lay specifically in the desire by the AG to seize the nationalist mantle in the Western region. In the event Enahoro's motion was lost amid uproar generated by Northern representatives fearing that the rapid self-government proposed by the AG would threaten Northern interests; given the North's educational backwardness compared to the South, independence simply threatened to replace British rule with rule by Southern politicians more versed in Western ways. 'The mistake of 1914 has now come to light', said the NPC leader, the Sardauna of Sokoto, ominously.[23]

This crisis had a number of consequences that seriously affected British policy. The most obvious was the deep cleavage the crisis revealed between North and South, and the NPC's overt willingness to stand against the demands of Southern nationalists for independence. To Southern nationalists, the Northern leaders had revealed their true colours as 'yes men', 'his master's voice' and 'government stooges', all descriptions that were hurled across the chamber at the NPC.[24] To NPC leaders, this episode confirmed their worst fears of the South's lack of understanding of Northern concerns. Shortly thereafter, in May, prompted by an AG plan to stage a rally in Kano, which would, said an AG leader, put Northern 'reactionaries' to flight, serious inter-ethnic rioting broke out in the city.[25]

However a second consequence, not often realised, was the way the affair destroyed the role of the Council of Ministers and thereby Macpherson's constitution; in this the AG achieved the aim they had spelt out in their 1952 ministerial-responsibility memorandum. Macpherson's idea of 'conciliar' responsibility for the Council – that Ministers had collective responsibility under the Governor for all government business – led him to insist that ministers should not speak in the debate on Enahoro's motion; he saw this as essential to maintain conciliar unity in a Council where all three parties were represented but often at loggerheads. In response the Western ministers in the Council resigned and thereby shattered his conception of conciliar responsibility.[26] The 1951 constitution was finished, less than two years after it had been inaugurated.

The third consequence of the episode was, again as the AG had hoped, its impact on the British timetable for self-government. Arguably the events of 1952–53 that culminated in the 31 March crisis, were the single most important turning point in British policy during the 1950s. On one level, the episode, simply by putting a date forward for discussion, meant that demands for self-government were now firmly on the agenda with a date that was clearly much more immediate than Macpherson had hitherto been prepared to acknowledge. The date of 1956 being out of the bottle, so to speak, could not be put back in it. The crisis thereby undermined the assumptions about a distant self-government on which Macpherson's policy since 1948, and indeed the CO's since 1943, had been predicated. This raised major questions for British policy. Given that Britain was not prepared to fight nationalism in West Africa, the ramifications of the crisis and thus, ironically, of the regionalism that had driven the AG to try to trump the NCNC, meant that self-government would now have to become a much more acknowledged and immediate feature of British policy towards Nigeria. Yet on another level, the crisis, by revealing Northern fears of independence, meant that reassurance would also simultaneously have to be given to the North that self-government was not imminent. The contradictions between these two approaches raised fundamental dilemmas for British policy. Clearly a reassessment of British options for Nigeria, as significant as that which had occurred in the early 1940s, would have to follow.

This was the moment the assumptions that had underlain British policy in Nigeria since the war had to be reconsidered. Although CO officials had already begun to review the Macpherson constitution in the light of the AG memorandum of 1952 and the Eastern 'sit-tight' crisis, the fall-out of the 31 March episode meant that this would have to involve a much more radical change than simply adjusting the mechanisms concerning dissolution of Houses of Assembly. During 1953 therefore, major debates about Nigerian policy, which reached the Cabinet on occasion, took place within the CO. Out of this a new policy towards Nigeria, one that was to characterise Britain's approach to the territory during the remaining years of colonial rule, emerged. Out of this too, came the CO's new emphasis on supporting the North.

In early 1953, before the crisis, CO officials realised that Nigerian demands for ministerial responsibility could no longer be resisted and that the constitution would have to be reviewed. Yet these proposals were at this stage couched in terms of legal modifications to the constitution rather than its full revision.[27] When consulted in March about the rapid political changes in the Gold Coast, Macpherson remained clear that in his view these developments were precipitate and should continue to be resisted in the case of Nigeria.[28] However the pace of constitutional review changed markedly following 31 March. The key moment came in mid-April when Macpherson and Sir Charles Arden-Clarke, Governor of the Gold Coast, were called to London for a series of meetings with officials and Oliver Lyttelton, the Secretary of State, to reconsider West African policy. A fundamental change in policy followed. Lyttelton made it clear to Macpherson that the constitution would now have to be 'radically recast'.[29] A Nigerian conference, probably in London, would need to be called to agree to the new constitution. While Lyttelton recognised that ministerial responsibility would have to be conceded, with all that that implied for the timetable to self-government, he also urged the need for much greater regional powers under the new constitution; regions would be given considerable autonomy with only very limited interference from the centre.[30]

The greater emphasis on regionalism that came out of these meetings was driven by the new importance given to the North by the CO. As Lyttelton, in a statement that underpinned British attitudes during this period, commented, the Muslim inhabitants of Northern Nigeria 'were more favourably disposed to this country than the Southern Nigerians'.[31] Throughout this crisis and the ensuing revision of policy, it is indeed striking how large the North loomed for all involved. Macpherson made the running. At a meeting in the CO on 15 April, he had stressed just how deep NPC anger with the Enahoro motion went: Northern views were, he said, 'hard, cold and implacable'. Northern leaders were thinking of separation from the South in reaction to these events, he felt, but he hoped they could be persuaded to avoid any drastic steps for the present. He added, in words that made his sympathies clear, that 'the people of the Northern Region had throughout been loyal, trustworthy and reasonable, although they were now beginning to wonder whether they might be let down by Her Majesty's Government. He felt it was unthinkable they should be so let down'. The meeting concluded that the North must be 'especially assured, as from the Secretary of State, that progress would not be made over their heads'.[32] Macpherson further emphasised this in May when he stressed the need for guarantees to the North. Britain 'should not leave the Northern leaders in doubt about their determination to fulfil their obligations to the seventeen million people of Northern Nigeria'.[33] His assessment of the situation concluded that Northern leaders did indeed want to secede from Nigeria, referring to his worries at the explosive 'magazine' situation in the region.[34] Macpherson's views were backed by Henry Hopkinson, the Minister of State, when he met Northern leaders in Nigeria in late April; he found them 'deeply disturbed' and seeing 'little purpose in continuing to attempt to work together' with the South.[35]

Macpherson's concerns were also reinforced by Sir Bryan Sharwood-Smith, Lieutenant-Governor and Governor of the Northern Region, 1952–57, who, it should be said, did little to assuage Northern leaders' fears.[36] He repeatedly made clear to the CO his own sympathies, stressing the popular support the NPC leadership had and emphasising the degree of corruption among politicians in the East and West, where 'the stench rose to High Heaven'.[37] Certainly AG descriptions of Northern leaders as 'a reactionary minority' and allegations that 'the British and the Northern political leaders were working hand-in-glove' in this period, along with demands that the British should 'compel the North to accept' self-government in 1956, played into his hands.[38]

These arguments had an impact in London. The danger of Northern secession had alarmed the CO since 31 March. A CO meeting in early May emphasised the need to use economic and financial inducements to encourage the NPC to stay in a united Nigeria. The 'disintegration of Nigeria' had to be avoided and this generated a marked shift in policy towards Northern interests.[39] When the issue reached the Cabinet on 27 May the new line was clear; it was agreed that while the constitution would be recast, arrangements 'would have to be such as to satisfy the North that their interests were effectively safeguarded'.[40] If reinforcement of the new CO policy were needed it had come the same month. On 21 May the Northern House of Assembly passed an 'Eight-points motion', demanding the break-up of Nigeria in all but name, with the regions having virtual autonomy and just a small central agency for central business.[41]

This new CO line of supporting NPC interests was very apparent in the run-up to the conference that met in London in July and August 1953. It was at first unclear if Northern leaders would even appear in London. Officials again emphasised the need to reassure NPC leaders that their interests would be protected in London. When T.B. Williamson, a senior CO official, visited Nigeria in June, his experience led him to urge that the Secretary of State in effect grant a 'veto'; he should stress to Nigerian leaders that Britain would not bring 'pressure to bear on the North to take self-government before they consider themselves ready'. In the next few weeks, he said, the CO would have to show the North that 'we are not going to let them down. ... We had better, while we still have the opportunity, go all out to secure the loyalty and faith in us of the North, rather than to lose the North, probably for ever, in an effort to placate an unreliable South'.[42] Shortly after, he urged the need to make any contemplated grant of self-government to Nigerian regions conditional on guarantees safeguarding the North's interests.[43] Macpherson echoed this. In a letter in July he repeated his view of the need for Lyttelton to make it clear that the CO 'will not bring any pressure whatsoever to bear on the North to accept any self-government in Nigeria ... before the North wish it to'.[44] These views were to shape CO policy thereafter.

When the conference met, with delegates representing all the Nigerian parties including the NPC, the CO's new approach was explicit. As anticipated, the 'Lyttelton' constitution that came out of the conference was one that granted greater autonomy to the regions and, in principle, ministerial responsibility in the Council of Ministers.[45] However the most critical issue the conference addressed was the question of 'self-government by 1956', the demand that had originally triggered the crisis. Lyttelton's approach was publicly to agree to *regional* self-government in 1956 – thus acknowledging in principle, eventual self-government for the Federation more broadly – while deferring a decision on the date of self-government for Nigeria as a whole. But in order to address Northern fears, he added that self-government would not come until *all* regions wished it; thereby explicitly granting a Northern 'veto' on independence. As Lyttelton stated to the conference, 'some of you may be tempted to murmur 'divide and rule'. I reject any such suggestion'.[46]

The importance of the 1953 conference and of Lyttelton's declaration on self-government cannot be gainsaid in the history of Britain's withdrawal from Nigeria. Just two years earlier the Macpherson constitution had come into effect with an implicit timetable for self-government that would take decades to achieve; by August 1953 this had been sharply curtailed. Promising regional self-government in 1956 did not, of course, imply full self-government would immediately follow but it was clearly now something that would be achieved within the foreseeable future. This was a turning point indeed. A new CO approach to Nigeria had emerged. It involved in essence, the concession of much greater power to Nigerian leaders and a recognition that self-government was now foreseeable, but also the prioritising of Northern interests within that process. Lyttelton spelt out his thinking to the Cabinet when reviewing the constitution in August. He stated how the leaders of the North were congenial to him, referring to their 'dignity, courtly manners, high bearing and conservative outlook which democracy and the *Daily Mirror* have not yet debased'. He compared them to the leaders of the South with 'higher education and lower manners ... somewhat intoxicated with nationalism', and added 'We cannot let the North down. They are more than half the population, more attached to the British and more trustful of the Colonial Service' than the South. Britain must not 'alienate our friends' and 'drive them into secession'.[47] The new CO line could hardly be clearer.

What was at the heart of this new policy therefore was the desire to reassure the NPC that the CO would defend Northern interests. That the CO would indeed do so could be seen very clearly in its reaction to a number of issues as they came forward in subsequent years. Not least in this were demands that the North should be broken up into two parts by creating a Middle Belt region, a long-term Southern demand. The NPC, as indeed the CO, feared this because it would remove the North's dominant position in the House of Representatives, where, because of its size, it continued to hold half of the seats. As early as May 1953 CO officials made it clear that a Middle Belt region would have to be avoided, despite attacks by the AG and NCNC on the 50 per cent representation of the North.[48] In preparing for the 1953 Conference CO officials again stressed their need to avoid a Middle Belt region and their desire to maintain the 50 per cent representation for the North.[49] The CO view, when it was spelt out again in 1955, was that avoiding a Middle Belt region was a necessity if Nigeria was to remain united and Northern secession be avoided.[50]

Sharwood-Smith, once again, was making the running on this issue. He made clear his belief that the AG and NCNC were trying to break-up the North simply for political advantage. This had to be resisted.[51] The administration in Nigeria agreed that if the idea of new regions were conceded in principle it would be difficult to prevent the creation of a Middle Belt and this could prompt the North to secede; by this stage resistance to new regions was almost an article of faith in the administration.[52] Sharwood-Smith in July 1955 stressed that the aim must be to maintain the unity of the North 'at all costs'.[53] When the CO began planning for the proposed 1956 London conference its papers emphasised that the NCNC were trying to break-up the North for political reasons and that this must be prevented.[54]

Yet the demands for a Middle Belt state were compelling, given the five million population of the area and their ethnic and religious differences from the 'Holy North'. They arose again in a major way at the 1957 London conference in the face of AG and NCNC pressures. The response of Alan Lennox-Boyd, Secretary of State, 1954–59, was to divert the attack by the appointment of the Willink Commission to examine the position of minorities in Nigeria more broadly.[55] When Sir Henry Willink reported in 1958, to the relief of the CO he recommended against the creation of new states, instead proposing measures to protect minorities.[56] When Nigerian leaders met at the 1958 conference this recommendation was endorsed, the key player being Azikiwe, who, because of the recent NPC–NCNC rapprochement, was now unwilling to antagonise NPC interests.[57]

If the CO were not prepared to challenge the NPC over a Middle Belt after 1953, nor where they prepared to push actively the cause of local government reform in the North. The CO recognised that the power of the ruling caste in the North, and thus the NPC, was based ultimately on its control of local government. Two-thirds of NPC leaders in 1959 were local government employees.[58] The CO recognised the prevalence of abuse within the system at a time when local government elsewhere in Nigeria was being reformed. Yet as early as 1953 Williamson had stressed the need to go gently on local government reform in the North, for fear of provoking the Islamic aristocracy.[59] He recognised none the less that the system was corrupt and that the region's rulers – or Emirs – influenced elections in favour of the NPC; he admitted that the electorate essentially did what the local Emir told them.[60] But the issue would not go away and another official, Maurice Smith, was by 1955 urging reform in the North and supporting a proposal by Sharwood-Smith that reform at the provincial level – the so-called '12 pillars' – would in practice preserve the power of the Emirs by cutting away demands from the South for the break-up of the North.[61] The CO set up an inquiry under R.S. Hudson, which reported in 1957 and endorsed Sharwood-Smith's ideas by proposing the creation of Provincial Authorities. None the less the CO, although welcoming the report, was realistic about the likelihood of real progress; Smith's view was that the Emirs would win out in the end by stonewalling change.[62] He was right. By 1958 it was clear that the Hudson Report was effectively being ignored; thereafter the administration soft-pedalled the idea of real reform of local government in the North.[63]

Nor was the CO willing to challenge NPC power in the electoral system after 1953. The desire for a uniform electoral law across the Federation, with standardised voting rights and voting systems, including direct elections in the North and votes for women, was pursued energetically by Southern parties in this period because they found it difficult, under existing arrangements, to break into the North. Yet CO officials remained cautious on this. Concern was expressed in 1955 by Williamson at the NCNC demand for the proposed 1956 conference to adopt a uniform electoral law for Nigeria or alternatively, if the North refused this, a reduction in the number of seats allocated to the North. His fear was that such a law would further open up the North's electorate to the AG and NCNC and this, he feared, would provoke a reaction by NPC leaders.[64] He urged the CO to defend indirect elections in the North and to refuse to give the vote to Northern women. The Nigerian government took a similar line.[65] This reflected wider concerns about Islamic sensibilities. While the AG argued that if the North did not give women the vote it was only fair the number of seats for the North should be correspondingly reduced, Sir James Robertson (Nigeria's Governor-General, 1955–60), stressed the position of Islam in relation to the electoral system and that Islamic concerns must be handled carefully; if Northern leaders felt concerned for the future of Islam it would drive the North out of Nigeria.[66]

Why did the CO take this line after 1953? Why did it attempt so assiduously to protect NPC interests on these issues? At its simplest, this derived from British fears of Northern secession. It is no exaggeration to say that this was the central determinant of British policy towards Nigeria after 1953. However it is also clear that NPC leaders were aware of CO concerns and were ready, for their own ends, to play on these fears; the collaborative relationship was never a one-way street. From the 31 March crisis onwards, the NPC leadership were never passive ciphers in the face of CO manipulation; nor were they 'yes men', 'his master's voice' or 'government stooges'. From 1953 it was effectively a three-cornered contest of North, South and CO, all three were fighting their corners effectively.

It is the view taken here that CO fears of Northern secession were real, as were NPC fears of Southern rule; but also real was the NPC's willingness to exaggerate the North's willingness to secede at the slightest threat from the South. That this leverage had worked in 1953 was incontrovertible. It was to work again thereafter. When elections were held in late 1954, and, to everyone's surprise, the NCNC won in the West as well as in the East, thus becoming the dominant party in the Council of Ministers (where portfolios were distributed on the basis of regional power), Macpherson was quick to note how the election result 'has severely shaken the North' with the threat now, he reported, that the NPC will either boycott the Council of Ministers or veto all legislation in the House of Representatives.[67] Its aim, he thought, was to create political gridlock in order to gain a separate North with only a weak central agency, as it had demanded in the 'Eight-points motion'. When H.R.E. Browne, the Civil Secretary in the North, met NPC leaders, they took a hard attitude to co-operating with the party.[68] Their obstinacy worked. Lennox-Boyd stressed the critical need to reassure Northern leaders by repeating to them that they would not be forced into self-government until they wished. The North had, he recognised, a 'veto' on Nigeria's independence. It must be made clear to the NPC, he felt, that the CO would defend their legitimate aspirations.[69]

In the event, the NPC agreed to co-operate, which suggests they were indeed using threats of secession as a negotiating counter. But their determination to use secession in this way continued thereafter. As the proposed 1956 conference approached fears of secession echoed among the administration. In June 1956, Sharwood-Smith reiterated his view that premature self-government for Nigeria if granted at the conference would lead to Northern secession.[70] His views were repeated by another official, K.P. Maddocks, who noted in late 1956 that among NPC leaders 'thoughts of ultimate secession are never far below the surface', while Tafawa Balewa, soon to be prime minister, made clear his view that 'there is little prospect of the continuance of a unified Nigeria after the attainment of full self-government'.[71] The CO's renowned 'skeleton plan' assessment in early 1957, which owed much to Macpherson, repeated the view that the North would, if self-government came too quickly, secede, particularly if the NCNC gained power in Lagos. 'If the British withdraw in the next half decade, it is quite on the cards that the North ... will secede.' It was essential Britain should move as slowly as possible therefore, and avoid any division of the North into two regions.[72]

Others reinforced these attitudes. Robertson in 1957 stated that 'the crux is the North. I don't really think the Northern right wing elements want independence', and he emphasised that there still was much talk of the East African High Commission model for Nigeria on the lines of the 'Eight-points motion'. When the idea of independence was explained to a meeting of Emirs in 1957, he said, 'they declared themselves astounded that their representatives in Lagos had agreed to it'.[73] Lennox-Boyd expressed fears in 1957 that the likelihood of 'bitter North/South friction' following independence meant that Britain must try to delay it at least to 1962–63.[74]

Officials, Sharwood-Smith in particular, encouraged these fears during these years. This had been seen at its most overt in 1953, when Sharwood-Smith played a critical role. His 'coloured-lights exercise' of early April 1953 appeared on one reading to suggest Northern secession was feasible.[75] Arguably too, he failed to prevent the moving of the 'Eight-points motion'. At a later date he seriously suggested secession in order to create a separate and sympathetic North modeled on Jordan – 'Muslim and friendly'.[76] He was patently encouraging Northern fears of Southern ambitions in this period. Before the 1957 conference he briefed Balewa to slow the move to self-government so that the North did not split up. His aim was to delay independence as long as possible in order to preserve 'a united Nigeria and a united North'.[77] He strongly argued for the CO to support the NPC in resisting 'fragmentation' or the creation of new regions; fragmentation would be a 'disaster'. If the North was broken up this would, he argued, lead to a unitary government based on Lagos and 'the effects of which on the North it is unnecessary to comment'.[78]

These fears suited British interests. C.G. Eastwood, a senior CO official, showed he recognised this when he expressed the hope that Sharwood-Smith would press the NPC not to demand regional self-government by 1959 at the conference; once the North gained regional self-government then self-government for the Federation as a whole would not be long in following and this needed to be made clear.[79] Yet it is difficult to suggest that NPC leaders were pawns of Sharwood-Smith or Britain more generally in this. The NPC leadership had their own agenda and were quick to use threats of secession to advance it as independence approached. Tafawa Balewa in 1957 stated to Sharwood-Smith that there were serious fears in the North at the idea of approaching self-government and that 'the ultimate answer must inevitably be separation', views Sharwood-Smith was quick to transmit.[80] Balewa, never the *ingénue* of popular mythology, reinforced this in comments to Robertson later that year that in his view there would probably be no central government after independence and Nigeria would break-up into separate regions.[81] The following year he was still talking of how it would be best if 'regions were left to get on with their own affairs' with just a small central agency; he coupled this with his rejection of votes for women in the North.[82] Indeed Gawain Bell, the Governor of the North after Sharwood-Smith, took the line that NPC leaders were so keen on secession that things were not propitious for an independent Nigeria and that it would quickly split apart on independence.[83]

It is unclear how far Tafawa Balewa and other NPC leaders genuinely considered secession feasible. Certainly by 1959 the dangers of secession were receding – as indeed was NPC reluctance to accept self-government – as NPC dominance in central politics became clearer. In this sense the threat had worked. The NPC–NCNC rapprochement of this period, although alarming the CO because of Azikiwe's likely influence, had the benefit of ensuring NPC victory in the 1959 elections, the last under British rule, with Tafawa Balewa, 'our very good friend' as Macleod described him, as the prime minister that led Nigeria to independence.[84] This was a victory for the NPC, but more importantly, it must be said, for the whole thrust of British policy since 1953. A CO memorandum in 1959 concluded that a Northern split from Nigeria was now unlikely, while a Foreign Office report suggested that by 1965 'the conservative North will probably be playing the major part in the Federal Government'.[85] Yet although Robertson felt confident in April 1960 that Nigeria would now hold together after independence and that the risks of secession had receded, NPC leaders continued to ostentatiously court Chad and Niger during 1960; rumours flourished of a possible Northern Nigeria–Niger union, though these links were described as merely 'a form of insurance'.[86]

Why was the CO so concerned at the danger of secession? Obviously the example of India–Pakistan was not a positive one. But the CO use of the danger of secession was not because it wished unduly to prolong British rule in Nigeria. This was simply not an option by this stage. Rather, the CO had positive reasons for supporting a united Nigeria. This was seen as being in Britain's interests and a united Nigeria, it was believed, could only be achieved at the price of Northern domination of the Federation. Once self-government became foreseeable, as it did from 1953, British policy was designed to maintain a united territory. Macpherson in 1953 stated that 'our objective is to keep united Nigeria in the Commonwealth of its own volition. This is good for Britain and good for Nigeria', a view echoed by Williamson.[87] Even as late as 1959 a CO memorandum defined British interests as 'being *primarily* (author's emphasis) to help Nigeria maintain a satisfactory unity'.[88]

What the CO wanted in Nigeria, as it accepted the inevitability of imminent self-government after 1953, was – as it had wanted in 1943 – a stable and prosperous territory which would be sympathetic to British interests. This was, however, only a first step in a broad vision for Africa. What the CO envisaged was a Nigeria that would be a major player in an Africa that as a whole, by the late 1950s, was approaching independence. One in four Africans lived in Nigeria. A united Nigeria, it was hoped, would certainly be the major state in West Africa and possibly, Africa north of the Limpopo more generally. 'Nigeria is potentially one of the great countries of Africa' ran one CO brief in 1956.[89] A divided Nigeria, or two separate Nigerias, would be weak and prey to rival

American and Soviet interests. If the Commonwealth was to be a means of preserving Britain's interests in Africa and if Nigeria was to be a major player in Africa, then Nigerian unity was necessary. 'There is no future worth considering for Nigeria unless she can remain united' said a CO appreciation in 1955; 'a united Nigeria with her large, vigorous and enthusiastic population will in time have no mean part to play in the Commonwealth ... and in world affairs'.[90]

Did this then, amount to a policy of 'divide and rule', the accusation which Lyttelton so sharply dismissed at the 1953 conference? Such an idea is too simplistic a description of British policy in these years. While it is true that British policy contributed to the divisions so characteristic of Nigerian politics, Britain's aim, after 1953, was far from 'ruling'. It was clear after 1953 that the idea of continuing 'rule' in Nigeria was a chimera. Britain's days in Nigeria were numbered and the CO soon realised this. On the contrary, one could perversely argue that British policy was designed thereafter to avoid dividing in order to rule: it was the unity of Nigeria that the CO wanted to maintain, because, once British rule had ended, it was clear that the unity of Nigeria was the best way for British interests to be protected in the long term. This was the conclusion that emerged out of the reassessment of Nigerian policy during 1953. This was a major turning point, as significant as that that had occurred in the early 1940s. Patently, this reassessment succeeded. The aim was to maintain a united Nigeria and bring it through to independence with as little challenge to British interests as possible. This it achieved. In this 'retreat' from Nigeria after 1953, British policy achieved a remarkably successful 'revival'.

Notes

1. The outcome of this re-assessment of policy was the 1943 memorandum by O.G.R. Williams, which set out a broad scheme of political change for the future, NA (National Archives, Kew), CO 554/132/20, no. 1, 'Constitutional development in West Africa'. For the Nigerian government's reaction see NA, CO 554/132/20, no. 13, Grantham to Dawe, 11 October 1943. Further, during 1943 a series of meetings at the CO were held with Governors Bourdillon and Richards to discuss Nigerian policy, see NA, CO 554/132/20, no. 16, CO record of a meeting with Richards, 19 November 1943. See also R.D. Pearce, *The Turning Point in Africa: British Colonial Policy, 1938–48* (London, 1982), pp. 17–41.
2. J.S. Coleman, *Nigeria: Background to Nationalism* (Berkeley, CA, 1971), pp. 251–67.
3. E.E.G. Iweriebor, *Radical Politics in Nigeria, 1945–50* (Zaria, 1996).
4. R.D. Pearce, 'Governors, nationalists and constitutions in Nigeria, 1935–51', *Journal of Imperial and Commonwealth History*, 9 (1981), 289–307; M. Lynn, 'Nigerian complications: The Colonial Office, the Colonial Service and

the 1953 crisis in Nigeria', in J. Smith (ed.), *Administering Empire: The British Colonial Service in Retrospect* (London, 1999), pp. 181–205.

5. NA, CO 554/260, no. 9D, Macpherson to Lloyd, 18 January 1952.
6. J. Smith, *Colonial Cadet in Nigeria* (Durham, NC, 1968), p. 6.
7. These constitutional changes can be followed in K. Ezera, *Constitutional Developments in Nigeria* (Cambridge, 1960) and Pearce, 'Governors, nationalists and constitutions'.
8. O. Awolowo, *Path to Nigerian Freedom* (London, 1947), p. 47.
9. A.E. Barnes, 'Evangelization where it is not wanted: Colonial administrators and missionaries in Northern Nigeria during the first third of the twentieth century', *Journal of Religion in Africa*, 25 (1995), pp. 412–41.
10. B.J. Dudley, *Parties and Politics in Northern Nigeria*, (London, 1968), pp. 12–39; C.S. Whitaker, *The Politics of Tradition: Continuity and Change in Northern Nigeria 1946–66* (Princeton, NJ, 1970), pp. 38–50.
11. Few nationalists in this period objected to the idea of regionalisation itself; the debate was over the number of regions it should involve, with the relative power of the North the critical issue.
12. NA, CO 554/262, no. 221, Nigerian government notes of a discussion with heads of department, 15 April 1953; J.T. Reynolds, *The Time of Politics (Zamanin Siyasa): Islam and the Politics of Legitimacy in Northern Nigeria 1950–66*, (Bethesda, MD, 1999), pp. 15–16, has useful detail on education and literacy rates in the North.
13. T. Clarke, *A Right Honourable Gentleman: Abubakar from the Black Rock* (London, 1991), p. 99.
14. R.L. Sklar, *Nigerian Political Parties: Power in an Emergent Nation*, (Princeton, NJ, 1963), pp. 88–101.
15. Ezera, *Constitutional Developments*, pp. 132–52.
16. S.O. Arifalo, 'The intensification of ethnic political consciousness in Nigeria: the rise of Egbe Omo Oduduwa 1947–71', *Geneve Africaine* 24 (1986), pp. 7–33; O. Awolowo, *Awo: The Autobiography of Chief Obafemi Awolowo* (Cambridge, 1960), p. 213; G.O. Olusanya, *The Second World War and Politics in Nigeria 1939–53* (Lagos, 1973), p. 139–41.
17. NA, CO 967/173, Macpherson to Lloyd, 8 January 1952.
18. K.W.J. Post and G.D. Jenkins, *The Price of Liberty: Personality and Politics in Colonial Nigeria* (Cambridge, 1973), passim, but esp. pp. 159ff.
19. NA, CO 554/313, no. 1, Macpherson to Lyttelton, 19 June 1952.
20. Sklar, *Nigerian Political Parties*, pp. 118–25.
21. NA, CO 554/313, no. 1, minute by Williamson, 4 July 1952 on Macpherson to Lyttelton, 19 June 1952.
22. NA, CO 554/260, no. 34, Macpherson to Lyttelton, 1 April 1953. This episode is detailed in Awolowo, *Awo*, pp. 238–42, A. Enahoro, *Fugitive Offender: An Autobiography* (London, 1965), pp. 124–31 and A. Bello, *My life* (Cambridge, 1962), pp. 115–34.
23. B. Sharwood-Smith, *Recollections of British Administration in the Cameroons and Northern Nigeria 1921–57: 'but always as friends'* (Durham, NC, 1969), p. 264.
24. Sharwood-Smith, *Recollections*, p. 262.
25. *Report on the Kano Disturbances 16–19 May 1953* (Kaduna, 1953).
26. NA, CO 554/260, no. 40, Macpherson to Lyttelton, 2 April 1953.
27. NA, CO 554/277, no. 1, Minute by I.B. Watt, 27 March 1953.

28. NA, CO 554/254, no. 20, Macpherson to Lloyd, 16 March 1953.
29. NA, CO 554/260, no. 76A, CO note on a meeting with Macpherson and Arden-Clarke, 15 April 1953.
30. NA, CO 554/260, no. 62, Conclusions of a meeting held at the CO under the chairmanship of Lyttelton, 15 April 1953.
31. NA, CO 554/261, no. 137, Cabinet conclusions, 27 May 1953.
32. NA, CO 554/260, no. 76A, CO note on a meeting with Macpherson and Arden-Clarke, 15 April 1953.
33. NA, CO 554/261, no. 98, Macpherson to Lyttelton, 9 May 1953.
34. NA, CO 554/261, no. 98, 'An assessment of the political situation in Nigeria on 9 May 1953', enclosure in Macpherson to Lyttelton, 9 May 1953.
35. NA, CO 554/260, no. 71, Hopkinson to Lyttelton, 24 April 1953.
36. Sharwood-Smith, *Recollections*, 258–78. His 'coloured-lights exercise' caused alarm in the CO, NA, CO 554/236, no. 51, Sharwood-Smith to Williamson, 1 May 1953.
37. NA, CO 554/236, no. 51, Sharwood-Smith to Williamson, 1 May 1953.
38. NA, CO 554/261, no. 98, 'An assessment of the political situation in Nigeria on 9 May 1953', enclosure in Macpherson to Lyttelton, 9 May 1953.
39. NA, CO 554/261, no. 92A, CO note of a meeting with Lyttelton, 5 May 1953.
40. NA, CAB 129/61, C(53)154, 'Constitutional developments in the Gold Coast and Nigeria', Cabinet memorandum by Lyttelton, 13 May 1953.
41. NA, CO 554/261, no. 127, Goble to Gorell Barnes, 21 May 1953; Sharwood-Smith, *Recollections*, p. 275.
42. NA, CO 554/262, no. 232A, minute by Williamson, 2 July 1953.
43. NA, CO 554/262, no. 262, CO note of a meeting of Lyttelton with Macpherson, 22 July 1953.
44. NA, CO 554/262, no. 250, Macpherson to Gorell Barnes, 15 July 1953.
45. NA, CO 554/312, no. 28, Lyttelton to Macpherson, 4 September 1953.
46. NA, CO 554/262, no. 296, draft statement by Lyttelton on '1956 and all that', 18 August 1953.
47. NA, PREM 11/1367, no. 375, Cabinet memorandum by Lyttelton, 17 August 1953.
48. NA, CO 554/261, no. 163c, minute by Huijsman, 22 May 1953; NA, CO 554/261, no. 139, Macpherson to Lyttelton, 29 May 1953.
49. NA, CO 554/262, no. 272, CO brief for Lyttelton, July 1953.
50. NA, CO 822/940, no. 3, Appreciation on Nigeria, March 1955.
51. NA, CO 554/846, no. 9, Sharwood-Smith to Williamson, 13 April 1955.
52. NA, CO 554/846, no. 10, Marshall to Lloyd, 18 April 1955.
53. NA, CO 554/997, no. 13, Sharwood-Smith to Marshall, 20 July 1955.
54. NA, CO 554/905, no. 45, 'Nigeria constitutional conference 1956: structure of the federal government', CO final brief, 27 July 1956.
55. J.D. Hargraves, *Decolonization in Africa* (Harlow, 1988), p. 162.
56. NA, CO 554/1521, minute by Smith, 10 October 1958.
57. NA, CO 554/2122, no. 82, Robertson to Macpherson, 2 December 1958.
58. Dudley, *Parties and Politics*, p. 118.
59. NA, CO 554/236, no. 69, minute by Williamson, 10 July 1953.
60. NA, CO 554/1183, no. 11, minute by Williamson to Eastwood, 20 April 1955.
61. NA, CO 554/1078, no. 10, minute by Smith, 31 May 1955.
62. NA, CO 554/1775, minute by Smith, 14 March 1957.

63. NA, CO 554/1775, no. 58, 'Provincial Administrations', memorandum by the Northern Region government, October 1958.
64. NA, CO 554/904, no. 6, Williamson to Robertson, 18 October 1955.
65. NA, CO 554/904, no. 13, Nigerian government brief on proposals concerning the electoral system, 19 December 1955.
66. NA, CO 554/1159, no. 17, Robertson to Lennox-Boyd, 26 June 1956.
67. NA, CO 554/1178, no. 3, Macpherson to Lennox-Boyd, 14 November 1954.
68. NA, CO 554/1178, no. 23, Browne to Lennox-Boyd, 29 November 1954.
69. NA, CO 554/1178, no. 4, Lennox-Boyd to Macpherson, 17 November 1954.
70. NA, CO 554/871, no. 13E, Sharwood-Smith to Robertson, 18 June 1956.
71. NA, CO 554/843, no. 7, Maddocks to Eastwood, 5 November 1956.
72. NA, CO 554/1533, no. 7, 'Skeleton Plan: Nigeria', March 1957.
73. NA, CO 554/1583, no. 23, Robertson to Williamson, 1 April 1957.
74. NA, CO 554/1583, no. 33, Lennox-Boyd to Robertson, 15 April 1957.
75. NA, CO 554/260, no. 73, Sharwood-Smith to Williamson, 7 April 1953.
76. J.N. Paden, *Ahmadu Bello, Sardauna of Sokoto*, (Zaria, 1986), p. 222.
77. NA, CO 554/1596, no. 1, Sharwood-Smith to Williamson, 14 May 1957.
78. NA, CO 554/1596, no. 1, 'The problem of safeguards for the North', in Sharwood-Smith to Williamson, 14 May 1957.
79. NA, CO 554/871, no. 7, Eastwood to Macpherson, 14 June 1956.
80. NA, CO 554/1583, no. 39, note by Sharwood-Smith on discussion with Malam Abubakar Tafawa Balewa, 15 April 1957; NA, CO 554/1596, no. 1, Sharwood-Smith to Williamson, 14 May 1957.
81. NA, CO 554/1583, no. 51, 'Note on a conversation with Malam Abubakar Tafawa Balewa' by Robertson, 23 April 1957.
82. NA, CO 554/2122, no. 37, Grey to Bell, 1 June 1958.
83. NA, CO 554/1841, no. 29, Bell to Lennox-Boyd, 4 December 1958.
84. NA, CO 554/2122, no. 82, Robertson to Macpherson, 2 December 1958; NA, PREM 11/3047, minute from Macleod to Macmillan, 9 May 1960.
85. NA, CAB 134/1353, AF(59)5, 'Prospects for the African territories': CO memorandum, 20 February 1959; NA, FO 371/137972, no. 24, 'Africa: the next ten years', FO confidential print.
86. NA, CO 554/2391, no. 2, Bell to Macleod, 31 March 1960; NA, CO 554/2391, no. 5, Robertson to Emanuel, 18 July 1960.
87. NA, CO 554/254, no. 20, Macpherson to Lloyd, 16 March 1953; NA, CO 554/236, no. 46A, Williamson to Sharwood-Smith, 18 April 1953.
88. NA, CO 554/1537, no. 15, 'Future of the posts of governor-general and regional governors and deputies', CO memorandum, 1959.
89. NA, CO 554/905, no. 45, 'Nigeria: constitutional conference 1956: structure of federal government', 27 July 1956.
90. NA, CO 822/940, no. 3, CO appreciation on Nigeria, March 1955.

8
Anglo-American Revival and Empire during the Macmillan Years, 1957–63

Nigel J. Ashton

In their seminal study, 'The imperialism of decolonization', Louis and Robinson postulated the notion that the British Empire was 'transformed as part of the Anglo-American coalition'.[1] They argued, in the effect, that both the renewal and subsequent divestment of the British Empire in the wake of the Second World War, took place as part of an Anglo-American *cooperative* enterprise. The worldwide role of the British during the post-war decades could not have been maintained without American money. This money was provided on the understanding that the empire would act as a bulwark for the West in the Cold War against the Soviet Union. Although they place the emphasis on co-operation, Louis and Robinson do not seek to gloss over instances of Anglo-American discord, such as the Iranian oil crisis of 1951–52, or the 1956 Suez crisis. Rather, they rationalise them as exceptional cases where the British defence of particular local interests clashed with the American conception of what was appropriate in terms of broader Cold War strategy.

There is much that is persuasive about this analysis. However, Louis and Robinson's account effectively ends in 1960, although an eye is cast forward briefly to subsequent developments.[2] The analysis offered here will seek to supplement their account by offering a re-interpretation of Anglo-American relations during the Macmillan years between 1957 and 1963, and by exploring other factors beyond broader Cold War strategy which may have influenced Anglo-American relations over the empire. In particular, it will seek to illuminate *British perceptions* of the role of US domestic politics in affecting Anglo-American relations over imperial issues. While domestic politics form no more than a sub-plot in the broader narrative of Anglo-American relations and the empire, as Jussi Hanhimaki has recently reminded us, they nevertheless need to be written back into our analysis of broader Cold War strategy.[3]

In the wider historiography of Anglo-American relations, the Macmillan years are normally portrayed as a period of revival, sandwiched in between the disastrous breach over the 1956 Suez crisis and the tensions engendered by the Vietnam war, the British financial crisis and the abandonment of the East of Suez role during the mid-to-late 1960s.[4] In John Dickie's phrase they were the 'golden days' of Anglo-American relations.[5] With respect to the opening phase of the Macmillan premiership during 1957–58, there is indeed some substance to this claim. Macmillan, whose talent for seizing political opportunities was second to none, pounced on the opening presented by the launch of the Soviet Sputnik satellite on 4 October 1957. During talks in Washington at the end of the month, he won both a new rhetorical and a new institutional commitment to the Anglo-American alliance from his former wartime comrade, President Dwight D. Eisenhower. Overriding the wishes of his more cautious Secretary of State, John Foster Dulles, Eisenhower agreed that the Anglo-American alliance should form the foundation of a new, much more closely integrated Western effort designed to meet the formidable Soviet challenge.[6] At a rhetorical level, this commitment found expression in the so called 'Declaration of Common Purpose', issued by the Prime Minister and President at the close of the summit, which stated that:

> The arrangements which the nations of the free world have made for collective defense and mutual help are based on the recognition that the concept of national self-sufficiency is now out of date. The countries of the free world are inter-dependent and only in genuine partnership, by combining their resources and sharing tasks in many fields, can progress and safety be found. For our part, we have agreed that our two countries will henceforth act in accordance with this principle.[7]

If this was the public, rhetorical commitment, to a renewal of the Anglo-American alliance, the parallel institutional commitment was kept largely secret at the time. Eisenhower agreed to the establishment of a range of Anglo-American Working Groups to study not only the resumption of nuclear co-operation, but also broader Cold War countermeasures in the fields of economics, trade and information, together with regional problems, including Syria, Hong Kong and Algeria.[8]

The main reason for the high level of secrecy accorded to this institutionalised system for Anglo-American consultation is not difficult to deduce. The Eisenhower Administration did not want other NATO allies, particularly the French and West Germans, to discover that new exclusive, bilateral Anglo-American consultative machinery had been established.

Initially, the fruits of this new Anglo-American partnership from the British perspective seemed impressive. True to his word, Eisenhower engaged in a successful effort to persuade Congress to amend the McMahon Act, opening the way to the July 1958 Agreement on Atomic Energy for Mutual Defence Purposes. But, in respect of the regional Working Groups established as a result of the Washington talks, progress over the same period was mixed. As ever in Anglo-American relations, the Middle East presented the thorniest problem. While the 'Syria Working Group', established in September 1957 when a communist coup in Damascus had seemed imminent, provided the prototype for the broader range of Working Groups, the follow-up work of what was now re-titled the 'Middle East Working Group' during the winter and spring of 1957–58 was disappointing. The British aimed at the drafting of detailed contingency plans, in which the logistics of combined Anglo-American military action in the region would be precisely worked out. Their hopes were thwarted by a mixture of bureaucratic inertia, an excessive preoccupation with secrecy and, most importantly of all, a difference in London and Washington's perception of the unfolding events in the region. Much as it had taken the crisis posed by the putative communist takeover in Damascus during August and September 1957 to bring about the creation of the original Syria Working Group, and the drafting of its 'Preferred Plan' for covert action against the Syrian regime,[9] so it now took the outbreak of civil strife in Lebanon in May 1958 to breathe life back into the Middle East Working Group.[10] Even then, events took an ironic, and, from the British perspective, most unfortunate turn. Instead of the expected contingency of the overthrow of the pro-Western régime of President Chamoun of Lebanon, London and Washington were confronted by the wholly unexpected contingency of the overthrow of the Hashemite Monarchy in Iraq on 14 July 1958.[11]

In Washington, Eisenhower drew the conclusion that the Iraqi coup was part of a Soviet-Nasserite plot to drive the Western powers out of the region. But, when it came to the question of implementing the existing contingency plan for intervention in the Lebanon, the President preferred unilateral American, to bilateral Anglo-American action. The reason offered by Eisenhower to Macmillan for this change of plan during a phone conversation on the evening of 14 July, was that the British might instead want to hold their forces in reserve for possible action in Jordan or Iraq itself. But, when Macmillan pressed him over a request for support which had been received from King Hussein of Jordan, Eisenhower was diffident and discouraging.[12] Although the American documentary record is not explicit on this point, the ghost of Suez still seemed to haunt the Anglo-American feast.[13] The Eisenhower Administration did not want to run the risk that its intervention in Lebanon might be tarred with the same imperialist brush as the Anglo-French action over Suez two years earlier.

Despite American discouragement, the Macmillan government now elected to despatch its own forces to Jordan. The key factors influencing this decision were: first, the thought that the presence of British forces might free up Hussein's own troops to make a move into Iraq; second a desire to salvage British prestige, which had been badly dented by the demise of the Hashemite regime in Baghdad; and third, a desire to bolster Hussein's own position. Although often presented as combined operations, the American intervention in Lebanon and the British in Jordan remained essentially little more than parallel actions. Macmillan's efforts to get the Americans to commit ground forces to Jordan met with blank refusal in Washington. Eisenhower and Dulles did not believe Jordan was a position which could be saved for the West in the face of what the US Secretary of State termed the 'flood tide' of Arab nationalism.[14] They were also suspicious of both British and Jordanian motives in trying to draw them into a military commitment.[15] Eisenhower feared, with some justification, that the British goal was really to manoeuvre Washington into launching a combined Anglo-American operation which would sweep through the whole region, extirpating Nasser's influence.[16]

British and American dealings over the Levant during 1957–58 established what was to be a pattern for their relations over the Middle East as a whole during the Macmillan premiership. On the one hand, there was a public front of co-operation and unity, together with extensive consultation in private. On the other, British and American analysis of the threat posed by Arab nationalism and communism to their interests in the region often diverged. This threw up frequent points of conflict. The attempts of both the Eisenhower and Kennedy Administrations to foster better relations with Nasser with a view to turning him against the Soviet Union were met with suspicion in London. Despite a tentative détente in Anglo-Egyptian relations between mid-1959 and 1961, suspicions ran deeply on both sides.[17] The outbreak of the Yemeni civil war in

September 1962 undermined what progress had been made in bilateral relations. By February 1963, both London and Cairo had largely reverted to their Suez mindsets, epitomised by Macmillan's scribbled annotation on a despatch from Ambassador Harold Beeley in Cairo: 'for Nasser read Hitler and it's all very familiar'.[18]

Not only did London and Washington's broader approach to dealing with Arab nationalism between 1957 and 1963 diverge, but successive administrations also kept British attempts to lure them into combined planning for action in defence of the Gulf essentially at arms length. Although an Anglo-American planning group,[19] and subsequently a formal Working Group,[20] were set up to look both at policy towards the Gulf and Iraq in the wake of the July 1958 revolution the practical results were once again limited. In London the hope was that the Americans might be drawn into joint planning for the defence of Kuwait against Iraq.[21] This was a development which the US military wanted to avoid at all costs, believing that it might limit American freedom of manoeuvre in a crisis.[22] Despite several personal interventions on the part of Macmillan with Eisenhower during 1959, his attempts to chivvy the planning process along came to nought.[23] The British government was forced to plan for the defence of Kuwait on the basis that only British military resources would be available. This dictated a pre-emptive strategy, since it was recognised that Britain did not have the troops available to evict an established Iraqi force from the emirate.[24] When, in response to the exchange of notes granting Kuwait independence on 19 June 1961, the Iraqi leader Abd al-Karim Qasim started to make bellicose noises, the Macmillan government took no chances with its significant economic interests in Kuwait. The planned 'Operation Vantage' was implemented, with the Americans remaining militarily on the sidelines.[25] This was despite that the fact that the Kennedy Administration came under pressure to take military action from representatives of Gulf Oil, which held a 50 per cent stake in the Kuwaiti concession.[26]

In view of the concerns in Washington about the communist connections of Qasim's regime, which had rumbled on for much of the period since the revolution, this American diffidence is perhaps surprising. In fact, Anglo-American relations over post-revolutionary Iraq had proven to be a classic illustration of the differences in their approach to dealing with Arab nationalism. While in Washington, the focus throughout 1959 and 1960 had been on the dangers posed by Qasim's links with the local Iraqi Communist Party, and the potential benefits of working with pro-Nasserite forces to counter this trend, in London the approach was different. Any victory for Nasser in Iraq would result in his dangerous aggrandisement and, quite possibly, an even graver threat to British interests in the Gulf than that posed by Qasim. The Macmillan government preferred instead to pursue the classic strategy of divide and rule in Arab politics, playing Qasim and Nasser off against each other. This approach was no where more clearly set out than in the conclusions of a special Cabinet Committee established to study Middle East policy in the wake of the Iraqi Revolution:

> Arab nationalism should not necessarily be looked upon as an indivisible movement. History had shown that Damascus and Baghdad and Cairo provided different focal points for the growth of national feeling. In the long-term, it might be possible to exploit the natural differences of outlook between the Iraqis and the Egyptians. There was much to be said for establishing good relations with the new Iraqi Government and building it up as a counterpart to the power of the UAR. In brief, coming to terms with the growth of Arab nationalism did not necessarily mean the establishment of a friendly relationship with Colonel Nasser.[27]

In Washington, by contrast, the emphasis shifted to the value of Nasser as an 'independent ally', willing to work with the United States to prevent the victory of communist forces in Iraq. As Eisenhower put it, 'Nasser can oppose Communists better than can the US in the three-cornered struggle of the Middle East.'[28] US officials reacted with astonishment to the British decision to tip Qasim off at the end of November 1958 about a planned coup against him.[29] When Eisenhower raised the problem posed by Iraq for Anglo-American relations at the Camp David summit of March 1959, the Prime Minister's response was a masterpiece of understatement: 'there might be a slight difference in emphasis' in their approaches he conceded. Foreign Secretary Selwyn Lloyd was at least candid about the continuing British suspicions of Nasser which underlay their concerns about the American strategy. 'Dining with the Devil called for a long spoon', he warned.[30]

The American reluctance to engage in detailed, joint contingency planning for intervention in the Gulf, whether in defence of Kuwait, or to counter a communist takeover in Iraq, was not only the product of a difference in assessment of the best way to deal with local nationalists. It reflected two further linked sentiments. The first was that the Gulf remained an area of British responsibility. US forces were sufficiently stretched in handling their other commitments around the globe for Washington not to want to take on further tasks, whether in partnership with the British or not. Second, as argued earlier, integrated Anglo-American contingency planning would limit US freedom of manoeuvre in a crisis. This was particularly important in view of the continuing differences of assessment as between London and Washington as to how best to handle Arab nationalism.

The civil war which broke out in Yemen at the end of September 1962 served as a vindication of Washington's reserved approach to the handling of Anglo-American relations in the region. In essence, the Yemeni crisis provided a focus for the tension between the British strategy based on the defence of local interests against the forces of Arab nationalism, and the American strategy which sought an accommodation with Nasser as a means towards the end of containing Soviet influence in the region. The Kennedy Administration had inherited the Eisenhower era idea of trying to encourage Nasser's anti-communist tendencies and, in typical 'New Frontier' style, re-packaged it as a fresh initiative.[31] Kennedy himself devoted some energy to the pursuit of a new relationship with Nasser, which he attempted to foster through personal correspondence with the Egyptian leader. The Yemeni civil war, in which Nasser's prestige was heavily engaged as the backer of the new Republican regime in Sanaa, threatened this initiative. The Macmillan government, which had always been sceptical as to the likelihood of Nasser being persuaded to moderate his ambitions, now focused on the threat his involvement in Yemen posed to the neighbouring Aden Colony and Protectorate, which was soon to be re-fashioned as the Federation of South Arabia. The Kennedy Administration's attempts to resolve the conflict by brokering a disengagement plan foundered on the reluctance of all parties, not least the British government, to accept the blow to their prestige which this might occasion. In a memorandum written just before the public announcement of the American disengagement plan, Harold Macmillan was candid about the dangers which co-operation with it might pose for the British position in the Gulf. As the Prime Minister saw things, recognition of the Republican regime in Sanaa might 'seem to have been forced on Her Majesty's Government by the Americans and may discourage the rulers and sheikhs in the Protectorate, Saudi Arabia and Jordan, and the Gulf who (like all Arabs) will be tempted to join the stronger side'.[32] Cognisant of the dangers posed by an open breach with the Kennedy Administration over Yemen, the British government instead adopted a strategy of prevarication, the aim of which was to wait until the Yemeni régime took some action which might justify a refusal to co-operate further in the disengagement plan. The Yemenis duly obliged, announcing the expulsion of

Christopher Gandy, the British representative in Taiz, in mid-February 1963.[33] Thereafter, there was to be no meeting of minds between London and Washington over how to handle the conflict. The state of Anglo-American relations over the Yemen and South Arabia by the end of the Macmillan premiership is best summed up in the words of Bob Komer, Kennedy's Middle East adviser on the National Security Council. The United States, wrote Komer, 'should beat up [the] UK to stop shafting us'.[34]

If the picture which emerges from this discussion of Anglo-American relations over the Middle East is one in which competition has to be given due weight alongside co-operation, there is always the danger that this particular regional focus might provide a distorted picture of Anglo-American relations over the empire during the Macmillan years. After all, the Middle East had already witnessed the worst bouts of post-war Anglo-American tension over Palestine, Iran and Suez. What evidence is there elsewhere of competition and disagreement over imperial issues disrupting the progress of Anglo-American 'interdependence'? Since there is space here only to discuss a limited range of examples let me pick out two for consideration: the Congo crisis; and the fate of the colony of British Guiana. While the former was without question the most important single problem of decolonisation affecting Anglo-American relations during this period, the latter also provides some interesting insights as to the factors affecting American views of this process. Both are, to some extent, ironic examples from the point of view of the study of Anglo-American relations and the empire. The Congo was not a British colony at all, although the crisis engendered by the precipitous unwinding of Belgian rule had far-reaching repercussions for the British position in Southern and Eastern Africa. British Guiana, by contrast, while relatively insignificant in terms of population and resources, became the British colony which occupied the most Anglo-American time and attention under the Kennedy Administration. The irony here is that the pressure exerted by Washington was for the *continuation* of British colonial rule, rather than for decolonisation. The explanation for this perverse state of affairs lay in the question of 'Castroism', and the potential domestic political damage which its perceived export to British Guiana might cause the Administration.

With regard to the Congo, Alan James, in his perceptive study, *Britain and the Congo Crisis*, has argued that 'in retrospect the unfolding of this Central African crisis constitutes an accurate international signpost to Britain's downhill destiny'.[35] In respect of Anglo-American relations and the defeat of the Katangan secession during the winter of 1962–63,

James describes the British government's approach thus: 'she would keep her head down and, if things came to the crunch, bow to the United States as a mark both of respect for her superior power and of remorse for having given way to it'.[36] James is right to stress the ultimate impotence of the Macmillan government in the face of the forcible re-integration of the secessionist Congolese province of Katanga. But his depiction of Anglo-American relations over the Congo needs to be set in a wider context. As will be outlined later, the Congo crisis was but one dimension of the broader 'crisis of interdependence' which affected Anglo-American relations at this juncture.

That Anglo-American relations over the Congo would end in the effective breakdown of discussion witnessed at the Nassau summit of December 1962 was far from clear when the crisis first broke out in June 1960. During the twilight months of the Eisenhower Administration, British and American policy over the Congo essentially pulled in the same direction. Both governments were suspicious of Patrice Lumumba, the post-independence Congolese Prime Minister. Macmillan described him as a 'witch doctor', while Eisenhower, apparently convinced that he was a drug addict by the discovery of hemp in Lumumba's Blair House bedroom, refused to meet him during his July 1960 visit to Washington.[37] The advent of the Kennedy Administration caused some greater concern in London over whether it would remain possible to co-ordinate the broader British and American approaches to decolonisation. As a senator, Kennedy had been a forceful critic of French policy in Algeria, and he had made the alleged indolence and lack of imagination of the Eisenhower Administration's policy towards Africa a key foreign policy theme of his presidential election campaign.[38] Mindful of the potential impact of this new emphasis on activism in the 'Third World' on Anglo-American relations, Macmillan included a passage in his first scene-setting message to the President-elect which stressed the importance of spreading confidence in free society to the 'uncommitted countries'.[39] The President's response, conveyed by Secretary of State-designate Dean Rusk to British Ambassador Harold Caccia, noted that with regard to colonialism 'the American people have some deep-rooted notions ... which make it important for us not to be constantly torn between loyalties to the Atlantic community and our genuine concern for the peoples of other continents'. Although Rusk added a gloss to the message indicating that this passage was not directed against Britain, the potential for conflict remained.[40]

Kennedy's key State Department appointments in the field of African affairs also did little to allay British concerns. The focal point of hostility proved to be the controversial Assistant-Secretary of State for African Affairs Mennen 'Soapy' Williams. Williams, whose nickname apparently derived from the business in which he had made his fortune rather than from any unusual concern for personal hygiene, displayed a great facility for stepping on British toes. An early high profile foray into Africa on the part of the former Governor of Michigan left Macmillan for one fuming. In conversation with Averell Harriman, who had been sent on a goodwill mission to Europe by the newly inaugurated President, the Prime Minister claimed that:

> the United Kingdom had been doing magnificent work in the last few years unwinding the British Empire. This was a much more difficult task than creating an Empire, but on the whole Britain was succeeding. The only people who could prevent her continued success were the Americans. It was deeply wounding to Britain when the United States Government or Americans individually accused the United Kingdom of being an evil reactionary influence and pilloried her in the United Nations or elsewhere. The activities of Governor Williams in Africa, unimportant though they were in themselves, were just the sort of thing which made Britain's task more difficult.[41]

Harriman attempted to pour oil on troubled waters, emphasising his own view that 'the British Commonwealth policy had been an outstanding example of statesmanship'. But Macmillan was not to be placated:

> this was all very well but ... Britain now had only influence left in Central Africa and no real power, and this was why the situation was so delicate. He begged Mr Harriman to tell the President that all that Britain wanted was to be left alone for a few years to finish the job. If American sniping at British policy went on, bitter feelings would be aroused in the United Kingdom which would do real damage to Anglo-American relations.

Despite British protests, Soapy's position at the State Department remained secure under Kennedy. The President admired his energy and no doubt felt that he contributed usefully to the Administration's reputation and profile with black Americans.[42] How far such sniping at Britain and other European powers over colonial matters served as a useful lightning rod for the President's initial failure to make significant domestic moves in respect of civil rights is a moot point. From the British perspective, the US position looked like pure hypocrisy. As Macmillan put it when commenting on a July 1962 article in *The Times* about the electoral politics of Mississippi:

> One cannot help being amused, as a poor British colonialist, at a State in which it is said that although 45% of the population is Negro, only a handful of Negro voters are on the roll. What does Soapy say to this sort of thing? But the ambivalences of American policies on colonialism are really past comprehension, and it is no use getting angry about it.[43]

In respect of the crisis in the Congo, it was not immediately apparent during the early months of the new administration that the issue would prove so divisive in Anglo-American relations. When the UN launched its first ill-fated attempt to reintegrate the rebel province of Katanga in September 1961, Macmillan and Kennedy agreed that the military operation was poorly timed and should be halted as soon as possible.[44] The launching of a second UN operation, in December 1961, proved more problematical. Macmillan, who was ever mindful of the hostility of the right wing of the Conservative Party to UN action against Katanga, worked himself up into a flap about the dangers of a major backbench revolt. He intervened personally with Kennedy to try to persuade him to support a call for a ceasefire.[45] Macmillan's pleas were reinforced at a private dinner by Ambassador David Ormsby Gore, a personal friend of the President. The result was that Kennedy picked up the phone to tell Ambassador Adlai Stevenson to intercede with UN Secretary-General U Thant to bring about a ceasefire.[46] In the event, Macmillan sailed through the House of Commons vote on the crisis on 14 December 1961 with a majority of 94, leaving Kennedy to comment dryly 'well, that was a pretty good majority; I wonder whether we needed to have gone to all that trouble the other night in order to get it?'[47]

In the aftermath of the so-called 'Second Round' of the UN's attempt to re-integrate Katanga, Macmillan mused in his diary about what he saw as the iniquities, both of that organisation, and of the American 'liberals' who used it as a platform to flaunt their anti-colonial opinions:

> [The] UN, driven on by the Afro-Asians & the 'unaligned', with their bitter 'anti-colonial' complex, and supported spiritually and financially by the US can do what they like. Of course, Britain can resign (as many Conservatives would prefer). But then we lose *all* influence. What we *can* do (and did very successfully in the last few days) is to

try to get the President & Secretary of State to exert themselves, instead of leaving the direction to the Adlai Stevensons and other half-baked 'liberals' whom they have put (for internal political reasons) at the UN. But it's a laborious process.[48]

During the course of 1962, the gap between the British government's position and that of the US Administration over the crisis widened still further. The US view of the crisis was conditioned above all by the desire to bolster the authority of the Congolese central government, under the leadership of the American client Cyrille Adoula. This, it was hoped, would prevent the Soviet Union capitalising on the crisis to advance its influence in Africa. The Macmillan government's approach, by contrast, was driven by a variety of considerations. These included the general hostility to the United Nations meddling in colonial affairs evidenced earlier, and a desire not to destabilise further the fragile Central African Federation, which bordered the rebel Congolese province of Katanga. The links between the Federation's Prime Minister, Sir Roy Welensky, and the right of the Conservative Party were part of Macmillan's domestic political problem.[49] However, British companies also had direct economic interests at stake in Katanga itself, including the significant shareholding in the *Union Minière du Haut-Katanga* held by Tanganyika Concessions. While these economic interests do not seem to have played a decisive role in the formation of British policy, Macmillan for one was convinced that parallel American interests played a key part in determining the Kennedy Administration's policy. The Prime Minister's fixation with what we might term the 'Congo Copper Plot' played an important part in fostering his growing frustration with the development of Anglo-American relations over the crisis. When the Kennedy Administration began touting sanctions as a possible way to put pressure on the Katangan regime to end its secession, Macmillan noted in his diary, on 3 October 1962, that 'the Americans are angry with us for not being willing to join in boycotting Congolese Copper. (We cannot help noticing that the Americans own most of the rest of world copper supplies and the market is rich)'.[50] In the same vein, on 27 November, with pressure for sanctions and/or forceful action on the part of the United Nations mounting, he wrote that 'I suspect the American copper interests in all this. They are equally jealous of Union Minière and of the N. Rhodesian copper companies.'[51]

The threat of sanctions against Katanga drew forth an even more intemperate response from Foreign Secretary Lord Home. Flaunting what can only be termed racist prejudices, he wrote to Secretary of State

Dean Rusk arguing that 'it may be logical that Tshombe should give way to sanctions, but he will not. He would rather go back to eating nuts than capitulate to the United Nations or Adoula ...'. The Foreign Secretary went on to expound what he saw as a broader 'truth' of African politics. 'The leading Africans, it is true, have their Cadillacs but they had nuts for much longer and are much nearer to them and they do not worry about returning to the jungle', he wrote.[52]

Fearing the collapse of Adoula's government, and mindful of the increasing agitation amongst the Afro-Asian group at the United Nations, the Kennedy Administration had reached the point by mid-December 1962 where it was giving active consideration to the despatch of a USAF squadron to bolster the UN forces in the Congo. It was against this backdrop that the intemperate debates over the Congo at the Nassau summit took place. If, a year earlier, Kennedy had been prepared to intervene personally to dig Macmillan out of a domestic political hole over the Congo, by December 1962 the President had reversed course. The newly proactive US policy aimed at ending the Katangan secession by force was decided at presidential level.[53] The Nassau discussions revealed just how far apart the two governments were in their approach to resolving the crisis. In response to Under-Secretary of State George Ball's comment that the United States was considering despatching an air squadron, Lord Home 'inquired dryly whether the United States Government was doing all this under any UN resolution'.[54] When Ball suggested that it might be necessary for Adoula to prorogue parliament and rule by decree, Home evidently lost his temper. 'Was the United States Government going to tell the world this? Personally speaking, he was all for the United States taking over a new African colony: "Best idea I have heard in years" '.[55] Picking up the debate in the same vein the Prime Minister weighed in with the sarcastic suggestion that 'of course if the United States would take over the Congo that would be very satisfactory. They could make Tshombe a maharaja with an American Resident'.[56]

Anglo-American co-operation over the Congo had thus effectively broken down. When, in line with the Kennedy Administration's policy, the United Nations launched its final, successful operation against Katanga on 28 December, the British government remained on the sidelines. By 15 January 1963, Tshombe was forced to announce his government's decision to end the secession. The manner in which the United Nations had eventually brought about its goal in the Congo was a clear defeat for British policy in the crisis, and a vindication of the US stance.[57] In terms of the argument advanced here about the limitations of Anglo-American co-operation over colonial questions, and the problems which beset the whole fabric of Anglo-American interdependence by the winter of 1962–63, the denouement of the Congo crisis provides much further grist to the mill. Not only that, but Macmillan's ready assumption that US policy was really driven by domestic commercial interests serves to illuminate further British perceptions of the wellsprings of American policy towards decolonisation.

US domestic politics also intruded into the conduct of Anglo-American relations over British Guiana. The nub of Kennedy's concern, particularly in the wake of the disastrous 'Bay of Pigs' landing of April 1961, was that the transfer of power to the nationalist leader, Cheddi Jagan, might be portrayed by his domestic political opponents as a further victory for the forces of 'Castroism' in the Western hemisphere. British and American assessments of Jagan were somewhat different. The British saw him, in Iain Macleod's memorable phrase, as a 'naïve London School of Economics Marxist', who was more likely to chart a neutralist, than an openly Castroist course in foreign affairs.[58] The Americans, by contrast, became more and more concerned that Jagan was a genuine fellow traveller, who might turn British Guiana into a Soviet satellite if he was allowed to achieve untrammelled power. During Macmillan's April 1961 visit to Washington, Secretary of State Rusk warned his counterpart Lord Home of the Administration's concern that in British Guiana, they might find themselves faced with 'another Castro-type situation'.[59]

By the beginning of February 1962, the Kennedy Administration had decided to adopt an active anti-Jagan strategy. One expression of this decision was the CIA's role in financing the protests and violence that broke out in Georgetown between 12 and 19 February.[60] Such actions were in contravention of a September 1961 intelligence gathering agreement with the British which had excluded covert operations.[61] At the same time on the diplomatic front, the British Government was pressed to take whatever measures were necessary to ensure that it did not hand over power in an independent British Guiana to Jagan. The new US policy was outlined by Rusk to Home in one of the more remarkable Anglo-American communications of the period:

> Dear Alex: ... I must tell you now that I have reached the conclusion that it is not possible for us to put up with an independent British Guiana under Jagan ... Partly reflective of ever growing concern over Cuba, public and Congressional opinion here is incensed at the thought of our dealing with Jagan. The Marxist-Leninist policy he

professes parallels that of Castro which the OAS at the Punta del Este Conference declared incompatible with the Inter-American system ... It seems clear to me that new elections should now be scheduled, and I hope we can agree that Jagan should not accede to power again. Cordially Yours, Dean Rusk.[62]

Rusk's message was met with incredulity in London. Macmillan himself could not believe it. 'I have just received a copy of a message to you from Mr Rusk about British Guiana', he wrote to Home. 'I am bound to say I have read it with amazement. One or two phrases are incredible.' Macmillan dwelt in particular on Rusk's references to not allowing Jagan to win power through due electoral process. He asked:

How can the Americans continue to attack us in the United Nations on colonialism and then use expressions like these which are not colonialism but pure Machiavellianism. Of course, it is nice to feel that they are partners with us and have such confidence in you as to send you a letter of this kind but it does show a degree of cynicism which I would have thought Dean Rusk could hardly put his pen to. He, after all, is not an Irishman, nor a politician, nor a millionaire: he has the reputation of being an honourable and somewhat academic figure.[63]

On a visit to London, the President's Special Assistant for Latin American Affairs, Arthur Schlesinger, found Colonial Secretary Reginald Maudling and his predecessor Iain Macleod voicing a mixture of puzzlement and amusement at Rusk's letter. Maudling apparently commented jovially 'if you Americans care so much about British Guiana, why don't you take it over? Nothing would please us more'.[64] In reality, Macleod at least should not have been surprised by Rusk's approach. He later recalled a meeting with Kennedy in the Oval Office during 1961 at which the president had pressed him hard not to move British Guiana too quickly towards independence. 'Mr President', Macleod had asked. 'Do I understand that you want us to go as quickly as possible towards independence everywhere else all over the world but not on your own doorstep in British Guiana?' Macleod recalled that Kennedy laughed and said 'well, that's probably just about it'.[65]

Home's response to Rusk's initiative was, as Ambassador Bruce put it, 'cold as the Arctic'.[66] The Foreign Secretary warned against the adoption of undemocratic and transparent devices designed to keep Jagan from power. He did agree though that there should be further Anglo-American consultation on developments in the territory.[67] These included discussions between Rusk and Home in Geneva on 12 March, during which Rusk emphasised to Home that 'the United States were really terrified of another Cuba on their continent'.[68] The feathers ruffled by their sharp exchange of letters were evidently somewhat smoothed over by the Foreign Secretary's acceptance that the British must not 'leave behind another Castro situation in this hemisphere'.[69]

After his own talks with the president in Washington in April 1962, Macmillan himself came round to recognising that, in view of the strength of American feeling on British Guiana, it was in Britain's interests to be 'as cooperative and forthcoming as we can'.[70] The Prime Minister, though, remained cynical about the American approach. 'They are ready to attack us as colonialists when it suits them. They are the first to squeal when "decolonisation" takes place near to them', he wrote in his diary.[71] In the event, although American concerns over the colony were to rumble on after the Cuban crisis, the British strategy during 1963 and 1964 was to be as accommodating as possible of the US position. This approach was to culminate in an election held under a system of proportional representation effectively framed to bar Jagan from power at the end of 1964.[72]

If the Middle East, the Congo and British Guiana all proved to be imperial and post-imperial problems where tensions often came to the fore, where do these issues fit into the broader pattern of Anglo-American relations during the Macmillan years? I have developed elsewhere in much more detail the concept of an Anglo-American 'crisis of interdependence' during the winter of 1962–63.[73] Briefly put, the roots of this crisis were a difference in the British and American perceptions of the nature of the new, 'interdependent' relationship to which Macmillan and Eisenhower had subscribed at their October 1957 summit. Macmillan believed they had established a new form of partnership, albeit one in which Britain would play the more junior role. This would involve, in the rhetoric of the 'Declaration of Common Purpose', the genuine 'sharing of tasks' across the entire range of defence and foreign affairs. In Washington, by contrast, the goal was more effective integration and co-ordination of the Western defence effort as a whole. This meant, in effect, more centralisation of decision-making in Washington, with the president taking ultimate responsibility for all of the most important tasks. This was put most succinctly by Kennedy, who, when discussing the mechanics of alliance nuclear policy, told Richard Neustadt that 'there had to be control by somebody. One man had to make the decision – and as things stood that had to be the American President. He couldn't share that decision with a whole lot of differently motivated and differently responsible people in Europe.'[74] The American desire for control in a crisis was nowhere more clearly brought home to Macmillan than at the Paris summit of May 1960. Eisenhower's unbending refusal to apologise for the U-2 fiasco, despite Macmillan's pleas, left the Prime Minister's hopes for East–West détente dashed. It was from his epiphany in Paris that Macmillan's personal turn towards full membership of the European Economic Community (EEC) was born. If the British Prime Minister's influence in Washington was unreliable, then Britain needed an alternative hedge to maintain her international position. Far from being an attempt to appease the United States, as Wolfram Kaiser has argued, the 1961 EEC application was an expression of British insecurity and lack of faith in the Anglo-American alliance.[75] This breakdown in trust between London and Washington came to a head during the winter of 1962–63 on the back of the crisis caused by the unilateral American decision to cancel the Skybolt missile system on which Britain depended for the continuation of her 'independent' nuclear deterrent. The crisis precipitated by Skybolt was wide-ranging, with Macmillan threatening to pull down the whole structure of Anglo-American cooperation worldwide. Imperial and post-imperial problems, particularly in the shape of the Congo crisis, tensions over the Yemeni civil war and disagreements about how to handle decolonisation in the Western hemisphere in the face of 'Castroism' contributed to this broader crisis of Anglo-American interdependence. In respect of Anglo-American relations, Dean Acheson thus not only hit the nail on the head, he hit it on the head at precisely the right time when he pronounced at West Point on 5 December 1962 that 'Great Britain has lost an Empire and not yet found a role'.[76]

Although the Anglo-American alliance was salvaged at the Nassau summit through Kennedy's decision to supply the Polaris nuclear delivery system to Britain, it was salvaged in a compromised form. Co-operation continued, but the realities of British dependence and American control in the nuclear field had been made apparent. Trust had also been seriously undermined. Less than a week after the Nassau summit, Macmillan could be found writing to the Minister of Defence, Peter Thorneycroft, warning that the Americans would have to be 'kept to the mark' to prevent them reneging on the agreement.[77]

How far should this 'crisis of interdependence' during the closing phase of the Macmillan premiership affect our broader view of Anglo-American co-operation over imperial matters? To be sure, the argument advanced here has highlighted elements of tension and competition in Anglo-American relations which were sufficiently serious to threaten the broader functioning of the alliance during the Macmillan years. But, in the end, the alliance was repaired and co-operation survived. What is clear, though, is that any thesis which postulates a smooth 'transfer of power' from Britain to the United States, neglects the tensions and mis-perceptions which beset this process.[78] Under Macmillan, the British government strove for an Anglo-American *partnership* which would act as a means of bolstering Britain's international position and preserving her vital interests. The Anglo-American relationship was not intended to act as a shroud for a graceful retreat from greatness. But the outcome of Macmillan's experiment in interdependence was an unhappy one. British expectations of genuine partnership were disappointed, and ulti-mately trumped by the hard-headed American reading of the balance of power underpinning their relationship.

Notes

1. Wm.R. Louis and R. Robinson, 'The imperialism of decolonization', *Journal of Imperial and Commonwealth History*, 22, 3 (1994), 462.
2. William Roger Louis has more recently offered further analysis of the Anglo-American context of the final phase of British decolonisation in the Far East in his article, 'The dissolution of the British Empire in the era of Vietnam', *American Historical Review*, 107, 1 (February 2002), 1–25.
3. J. Hanhimaki, 'Global visions and parochial politics: the persistent dilemma of the "American Century" ', *Diplomatic History*, 27, 4 (September 2003), 423–47.
4. This observation applies to all textbook descriptions of Anglo-American relations during the Macmillan years of which I am aware. See for example: C.J. Bartlett, *The Special Relationship: A Political History of Anglo-American Relations since 1945* (London: 1992); J. Dickie, *Special No More: Anglo-American Relations: Rhetoric and Reality* (London: 1994); A.P. Dobson, *Anglo-American Relations in the Twentieth Century: Of Friendship, Conflict and the Rise and Decline of Superpowers* (London: 1995); J. Dumbrell *A Special Relationship: Anglo-American Relations in the Cold War and After* (Basingstoke: 2001); R.M. Hathaway, *Great Britain and the United States: Special Relations Since World War II* (Boston, MA: 1990); R. Ovendale, *Anglo-American Relations in the Twentieth Century* (Basingstoke: 1998); D. Reynolds and D. Dimbleby, *An Ocean Apart: The Relationship between Britain and America in the Twentieth Century* (London: 1988).
5. Dickie, *Special No More*, p. 105. Dickie refers here specifically to the Kennedy–Macmillan years.
6. N.J. Ashton, *Eisenhower, Macmillan and the Problem of Nasser: Anglo-American Relations and Arab Nationalism, 1955–59* (Basingstoke: 1996), pp. 134–6.
7. Declaration of Common Purpose, 25 October 1957, quoted in H. Macmillan, *Riding the Storm, 1956–1959* (London: 1971), pp. 756–9.
8. For more detail on the Working Groups see Ashton, *Eisenhower, Macmillan and the Problem of Nasser*, pp. 136–9; and M. Jones, 'Anglo-American relations after Suez, the rise and decline of the Working Group experiment, and the French challenge to NATO, 1957–59', *Diplomacy & Statecraft*, 14, 1 (March 2003), 49–79.

9. For further discussion of this see M. Jones, 'The "Preferred Plan": The Anglo-American Working Group Report on Covert Action in Syria, 1957', *Intelligence and National Security* 19, 3 (September 2004), 401–15.

10. Ashton, *Eisenhower, Macmillan and the Problem of Nasser*, pp. 151–4.

11. For discussion as to why the US intelligence community did not predict the coup see 'Intelligence indications of coup in Iraq', *FRUS*, 1958–60, Vol. XII, (Washington, DC: 1993), pp. 322–3.

12. Record of a conversation between the Prime Minister and the President, 14 July 1958, NA, PREM11/2387.

13. See for example the advance warning issued by Admiral Burke, Chief of Naval Operations, about the implications of joint Anglo-American military intervention in the Levant: 'this would be a military campaign with political overtones comparable in many respects to the United Kingdom-France-Israel debacle of 1956 ...'. (US Joint Chiefs of Staff History, 432, RG218, USNA). Note also, UN Ambassador Henry Cabot Lodge's comment: 'if we go in alone the contrast with Suez would be brought out.' (Lodge to Dulles, 23 June 1958, *FRUS*, 1958–60, Vol. XI, pp. 168–9.)

14. Conference with the President, 23 July 1958, Box 35, DDE Diary Series, Ann Whitman File, Dwight D. Eisenhower Library, Abilene, Kansas [hereafter DDEL].

15. Hood to Lloyd, 15 July 1958, NA, PREM11/2380; Meeting re Jordan, 15 July 1958, Box 16, John Foster Dulles, Chronological Series, DDEL.

16. Meeting between Eisenhower and Twining, 15 July 1958, Box 35, DDE Diary Series, Ann Whitman File, DDEL.

17. See R. McNamara, *Britain, Nasser and the Balance of Power in the Middle East, 1952–67* (London: 2003) for a recent account which takes a more positive view of the extent of the Anglo-Egyptian détente during this period.

18. Macmillan's annotation, Beeley to Home, 25 February 1963, NA, PREM11/4173.

19. Whitney to Dulles, 8 August 1958, 780.00/8/858, Central Decimal File, RG59, USNA.

20. Memorandum of Conversation, Camp David, 22 March 1959, *FRUS*, 1958–60, Vol. XII, pp. 217–18.

21. 'Anglo-American Planning in the Middle East', 25 July 1959, NA, CAB131/21.

22. JCS to Holloway, 23 August 1958, JCS Central Decimal File, 'US/UK Planning', CCS381 EMMEA.

23. For example, Macmillan to Eisenhower, 14 May 1959, NA, PREM11/3427.

24. Watkinson to Home, 17 January 1961; and Home to Watkinson, 8 February 1961, NA, PREM11/3427.

25. On the Kuwaiti crisis see M. Alani, *Operation Vantage: British Military Intervention in Kuwait, 1961* (London: 1990); N. Ashton, 'Britain and the Kuwaiti crisis, 1961', *Diplomacy and Statecraft*, 9, 1 (1998); S. Smith, *Kuwait, the al-Sabah and Oil* (London: 1999); M. Snell-Mendoza, 'In defence of oil: Britain's response to the Iraqi threat towards Kuwait, 1961', *Contemporary British History*, 10, 3 (1996).

26. State to Kuwait, D.10.23pm, 30 June 1961, 786D.36/6-3061, Central Decimal File, RG59, USNA.

27. GEN658, first meeting, 22 July 1958, NA, CAB130/153.

28. Conference with the President, 23 December 1958, Box 3, State Department Series, Office of the Staff Secretary, White House Office, DDEL.
29. Stevens to Lloyd, 29 November 1958, NA, FO371/133074.
30. Memorandum of Conversation, Camp David, 22 March 1959, *FRUS*, 1958–60, Vol. XII, pp. 217–18.
31. For a variety of views on the novelty of Kennedy's policy towards Nasser and Arab nationalism see: W. Bass, *Support Any Friend: Kennedy's Middle East and the Making of the US-Israel Alliance* (Oxford: 2003), pp. 64–97; F.A. Gerges, 'The Kennedy Administration and the Egyptian–Saudi conflict in Yemen: Co-opting Arab nationalism', *Middle East Journal*, 49, 2 (Spring 1995), 292–311; D. Little, 'The new frontier on the Nile: JFK, Nasser, and Arab nationalism', *Journal of American History*, 75, 2 (September 1988), 501–27; A. Ben-Zvi, *Decade of Transition: Eisenhower, Kennedy and the Origins of the American–Israeli Alliance* (New York: 1998), pp. 131–2.
32. Memorandum, 'United Kingdom recognition of the Yemen regime', 12 December 1962, NA, PREM11/4356.
33. N.J. Ashton, *Kennedy, Macmillan and the Cold War: The Irony of Interdependence* (Basingstoke: 2002), p. 102.
34. Komer to Kennedy, 20 September 1963, *FRUS*, 1961–63, Vol. XVIII, pp. 710–13.
35. A. James, *Britain and the Congo Crisis, 1960–63* (Basingstoke: 1996), p. 207.
36. Ibid., p. 176.
37. H. Macmillan, *Pointing the Way, 1959–61* (London: 1972), p. 431; T.J. Noer, 'New frontiers and old priorities in Africa', in T.G. Paterson (ed.), *Kennedy's Quest for Victory: American Foreign Policy, 1961–63* (Oxford: 1989), p. 261.
38. Noer, 'New frontiers', p. 256.
39. Macmillan to Kennedy, 19 December 1960, T.736/60, NA, PREM11/3326.
40. Caccia to Macmillan, 3 January 1961, Washington telegrams nos 19 and 20, NA, PREM11/3326.
41. Record of a conversation at dinner at Admiralty House on Monday 27 February 1961, NA, PREM11/4590.
42. Noer, 'New frontiers', p. 259.
43. Macmillan to Ormsby Gore, 3 July 1962, Fol. 591, dep.c.333, Harold Macmillan Archive [hereafter HMA], Bodleian Library, Oxford.
44. Macmillan, *Pointing the Way*, p. 442; State to Brussels, 16 September 1961, *FRUS*, 1961–63, Vol. XX, p. 221.
45. Record of a telephone conversation between the Prime Minister and President Kennedy, 7.08pm, 13 December 1961, NA, PREM11/3193. The American record is in *FRUS*, 1961–63, Vol. XX, pp. 310–11.
46. Lord Harlech, 1964 Oral History Interview, John F. Kennedy Library, Boston, MA [hereafter JFKL]; Ormsby-Gore to Macmillan, 14 December 1961, NA, PREM11/3193; A. Horne, *Macmillan, 1957–86* (London: 1989), p. 402.
47. Lord Harlech, *1964 Oral History*, p. 38, JFKL; Horne, *Macmillan, 1957–86*, p. 403.
48. Harold Macmillan Diary [hereafter HMD], 20 December 1961, dep.d.44, pp. 82–3, Bodleian Library, Oxford.
49. J. Turner, *Macmillan* (London: 1994), 185; R. Shepherd, *Iain Macleod* (London: 1994), pp. 211, 216–17, 222–4.
50. HMD, 3 October 1962, dep.d.47, p. 40, Bodleian Library, Oxford.
51. HMD, 27 November 1962, dep. d. 47, p. 115, Bodleian Library, Oxford.

52. Home to Rusk, 10 August 1962, NA, PREM11/3629. The editors of the *FRUS* series were evidently denied permission to publish this message in their Congo crisis volume (see *FRUS*, 1961–63, Vol. XX, p. 537).
53. Memorandum for the Record, 20 December 1962, *FRUS*, 1961–63, Vol. XX, pp. 768–9.
54. Memcon, 6pm, 19 December 1962, *FRUS*, 1961–63, Vol. XX, p. 762. The British record is in NA, PREM11/3630 (hereafter 'British record').
55. Memcon, 6pm, 19 December 1962, *FRUS*, 1961–63, Vol. XX, p. 762.
56. Ibid; British record, p. 3.
57. Noer, 'New frontiers', pp. 268–9, (in common with S.R. Weissman, *American Foreign Policy in the Congo, 1960–1964* (Ithaca, NY: 1974), pp. 192–3) argues that Kennedy's policy had been one of indecision. However, this interpretation does not sit too easily with the evidence of presidential activism on the issue in the second half of December 1962.
58. Schlesinger to Bruce, 27 February 1962, *FRUS*, 1961–1963, Vol. XII, p. 549; London to State, 17 August 1961, Folder British Guiana General 5/19/61–8/23/61, Box 14a, NSF, JFKL; London to State, 7 September 1961, Folder British Guiana General 9/7/61–9/28/61, ibid.
59. Record of a conversation held in the State Department, 11am, 6 April 1961, NA, PREM11/3666. There is a brief account of this meeting in Battle to Bundy, 19 May 1961, *FRUS*, 1961–1963, Vol. XII, pp. 517–18. See also C. Fraser, 'The "New Frontier" of empire in the Caribbean: the transfer of power in British Guiana, 1961–1964', *International History Review*, 22, 3 (September 2000), 585–6.
60. S. Rabe, *The Most Dangerous Area of the World: John F. Kennedy Confronts Communist Revolution in Latin America* (Chapel Hill, NC: 1999), pp. 88–9.
61. For references to this agreement see: Rusk to Bruce, 4 September 1961, *FRUS*, 1961–1963, Vol. XII, pp. 528–9; 5 September 1961, ibid., p. 530; Record of a Meeting held at the White House, 5.15pm, Saturday 28 April 1962, NA, CAB133/246.
62. Rusk to Home, 19 February 1962, *FRUS*, 1961–1963, Vol. XII, pp. 544–5; also NA, PREM11/3666.
63. Macmillan to Home, 21 February 1962, M.51/62, NA, PREM11/3666.
64. Schlesinger to Bruce, 27 February 1962, *FRUS*, 1961–1963, Vol. XII, p. 549.
65. Shepherd, *Iain Macleod*, p. 239.
66. David K. E. Bruce Diary, 27 February 1962, Vol. 39, Virginia Historical Society, Richmond, Virginia.
67. Home to Rusk, 26 February 1962, NA, PREM11/3666; *FRUS*, 1961–1963, Vol. XII, pp. 546–8.
68. Record of a conversation between the Secretary of State and Mr Rusk in Geneva, 12 March 1962, NA, PREM11/3666.
69. Rusk to State, 13 March 1962, *FRUS*, 1961–1963, Vol. XII, p. 553. See also Fraser, 'The "New Frontier" in British Guiana', p. 599.
70. Macmillan to Brook, 3 May 1962, M.112/62, NA, PREM11/3666.
71. HMD, 27 September 1962, dep.d.47, pp. 28–9, Bodleian Library, Oxford.
72. Shepherd, *Iain Macleod*, p. 239; Rabe, *The Most Dangerous Area of the World*, pp. 90–5.
73. See Ashton, *Kennedy, Macmillan and the Cold War*.

74. Memcon with the President, 27 April 1963, Folder Memcons US, Box 20A, Richard E. Neustadt Papers, JFKL.
75. For Wolfram Kaiser's views see *Using Europe, Abusing the Europeans: Britain and European Integration, 1945–63* (Basingstoke: 1996).
76. For discussion of Acheson's speech see D. Brinkley, *Dean Acheson: The Cold War Years, 1953–71* (New Haven, CT: 1992), p. 176.
77. Macmillan to Thorneycroft, 26 December 1962, M.343/62, NA, PREM11/4147.
78. For this interpretation see Ritchie Ovendale's *Britain, the United States and the Transfer of Power in the Middle East, 1945–62* (Leicester: 1996).

9
Public Enemy Number One: The British Empire in the Dock at the United Nations, 1957–71

Wm. Roger Louis

I don't think they play at all fairly', Alice began, in rather a complaining tone 'and they all quarrel so dreadfully one can't hear oneself speak – and they don't seem to have any rules in particular; at least, if there are, nobody attends to them.[1]

Or, to use another literary allusion, as did Sir John Martin, the Deputy Under-Secretary of State for the Colonies in 1964, 'No man is an island'.[2] The Colonial Office drew up plans for territorial and economic configurations affecting millions throughout the world; nationalist leaders in Asia, Africa and the Caribbean made decisions attempting to set the pace for decolonisation; and the United States and the Soviet Union drew conclusions influencing the course of the Cold War. In these interlocking circumstances, it is useful at the international level to focus on the United Nations as a microcosm in which to study, in the British case, the relative weight of metropolitan infirmity, nationalist insurgency and international interference.[3] The British public as well as successive governments, on the whole, endorsed the idea of the United Nations as 'the finest conception that has yet been born among mankind'.[4] But by 1960, if not indeed five years before when the membership had expanded from 51 to 67, the United Nations was a quite different organisation from the one its founders had created in 1945. To add Mary Wollstonecraft Shelley to Lewis Carroll and John Donne, the United Nations in its colonial guise had become a Frankenstein's monster. In 1960 the General Assembly passed the notorious (at least to the British) Resolution 1514 calling for a speedy and unconditional end to colonialism.

In the United Nations no less than in Britain, the post-war history of the British Empire divides into two phases, pre-Suez and post-Suez. But the antecedents of the colonial problem at Turtle Bay (the location of the United Nations on the East River in New York City) can be traced to the founding of the organisation itself. Sir Hilton Poynton, the Permanent Under-Secretary at the Colonial Office (1959–66), had attended the San Francisco conference that had created the United Nations. He had wholeheartedly agreed with the Colonial Secretary of the time, Sir Oliver Stanley, that the United Nations must be kept out of the affairs of the British Empire. 'A motley international assembly' – Stanley's phrase – must not be allowed to put the empire in the dock.[5] No one was more consistent or adamant than Poynton in the view that the United Nations must not be allowed to interfere in British colonial administration. 'I have always been, and unashamedly remain, on the extreme right wing over this', he once wrote.[6] Even so, the commitment made by Britain to the United Nations was minimal. Under the UN arrangements (chapters XII and XIII of the Charter), the British agreed to submit reports, hear petitions and accept visiting missions to the trust territories. Tanganyika was the only British trusteeship dependency of any consequence, though British Togoland and British Cameroons had a certain relevance to the independence of the Gold Coast and Nigeria. Despite the negligible significance of most of the trusteeship territories, the debates were often acrimonious – especially those regarding visiting missions. The Afro-Asian bloc, as it became known, insisted that UN missions should be despatched to as many colonial dependencies as possible and not merely to the trust territories. On this issue as on others, and above all on the invasion of Egypt in 1956, the British inevitably found, in perhaps an understatement, that 'public debate at Turtle Bay exacerbates rather than assuages'.[7]

In 1945 the British had also acquiesced in the Declaration regarding Non-Self-Governing Territories (chapter XI of the Charter). They agreed to submit information on economic, social and educational progress in British colonies; but, as in the case of the trusteeship provisions, the Afro-Asian bloc insisted that the colonial powers also provide plans for independence. Here Poynton held a rigid view that 'independence' and 'self-determination' – phrases the British in 1945 had managed to keep to a subdued use in the UN Charter – should not be admitted into UN discourse. To Poynton's mind, emphasising independence would encourage colonial subjects to break away from the empire rather than to become self-governing within the empire as a step towards dominion status within the Commonwealth. Recalling his early involvement, he stressed Britain's minimal obligation:

> I have a special personal interest in this in that I was myself repre-
> senting the Colonial Office as an Adviser (Assistant Secretary) at the ...
> San Francisco Conference and all the earlier meetings of the United
> Nations and the Trusteeship Council.
>
> The charter obliges us to transmit such information on social,
> economic and educational conditions, but not on political and
> constitutional progress. ... I confess I should be very sorry to see this
> point surrendered during my period as Permanent Secretary of the
> Colonial Office.[8]

On another occasion he remarked: 'I do not accept that the United
Nations should have a right to meddle in our Colonial affairs.'[9] What
Poynton feared most of all was that pressure by the United Nations
would cause the British to grant independence before adequate political,
economic, social and educational preparation. His judgment on UN oratorical extravagance was unequivocal and emphatic: 'dangerous balder-
dash'.[10] But whatever the rhetoric, the UN Charter itself, even in its
measured language, was, and is, a profoundly anti-colonial document.

One of the ironies of the process of decolonisation is that in 1945 – as
in 1919 at the time of the creation of the mandates system – the British
had fiercely resisted the principle of self-determination, or, in the
language of the UN Charter, 'the freely expressed wishes of the peoples
concerned'.[11] Ultimately however the British came to rely on the
formula of self-determination as an answer to their critics. In the rocks,
shoals and other remnants of empire, what made more sense than to
allow the inhabitants of Gibraltar or the Falklands to determine their
own future? (Hong Kong was a unique exception.) In 1945, however, the
wave of the future, to the British at least, seemed to lie in large economic
and territorial units. Federations became the grand design of the two
post-war decades. Whether in the West Indies, Nigeria, Central Africa,
Aden or Malaysia, the aim would be to make economic sense out of the
arbitrary territorial boundaries by forging dependencies into viable
nascent states. The British wanted to avoid the fragmentation that the
United Nations seemed to be encouraging with its emphasis on individual
sovereign states whatever their size or capacity to stand on their own.
Christopher Eastwood in the Colonial Office asked, where would it all
end? The logical progression, or absurdity, seemed to point to Pitcairn
Island, a possibility he dismissed out of hand. 'Pitcairn Island, with
70 or 80 inhabitants, cannot really become independent.'[12] By the time

of the decision to recall all British troops East of Su
Nations had grown to 133 (as compared with 191 in
future lay with the wave of independent states, but
Suez crisis in 1956 the United Nations had not yet acqu
tion as an aggressive anti-colonial champion of self-deter
characterised it in the subsequent decade.

The public in Britain remained generally oblivious to the
which the United Nations in the mid-1950s was already being
formed into an organisation whose purpose would be, in Conor C
O'Brien's classic formulation, multiracialism and decolonisation as w
as peace.[14] The moral authority of the United Nations endowed it with a
charisma and quasi-religious quality – with Dag Hammarskjöld as the
secular Pope on the East River – that seemed, to those following its
evolution closely within the British government, to be irrational yet
compelling and thus dangerous. This 'theological' quality was clearly
detected in the Colonial Office.[15] In late 1954 Will Mathieson, who had
previously served as the colonial adviser in the British delegation at the
United Nations, commented that the UN membership would continue
increasingly to reflect an anti-colonial and especially an anti-British
bias. Mathieson later became head of the East African Department in the
Colonial Office and still later served on the Executive Board of UNESCO.
His minute of December 1954 reveals a certain intellectual acumen in
dealing with the mythology of colonialism at the United Nations. Such
was the power of UN emotional rhetoric that it could not 'be neutralised
by rational argument'. There were five components:

The myth that sovereign status is a sovereign remedy for all ills and that
poverty and social injustices in dependent territories are attributable
solely to their dependent status.

The myth that expansion overseas is 'aggressive imperialism' whereas
the assimilation of territory overland is the rightful and admirable
prerogative of a vigorous state.

The myth that 'colonialism', a term of abuse with historical origins
in the relationship between metropolitan governments and peoples
of the same stock in overseas settlements, still merits emotional application to the relationship between the remaining colonial powers and
their wards of different race in their dependencies.

The myth that professed altruism by Europeans towards coloured
peoples must mask determined exploitation.

And the myth that the major cause of war is the political subjection of
one people by another of different pigmentation.[16]

conclusion. 'Perpetuating all these
...hobia or reverse colour prejudice of
...ley crew' (the phrase had become
...had become 'hag-ridden by prej-
...operating under a system which
...national units whatever the[ir]
...emarked when the anti-colonial
...e nothing but 'trouble ahead'.[18]
...underclap with Gamal Abdel
...Company on 26 July 1956.[19]
...urtle Bay until several months
...thony Eden and John Foster Dulles, were
...united Nations, the latter because the United States
...o longer control it, at least not always, the former because he was
planning military action against Egypt. But Eden needed to prove that
he had exhausted all peaceful remedies before using force. In September
he decided to refer the Suez issue to the United Nations. Such was the
nature of the secret planning that virtually no one in the Colonial
Office and few in the Foreign Office besides Sir Ivone Kirkpatrick, the
Permanent Under-Secretary, along with a handful of others, were privy
to Eden's plot to depose Nasser by force. When the news of referral
reached the United Nations, Sir Pierson Dixon, the Ambassador, was
uncertain whether to regard it as a genuine effort to resolve the issue or
to view it as a smokescreen.[20] Ironically the British, French and Egyptian
delegates came close to finding a solution but at the same time Eden
plunged further into secret plans – collusion – with the French and
Israelis for a co-ordinated invasion.[21] Those in the British delegation,
which included Peter Ramsbotham (later Ambassador in Washington)
and the young Douglas Hurd (later Foreign Secretary), though they had
their suspicions, knew nothing until the Israeli attack on Egypt on
29 October.[22] The next day Britain and France delivered an ultimatum to
Israel and Egypt to withdraw from the Canal Zone. The Egyptians, if
they complied, would be withdrawing from Egyptian sovereign territory. It was clear to most observers that the ultimatum was contrived
and that it would be impossible for Egypt to accept it.

The world now witnessed the drama of Britain and France defying the
United Nations by casting vetoes against an American resolution in the
Security Council calling for the withdrawal of Israeli troops and – in an
event unique in the annals of the Cold War – of the Soviet Union intro-
ducing virtually the same resolution only to have it again vetoed by
Britain and France. On 31 October Britain and France launched air

attacks on Egypt. Two days later the General Assembly (where the veto does not apply) voted 65 to 5 (with 6 abstentions) to call for an immediate ceasefire and the withdrawal of Israeli troops. Only Australia and New Zealand voted with Britain and her two collusionist allies against the resolution. The resolution itself constituted one of the most emphatic censures ever voiced by the General Assembly. Only a few days later, with the deterioration of the pound sterling and under heavy pressure from the United States, Eden halted the advance of British troops in the Canal Zone. The Suez war thus ended abruptly. The immediate crisis was over, but at an immense cost to Britain's reputation at the United Nations. The *New Statesman* perhaps best summed it up by stating a glaring truth: 'The British government has broken the Charter of the U.N.'[23]

The Suez crisis had two far-reaching consequences for the British Empire in the international community. One was short term, the other longer lasting. Both have to be understood in the temper of the time, when the United Nations still represented the hope of the world in an era under the enduring shadow of the Second World War. The first consequence was that the debate about the Suez Canal and the invasion of Egypt became transformed into a full-blown polemical yet searching discussion about colonialism. The British Empire was now not merely in the dock but reviled as a renegade. In a manner that previously would have been regarded as inconceivable to most people in Britain, at least in its intensity, the British Empire was now denounced as just as immoral and vicious as the Soviet Empire in Eastern Europe and Central Asia. The Suez crisis occurred at the same time that Russian tanks rolled through Budapest to crush the Hungarian uprising. The British bombing of airfields in and around Cairo caused John Foster Dulles to remark that British and French methods were as brutal and barbaric as Russian tactics.[24] The moral turmoil of Sir Pierson Dixon spilled over into a telegram to the Foreign Office: 'We are inevitably being placed in the same low category as the Russians in their bombing of Budapest. I do not see how we can carry much conviction in our protests against the Russian bombing of Budapest, if we are ourselves bombing Cairo.'[25] Britain's ethical position at the United Nations had been shattered.

A few months later I.T.M. Pink of the Foreign Office assessed the damage. Pink had served in Tokyo and Berlin as well as Tehran and thus had perspective on the historical evolution of the British Empire in world affairs. He reflected on the loss of Britain's good name:

> Our recent troubles over the Suez affair have seriously weakened our position in the United Nations, which was based not so much on our

material power as on our reputation for wisdom, honesty, fair dealing and restraint. We may hope to regain the ground we have lost, but it will take time to re-establish our position.[26]

Ivor Pink was certainly right about the long-term implications. It was now clear, as if in a moment of revelation, that Britain could not act independently of the United States, nor did the British state possess the economic or military strength to be ranked as a great power. At the United Nations, the British Empire seemed to have revealed its true colors as a marauding, reactionary force. Here was the other consequence, which was entirely unexpected. For the next 15 years or so, Britain became Public Enemy Number One at the United Nations.

Colonialism as a menace to world peace

International notoriety can be exhilarating, but in unpredictable ways. At the United Nations during the Suez crisis the members of the British delegation were shunned. Scornful and embarrassed silence sometimes concealed genuine grief. Sir Pierson Dixon recalled the emotionally tense general mood: 'Flanked by our faithful Australians and New Zealanders, we wandered about the U.N. halls like lost spirits. Our best friends averted their gaze or burst into tears as we passed.'[27] Britain, one of the principal founders of the United Nations, had undermined the purpose of the organisation itself. The memory of the British acting true to form by invading Egypt persisted through the next decade. During the Middle East war of 1967, Israeli forces defeated the armies of Egypt, Syria and Jordan. The Arabs did not believe that the Israeli victory could have been possible without British (and American) assistance. This time, however, their suspicions were entirely unfounded. Their allegations were denounced by Britain and the United States as 'The Big Lie'. But Arab assumptions about British motives were easy to understand. British credibility had been destroyed in 1956. It was not until 1967, however, that the British paid the ultimate price for the Suez adventure. Apart from a few Commonwealth stalwarts, very few non-Western representatives at the United Nations were willing to give the British the benefit of the doubt when it came to motive. The Suez crisis thus provided the context for the anti-colonial movement as it gained momentum at the United Nations in the early 1960s.

The anti-colonial debate forced the British to centre stage. It compelled them to concentrate on large issues such as the purpose of colonial rule and the fate of the non-Western world. The British of course were not alone, though the British Empire was still far and away the largest of the remaining Western maritime enterprises. The French were equally notorious, but with a difference. No one at the United Nations expected anything but colonialist behaviour from the French. By contrast the British achievement beginning with India in 1947 had demonstrated consecutive transfers of power conferring sovereign equality. 'Our colonial record tends to be forgotten', lamented the British delegation at the United Nations.[28] As if in the worst of all possible worlds, the French continued to command the loyalty of their former colonies whereas 'some of the Commonwealth countries are our most dangerous opponents in New York'.[29] Was this, asked John Beith in the Foreign Office, an example of 'French toughness and British flabbiness'?[30] The Foreign Office came to the conclusion that the French drew strength from their former colonies because of a greater willingness to continue a much higher degree of economic and military assistance than the British themselves were able or willing to provide. As the decade progressed the British shared the colonial spotlight not only with the French but also with the South Africans and the Portuguese. In what was known as the 'Unholy Alliance' the British were suspected of indirectly supporting South African apartheid on the one hand, and the antiquated Portuguese system on the other. According to the anti-colonialists, the British aimed to preserve the Central African Federation and with it the profits of the mining industry as well as the supremacy of kith and kin in Southern Rhodesia.[31] Virtually no one would accept the explanation that the British hoped to achieve harmonious race relations based on equality and then to disengage. Being Public Enemy Number One was exhilarating but also exasperating.

The non-Western members of the United Nations appeared to have the long collective memories of the oppressed. They criticised British motives during and after the Suez crisis. They never allowed the British to minimise their buccaneering past or the exploitative nature of the British Empire. Nor did Britain's record of decolonisation seem to hold up very well according to the doctrine of 'neo-colonialism', the theory that the metropolitan countries still held the colonies in thrall economically even after independence.[32] Much later, in the 1970s, Sir Colin Crowe reflected that the widespread obsession with colonialism could be traced to the decade before the First World War and the early years of British rule in Africa: 'At the turn of the century the British nanny was individually one of the most potent educative influences around the world, but what may be tolerable in the nursery causes resentment in international organisations and far too often we take on the role of universal governess.'[33]

There certainly seemed to be a psychological dimension to the anti-colonial campaign of the 1960s. According to one of the most interesting explanations, the former colonial subjects still, on the whole, preferred the extended hand of the former nanny to the embrace of the Americans. Anti-colonialism, at least in Asia, was a cultural as well as political phenomenon:

> It is a frame of mind, resentment at patronage, resentment at fancied Western assumptions of superiority whether in social status or culture, reaction to the Western impact on Asia in past centuries. This frame of mind, expressed in terms of opposition to Western control or interference, explains the paradox of 'anti-colonialism' in countries that have never been colonies, directed against countries that have never had them.
>
> Americans are sometimes baffled to find that Asian sentiment towards Britain, the greatest colonial power of all, is apt to be more cordial than towards the United States, despite their remarkable record of generosity and altruism in dealings with Asia.[34]

Looking suspiciously at Britain's place in the world as an imperial power, the anti-colonialists not only condemned the British because of their colonial past but also despised them because of their post-Suez weakness and indecision. The enemies of imperialism would not let it be forgotten, as Sir Evelyn Shuckburgh summed it up, that the British had been 'great marauders in the past and are still a long way from having abandoned ill-gotten acquisitions' – while on the other hand, the lesson of Suez seemed to be that 'we are a poor, sad shadow of an influential past'.[35]

'It is important to us in all sorts of ways', wrote Sir John Martin, whose balanced judgment attracted respect throughout Whitehall, 'that the image of Britain should be that of a progressive modern State rather than of a feeble senescent power living in the past'.[36] What the British thought of themselves had a bearing on the Cold War and the Russian efforts to dismantle the British Empire as well as on colonial nationalism and the attempts by nationalists, especially in Africa, to force the pace of decolonisation. There were two widely held assumptions that are important to understand why the British acted as they did in trying to regain the initiative at the United Nations and elsewhere after the Suez crisis. The first was the common belief that the British Empire would last a good deal longer than it in fact did. As late as 1959 the projected timetable for independence in East Africa was 1970 for Tanganyika,

1971 for Uganda and 1975 for Kenya – as opposed to the actual dates of the early 1960s.[37]

The second assumption was that the international system at the United Nations was rigged against the British because of what was known as the 'double standard'. Representatives of the non-Western countries, above all India, held the Soviet Union to one standard, which was tolerant and forgiving, and Britain to another that was harsh and exacting. Jawaharlal Nehru had been slow to criticise the Russians in Hungary but quick to condemn the British at Suez. At the United Nations, the anti-British and anti-American tone had been set by India's legendary representative in the 1950s, Krishna Menon, who spoke, according to a slightly jaded British description, as 'the mouthpiece of the world's conscience'. His unbridled and eloquent passion was usually directed, often to the relief of the British, towards the United States.

> The long curved fingers, the curling lip, the limp and the stick, the sometimes almost incomprehensible but always earnest speech, seem to set him apart from other delegates. In some people ... he inspires an instinctive dislike and mistrust. Almost all Americans regard him with intense suspicion. ... His anti-Americanism ... sometimes verges on the hysterical.[38]

The first assumption on the longevity of the colonial system was shaken in 1960 by UN Resolution 1514 calling for immediate liberation of all colonies. The second assumption continued to prove all too true. Resolution 1514 quickly gained a momentum in which the 'double standard' seemed conspicuous.

The year 1960 was the critical juncture between the Suez crisis and the end of the British colonial era. In May riots broke out in South Africa in the town of Sharpeville leaving 69 dead and 180 injured. The Sharpeville massacre marked the beginning of the 30-year international campaign against apartheid. In June the Belgians left the Congo. The tempestuous events of 'Congo chaos' proved to Sir Hilton Poynton and others in the Colonial Office the lessons of premature independence. The Congo became a cock pit of the Cold War. In September Nikita Khrushchev visited Turtle Bay. He was followed by Harold Macmillan. In deciding to reiterate the message of the 'Wind of Change' blowing through Africa (the theme of his speech delivered earlier in the year in Cape Town), Macmillan deviated from usual UN procedure. Instead of reading a verbatim text, he deployed to memorable effect the House of Commons technique of directly addressing his audience and making references to previous speakers. He demonstrated a spontaneous and devastating wit, reaching one of the peaks of his occasional comic genius. It occurred when Khrushchev banged on a desk with his shoe. Macmillan paused. He said he had not quite understood. Could he please have a translation?[39] The General Assembly erupted into hilarity. Public Enemy Number One could be entertaining as well as courteous and unflappable, though his inner thoughts in the archival records reveal an anguished soul.

By the end of the year the number of new African states in the United Nations increased by 17 members.[40] The Colonial Office felt the time had come to warn Colonial Governors of adverse international circumstances and the unprecedented menace in the shape of the United Nations. 'Recent events in Africa and in the U.N.', Poynton wrote in September 1960, 'have been forcing us to think about the role which the United Nations is likely to play in future in relation to British territories'. He mentioned the Algerian revolution as well as the Sharpeville massacre and the disaster in the Congo. He emphasised the changing 'international climate'. He believed the British themselves had consequently entered a period in which the United Nations would be 'a more decisive factor' in decolonisation.[41] Poynton wrote only a few weeks before Resolution 1514, which echoed Khrushchev's demand for colonial liberation. The Russians helped to sponsor the resolution, but the Africans themselves were now in full voice. According to another Colonial Office official: 'The Russians no longer need to push the band wagon, it rolls on without them.'[42]

Having resolved to end colonialism, the General Assembly in 1961 created what became known initially as the Committee of 17.[43] In the next year the Colonial Office, with considerable alarm, saw its membership increase to become the Committee of 24.[44] Though the British were represented, their frustration was palpable. The committee became famous in the history of the United Nations for its persistent, voluble and impassioned attacks on the Western colonial powers, especially Britain. To the Colonial Office it was, in Christopher's Eastwood's phrase, 'an infernal nuisance'.[45] It could become an outright danger by despatching visiting missions that would whip up anti-British nationalism. Eastwood warned in January 1961 that 'colonialism' was now 'in the mainstream of United Nations affairs' and that colonies 'have become an international issue in a sense which they have not been hitherto'.[46] Later in the same year he wrote that there would be 'a harder and more sustained onslaught against the colonial powers' than ever before.[47]

As long as the United Nations remained one of Britain's principal obligations in international affairs, then the British delegation felt compelled to support all of its activities – even though the Colonial Office viewed the Committee of 24 as obnoxious. Loyalty to the higher purpose of the United Nations thus overrode the urge to walk out. Only with great reluctance did Sir Hilton Poynton concede that the advantages of remaining in the committee outweighed those of leaving it. Sir Hugh Foot summed it up by writing of an anti-American, anti-United Nations bias at the Colonial Office. 'Poynton in particular seems entirely obsessed by the need to resist any attempt by people at the U.N. to interest themselves in British colonial affairs.'[48]

Sir Hugh Foot – elevated to the peerage in 1964 as Lord Caradon – was a former Colonial Governor who believed passionately and indefatigably in the cause of the United Nations. In the 1960s the phrase 'Caradonian' came to signify total commitment to peace and decolonisation. He came from a family of devout Christian outlook tempered by philosophical radicalism. His brothers included the lawyer Dingle and the Labour politician Michael. He served in Palestine and Nigeria before becoming Governor of Jamaica (1951–57) and then Governor of Cyprus (1957–60).[49] In 1960, after some 30 years in the colonial service, he succeeded Sir Andrew Cohen (another Colonial Governor) as British representative on the Trusteeship Council.[50] Foot was a man of goodwill and indestructible optimism. He would reply point by point to the allegations and denigration of British motive by the Committee of 24 in the belief that every opportunity should be taken to establish the accuracy of the colonial record, of which the British had every right to be proud and not ashamed. In 1961 he resigned over the Rhodesian issue, a decision that revealed his uncompromising commitment, in his own phrase, to African freedom. He stayed on at the United Nations to guide its development programme. In 1964 the Harold Wilson government appointed him as Ambassador to the United Nations. He now rejoined the battle against the Committee of 24. He described his own determined tactic in Churchillian rhetoric: We shall fight on the resolutions. We shall fight in the corridors. We shall fight in the Committees. We shall never abstain.[51]

Sir Hugh Foot won the confidence of the US delegation while gaining the respect of the Africans and other anti-colonialists by speaking to them without condescension. He also struck up a close friendship with Ralph Bunche in the UN Secretariat.[52] But one of the problems of the United Nations after the death of Hammarskjöld in 1961 was the quality of leadership of the Secretary-General, U Thant, and of the

US Ambassador, Adlai Stevenson.[53] And, just as the UN Secretariat could do very little to curtail the extremism of the Committee of 24, so the American delegation seemed paralysed because of what the British described as 'the revolt of the American negro'. Against the background and 'shocking impact' of 'dogs and fire hoses being turned on negro demonstrators', the members of the American delegation found it diffi-cult to stand up to African nationalists. 'I regret', wrote Denis Greenhill of the British Embassy in Washington in 1963, 'that the present racial crisis has taken some of the stuffing out of the [US] Administration's will to resist African nationalist demands'.[54]

On the other hand the British found active support in the middle ranks of the State Department and other parts of the bureaucracy in Washington. The inspiration of the British District Officer in Africa and elsewhere was apparent in the younger cohort of the Kennedy adminis-tration. The idealism and the 'same uncritical faith and hope' that had originally inspired the League of Nations spilled over into the Peace Corps of the 1960s. On issues affecting the British Empire, wrote the British Colonial Attaché in Washington, the Kennedy administration 'is shot through with a fundamental goodwill towards us'.[55] So it remained, more or less, in the LBJ era, but the American 'endemic naivety towards the Africans' began to wear off in the face of the onslaught of the Committee of 24, which from time to time could be as hostile to the United States as to Britain.[56] The Americans had helped the Africans along the path towards independence but now felt 'the sharp knife of ingratitude'.[57] Like the British, their patience began to wear thin. As for Public Enemy Number One, enough was enough. It was time for a tougher line.

The British revolt against the Committee of 24

'KEEP OFF THE GRASS', according to one observer of the Colonial Office attitude towards the United Nations, would be a good way to sum up a traditional outlook.[58] The Colonial Office had seen its position deterio-rate, however, to the point of accepting visiting missions not merely to trust territories but to other British dependencies, even though there was real enough risk of bloodshed. To some extent the later stages of this development can be traced to Lord Caradon (Sir Hugh Foot). His ener-getic and persuasive tactics carried considerable weight within the British government. But the erosion of the Colonial Office position also reflected the dominance of the Foreign Office as well as the general con-sensus in official circles on the relationship between the United Nations and the British colonial empire. Caradon for example, always held that Britain could not share or shift responsibility for the administration of colonial territories. But he nevertheless believed that the British should co-operate with the United Nations to the fullest extent possible for pragmatic as well as other reasons. Only by remaining on good terms with the United Nations in general could the British hope to minimise interference in colonies, where tensions would continue to mount. He wrote in 1965: 'We are no doubt in for a very rough time in the United Nations this year since we shall not be able to move in the directions which the Afro-Asians wish on southern Africa, questions on which they feel intensely.'[59]

The anti-colonialists aimed increasingly at overthrowing the South African government, liquidating the Portuguese Empire, and (after the declaration of unilateral independence by Southern Rhodesia in 1965) liberating Africans held in the grip of the Rhodesian white settlers. The majority on the Committee of 24 embodied those ambitions. Caradon hoped to blunt the attack and to mediate. But the Committee would not be appeased. By early 1966 the Permanent Under-Secretary at the Foreign Office, Sir Paul Gore-Booth, believed the Committee to be so dishonest and dangerous that it was a disgrace for Britain any longer to be associated with it. He moved towards withdrawal, thus endorsing the position of the majority in the Colonial Office; but thereby he brought into play the larger issue of Britain's relations with the United Nations. The decision in 1966 was to soldier on with the Committee of 24, but in late 1967 Gore-Booth returned to the charge.

The problem was that the Committee of 24 was obsessed – in the British view to a psychotic degree – with decolonisation. As if reverting to an explanation that had endured since the late nineteenth century, the British believed that fundamental trouble in Asia and Africa could usually be traced to the French. At the centre of the ideological drive of the Committee of 24 stood the Tunisians. They viewed the worldwide quest for national liberation as a mirror reflection of the Tunisian and Algerian struggle against France. The Tunisians 'enjoy twisting our tail', according to Sir Herbert Marchant, the British Ambassador in Tunisia; but the fixation also revealed 'a national state of mind':

> For the last thirty years they have been engaged in an unhappy fight against the French. There have been some ugly incidents which have not reflected much glory on the colonialist power in question and they have had a ringside seat for the seven years' war in Algeria, where things have been even less savoury.

Against this background British military bases, be they in Gibraltar, Malta, Cyprus, in the Middle East or in South East Asia, bear a strong resemblance in Tunisian eyes to French troops in Bizerta. They see in any country that has not yet got complete independence the image of themselves fighting their way to freedom – however dissimilar the cases may be. The whole emotional background makes this, I think, inevitable – and we are dealing with emotion rather than reason.[60]

Within the Committee, to give only a partial example, the Tunisians and Iraqis were cheered on by the Bulgarians and Poles while the Chileans and Venezuelans usually added their applause. The British could rely on firm support only from the Australians and the Danes, but alas the stalwart Danes eventually withdrew from the Committee. Within a single year, 1963, the Committee discussed Southern Rhodesia, Aden, Malta, Fiji, British Guiana, Kenya, Northern Rhodesia, Nyasaland, Zanzibar, Basutoland, Bechuanaland, Swaziland, Gibraltar and the Gambia. One of their resolutions called for immediate independence for the Gambia.[61] On a much more serious note, they demanded visiting missions to, among other places, Aden, Fiji and British Guiana, all of which had problems that could only be described, in the word of the Colonial Secretary, Reginald Maudling, as 'explosive'.[62]

'The wretched Committee of Twenty-Four', wrote David Jerrom, the head of the International Relations Department in the Colonial Office, had forced its way into a position of influence on all questions of decolonisation. Here is a key passage from one of Jerrom's Minutes on the extent to which international interference must be taken into account in the general process of decolonisation:

> Many people still tend to look on the Committee as an anti-colonial pressure group divorced from the serious business of life. I think that this was a pretty sound view until the Committee took up Aden in 1963, since when *it has become a political factor of importance in all delicate colonial situations*.[63]

In Aden, British colonial officers could not but recall the visit, catastrophic in their view, by the United Nations Special Committee on Palestine in 1947. The Arabs had boycotted the mission but the members of the Committee themselves prepared the way for a debate in the General Assembly and the end of the British mandate. In places such as Fiji or British Guiana, a visiting mission could easily upset, with violent results, the intricate ethnic balance between the indigenous inhabitants and immigrant populations. Visiting missions were thus, in Jerrom's phrase, the 'crux of the issue'.[64] What the Colonial Office feared was that a visiting mission to Aden, for example, might set the precedent for another mission, this time to Southern Rhodesia.[65] Would the British thus not be shifting the very basis of colonial rule from accountability to parliament to accountability – in the Colonial Office phrase – to the motley international assembly? In such a way did the problem of visiting missions go to the heart of the British colonial system. It was an issue that had to be taken seriously in the Foreign Office, where the question of accountability ran in the direction of fulfilling the commitment to the United Nations.[66]

The counterpart of David Jerrom in the Foreign Office was Sam Falle, the head of the UN Department. Falle had extensive Middle East experience and was thus sensitive to the drift towards civil war in Aden. He had served in Iran, where he had formed close connections with MI6 and the CIA, and in Iraq, where he had been one of the few to predict the 1958 revolution. He viewed himself as a UN man, not quite a Caradonian, but one of Caradon's admirers.[67] Falle concurred in the Colonial Office's strongly held point that the Committee of 24 must not be allowed to dictate colonial policy. But he also agreed with Caradon on the enlightened nature of British colonial rule: 'if we have nothing in the colonies of which we are ashamed, we ought to welcome visits by United Nations bodies, to whom we could explain our problems'.[68] In the case of the Committee of 24, Falle proved to be far too optimistic, but it seemed to be a reasonable assumption that a UN visiting mission would be willing to listen and thus not take the extremist view echoed in the chambers of Turtle Bay. Falle also recognised that the Committee resembled, in the words of the British UN delegation 'a whale stranded on a beach, imposing in its bulk but helpless in action'.[69] In this view, it was better to let the Committee rot away or self-destruct rather than to declare war against a major body of the United Nations. This solution proved futile because of the Committee's own activist behaviour. Its members neither listened nor learned but took an ever-increasing theoretical or 'theological' view of British colonialism.

Sam Falle eventually became appalled at the violence of the rhetoric and the virulence of the personal insults, as did the Deputy Under-Secretary, Sir Martin Le Quesne. Falle prided himself on being thick-skinned, and his wartime service in the Royal Navy had made him about as tough as they came. But when he read of the experiences of Francis Brown, a member of the British delegation in New York who had helped escort the Committee of 24 on its travels in Africa, he confessed to David Jerrom: 'Even after 3½ years in this Department and the almost impenetrable hide I have grown during this time, this ... brought tears to my eyes.'[70] In similar vein Le Quesne commented that the time had come to depart from the Committee of 24. Le Quesne, like Falle, had Middle East experience but had also served as Ambassador to Mali and had become the Foreign Office's expert on radical African nationalism. He later served as Ambassador in Algeria. In retirement he achieved glory as Chairman of the Reform Club. At the time of the confrontation with the Committee of 24, he had definite ideas about gentlemanly behaviour and where to draw the line. He too commented on Francis Brown's experience with the Committee:

> The Committee's visit to Africa last year placed Mr. Brown in an intol-erably difficult and embarrassing position, in which he conducted himself with superhuman patience and dignity. I do not believe, however, that, apart from such favourable impression as his display of British steadiness under fire may have created, he did us the slightest good so far as the question of securing understanding and sympathy for our problems and policies goes.[71]

Indignation began to mount from the middle ranks of the Foreign Office to the top. From early 1966 onwards the insults of the Committee of the 24 began to catch the attention of the Permanent Under-Secretary, Sir Paul Gore-Booth.

Gore-Booth held strong convictions about the purpose of the United Nations. He had participated in its planning during the Second World War while at the British Embassy in Washington. He had attended the San Francisco conference in 1945. He viewed the Committee of 24 not only as a caricature of the United Nations but at variance with his own sense of civilised international society. He had developed a set of ethics based on Christian Science, though with a detectible Eton and Balliol influence. His career had embraced long periods in Asia and other parts of the world. His early posts before the Second World War had included Japan and he had learned Japanese. As Ambassador to Burma during the early 1950s he and his wife had adopted the daughter of the assassinated nationalist leader, Aung Sang (Suu Kyi Aung San, the present-day Burmese prisoner of conscience). In India as High Commissioner a decade later he had been treated with great respect by Nehru, in part because Nehru knew that he had opposed the Suez expedition. Gore-Booth became Permanent Under-Secretary in 1965, at about the time that Sam Falle began to write, by implication at least, of the moral obliquity of the

Committee of 24. In February 1966 Falle recorded such acts as encouraging hostile petitioners, drumming up extremist groups and calling for violence.[72] Gore-Booth at this stage noted that the British should either walk out of the Committee or themselves become more aggressive. 'The time for quiet reasonableness has passed.'[73]

Despite Gore-Booth's nudge towards withdrawal, the move to terminate Britain's connection with the Committee of 24 made no progress during the rest of the year. In a pattern that would recur, the combination of Lord Caradon and Eirene White, the Minister of State, prevailed over the UN Department and the Deputy Under-Secretary, Sir Denis Greenhill, as well as Gore-Booth. Sam Falle wrote in July 1966: 'As a determined U.N. man I am in favour of entering the ring on every possible occasion and defending our policy with vigour.' But Falle was also impressed with the 'violence of the debates' and the radical dissidence as well as the 'inverse racism' affecting the United Nations itself. Falle therefore recommended withdrawal.[74]

The advice did not commend itself to Lord Caradon, who held the rank of Minister of State as well as Ambassador to the United Nations. At the ministerial level of the Foreign Office, he effectively argued that withdrawal would be interpreted as a 'complete reversal' of British policy of co-operation with the United Nations on one of its most important missions - the mission that affected the British most directly: decolonisation. This point had ramifications for parliament as well as the British public. Here the influence of Eirene White, another Minister of State, was significant because she too was passionately committed to the United Nations, though not so much as Caradon.[75] To her and Caradon the act of withdrawal would stand symbolically as Britain reverting to true form - at least in the eyes of the enemies of British imperialism - to the Britain of Anthony Eden and the invasion of Egypt. So powerful was the memory of the recent past that no Labour government could endorse a proposal that seemed to reverse course and to reestablish Britain as a reactionary power. The British would take a tougher line with the committee and 'soldier on', not withdraw.[76]

The decision to leave the Committee of 24

The US government, above all Ambassador Arthur Goldberg (Stevenson's successor), held the Committee of 24 in part responsible for this adverse turn in the Cold War.[77] Goldberg told Caradon in December 1967 that 'the Committee was being used as an instrument to attack the United States Government'. The time had come, Goldberg said, for the British and Americans to withdraw from the Committee. 'It had been largely captured by the radical elements amongst the Afro-Asians and instead of being used for its proper purposes of encouraging and facilitating decolonisation it was being turned into a vehicle for vituperous attacks, principally on Western powers.'[78]

Caradon, knowing that American withdrawal from the Committee would provoke another round of debate in London, wrote as always in robust language in favour of the British remaining loyal to the principle of honestly defending the British colonial record come thick or thin. 'I do not believe in walking out or running away', he declared. The ill-informed and malicious attacks on the British Empire would continue, and, if Britain left the Committee, the slander would remain unchallenged. 'We have stood our ground for many years and stated our case and answered back when attacks have been made. I should like to see this thing through.' With considerable eloquence Caradon in short argued in favour of staying the course and debating the issue of British colonialism 'even with the wildest men amongst the Afro-Asians'.[79]

The question of the Committee of 24 now moved into its most dramatic phase. Sir Paul Gore-Booth returned to the charge, once again bringing into play the larger stakes of Britain's support for the United Nations. Like others in the British government, Gore-Booth was appalled at the 'futile' mission to Aden and its attempt to cast a slur on the record of British rule. He believed that the time had come, once and forevermore, to put an end to Britain's participation in 'unfair, destructive nonsense'.[80] He found a powerful ally in presenting the case for withdrawal in George Thomson, later Lord Thomson, the head of the Commonwealth Office before the new Foreign and Commonwealth Office was created in October 1968. Thomson also protested against the Committee's 'dogmatic anti-Colonialism'. Though some of the principal colonial difficulties had been resolved, there were still many British dependencies vulnerable to UN interference:

> We have now come practically to the end of our programme of decolonisation and we shall soon be left with territories too small and unviable to achieve independence and with a limited number of extremely difficult and delicate questions – the disputed territories of Gibraltar, Falklands, British Honduras, Fiji with its deep racial problem, Hong Kong and New Hebrides.
>
> Our continued presence in the Committee of 24 erodes our authority and confuses responsibilities.[81]

Sir Hilton Poynton could not have put the case better, but again it was a vain protest. The attempt to cut the connection with the Committee of 24 failed, not least because of the tenacious, persuasive and eloquent Lord Caradon.

In the final confrontation, Caradon found an ally in Goronwy Roberts, Minister of State in the Foreign Office and one of the few who could consistently influence the erratic Foreign Secretary, George Brown. Caradon and Brown proved to be an unbreakable combination. Brown himself took only a fleeting grasp at the issue, but his intellect penetrated to its heart. He grasped immediately, though 'reluctantly' and irritably, that Britain could not leave the Committee.[82] 'Our difference on these questions', he wrote, 'is not just with the Committee but with the majority at the United Nations'.[83] Brown's instinct was to remain loyal to the United Nations. The decisive words – indeed the rationale for the decision itself – were written by Goronwy Roberts: 'I do not wish you of all people to be the first Secretary of State to be associated with a retreat by Britain from full United Nations participation – for this is how it would look and how it would be regarded in this country and abroad.'[84] The Caradonian principle thus prevailed.

Gore-Booth did triumph on one point. He managed to persuade the Foreign Secretary to buck up Lord Caradon and to urge the delegation in New York to take a much more aggressive stance in the Committee – to 'play it tougher', in Gore-Booth's words.[85] But Gore-Booth did not think Caradon temperamentally capable of a sufficiently pugnacious attitude, even under direct order. This advice suited Brown's own belligerent disposition, drunk or sober.[86] They thus turned to Evan Luard (Parliamentary Under-Secretary at the Foreign and Commonwealth Office, MP for Oxford and Supernumerary Fellow of St. Antony's College), who recently had been enlisted to help Caradon in the Committee of 24. Luard was a true believer in both the United Nations and the British Empire, though in a particular sense. He had been one of the few members of the Foreign Office to resign at the time of Suez in protest at Britain's flouting of the United Nations. He was second to none in defending Britain's colonial record, but he also upheld the principle of orderly liquidation of the Empire and its transformation into the Commonwealth. In fact his attitude was identical with Caradon's though he employed a more rough and tumble House of Commons debating technique and his comments had a confrontational edge. His earnest, plain speaking was much more to the taste of both Gore-Booth and Brown than Caradon's congenial rebuttals. Brown had written to

Luard earlier: 'it was good to know that we had ... someone who defended resolutely and counter-attacked boldly ... . It is certainly a tribute to you that, while giving no quarter, you were able to make and preserve many friendships among even our sharpest critics.'[87] With Luard speaking out at the United Nations, the Committee at least got, though not quite, the comeuppance that Gore-Booth thought it deserved.

The break with the Committee of 24 did finally occur, as Gore-Booth and others hoped it would, on 11 January 1971. The main reason was obvious to everyone at the time. Lord Caradon had retired after distinguished service as British Ambassador to the United Nations after the Conservative victory in the election of 1970. But there were other fundamental reasons as well. By the end of the 1960s the anti-colonial movement had begun to run out of steam. Nasser's death in 1970 symbolised the end of the post-Suez era. By the beginning of the new decade many of the problematical colonies such as Fiji had achieved independence or were on their way to it. There remained of course Hong Kong, Gibraltar and the Falklands as well as an array of island dependencies such as St. Helena and Pitcairn, but even at the United Nations these were generally recognised as 'outposts without an empire'.[88] Britain remained 'shackled by the ball-and-chain of Rhodesia'.[89] But by the early 1970s the Committee of 24 itself had begun to suffer from a grave and deadly affliction: public boredom.

As if they were mates in a long-enduring but mismatched marriage, Britannia lost her reputation as an ongoing colonial predator while the Committee became 'pretty impotent'.[90] Not only was there a general view that the Committee of 24 had run its course but in Britain there was an increasing disillusionment with the United Nations itself.[91] 'I am not at all a "Caradonian" ', wrote F.A. Warner of the British delegation in New York in 1970, but it would be good, he argued, to keep things in perspective, neither overvaluing the United Nations nor writing it off as representing only 'a lot of hot air'.[92] The decision to leave the Committee reflected a balanced and hard-headed assessment that the British could now cautiously depart, safe in the knowledge, in the words of a much earlier Colonial Office judgment, that 'a rump committee composed of Communists, Afro-Asians and Latin Americans should not cause us much trouble'.[93] The British could thus listen more indifferently to such accusations, in the mantra of the Committee of 24, that colonialism in any form is a crime against humanity. The British could now breathe easier, but without the exhilaration of being Public Enemy Number One.[94]

Notes

1. Quoted in Report on the Proceedings in the Fourth (Trusteeship and Colonial) Committee at the 21st Session of the United Nations, enclosed in Lord Caradon (Ambassador to the United Nations) to FCO, Confidential, 15 February 1967, FCO 58/87. John Sankey, 'Decolonisation: cooperation and confrontation at the United Nations', in Erik Jensen and Thomas Fisher (eds), *The United Kingdom – The United Nations* (London: 1990), is an indispensable work of reference. Sankey for many years was the colonial adviser to the British delegation in New York and later UK Permanent Representative to the United Nations in Geneva.

2. Minute by Martin, 6 October 1964, CO 936/925.

3. See W.R. Louis and R.E. Robinson, 'The imperialism of decolonization', *Journal of Imperial and Commonwealth History*, 22, 3 (September 1994); John Darwin, 'Decolonization and the end of empire', in Robin W. Winks (ed.), *Historiography* (vol. 5 in the *Oxford History of the British Empire*, Oxford: 1999).

4. Sir Alec Douglas Home in the House of Commons, 4 March 1965, *Parliamentary Debates* (Commons), col. 1551, from which Christopher Eastwood in the Colonial Office drew the conclusion that 'there is no great division between the parties on this'. Minute by Eastwood, 5 March 1965, CO 936/927.

5. See W.R. Louis, *Imperialism at Bay* (Oxford: 1977), chs 33 and 34, esp. p. 531 on Poynton's dismay at the creation of the UN's Trusteeship Council empowered to examine annual reports, receive petitions, and despatch visiting missions. 'I am ... disheartened over the whole thing', he wrote to Kenneth Robinson in the Colonial Office. 'I'm afraid we've got ourselves into a ghastly jam. I expect you are all seething with rage in London.' On Poynton's views see also especially Sankey, 'Decolonisation and the UN', pp. 114–15.

6. Quoted by Ronald Hyam in Ronald Hyam and W.R. Louis (eds), *British Documents on the End of Empire: The Conservative Government and the End of Empire 1957–1964* (2 vols., London: 2000), pp. I, lxxi.

7. Caradon to FCO, Confidential, 26 January 1965, FO 371/183521.

8. Minute by Poynton, 28 July 1961, CO 936/681.

9. Minute by Poynton, 9 May 1962, CO 936/727.

10. Minute by Poynton, 2 November 1961, CO 936/683.

11. The UN Charter does not refer explicitly to the principle of self-determination but rather to 'a full measure of self-government' (Chapter XI) and 'self-government or independence' (Chapter XII). Resolution 1541 of 1960 stated that non-self-governing territories could achieve a full measure of self-government either by independence or by free association or integration with an independent state. See Sankey, 'Decolonisation', pp. 99–100.

12. Minute by Eastwood, 20 October 1964, CO 936/925. Despite Eastwood's fears, Pitcairn Island, with a declining population – 47 in 2003 – has not yet become a member of the United Nations.

13. To those within the British government watching the growth of the United Nations, there seemed to be a sort of Parkinson's law at work: the number of 'oppressed' would increase indefinitely in inverse proportion to the constant number of 'oppressors'. (See for example, the minute by the young Philip Ziegler in the Foreign Office, 23 February 1962, FO 371/166850.)

14. See Conor Cruise O'Brien, *'The United Nations: Sacred Drama* (New York: 1968). On the decade of radical chic following the Suez crisis, O'Brien writes that 'these were the years when fair British royalty would be photographed dancing with jet-black African potentates' (p. 33, O'Brien, quoting the Brazilian journalist Hernane Tavares de Sá, who had Princess Margaret in mind). On the significance of O'Brien's book see Adam Roberts and Benedict Kingsbury, *United Nations, Divided World* (Oxford: 1993), p. 21.

Here and in a few other passages I have drawn on a paper presented to a conference on the United Nations in Hokkaido, Japan, in December 2003. I have benefited from Asahiko Hanzawa, 'An invisible surrender: The United Nations and the end of the British Empire, 1956–1963' (Oxford D. Phil. thesis: 2002).

15. 'Theological' was the word used by Christopher Eastwood in a letter to John Tahourdin of the Foreign Office, Confidential, 16 October 1959, FO 371/145269.

16. Minute by Mathieson, 31 December 1954, CO 936/319. Mathieson's minute reflected many of the assumptions developed by Poynton, since late in the wartime period, that had become firmly established in departmental lore. See Louis, *Imperialism at Bay*, ch. 25.

17. The motley crew moreover seemed to suffer from 'a colonial hangover' – another phrase used by Mathieson to sum up his conclusions. He went on: 'To put this in terms of Latin American oratory, in the lobbies of the United Nations the ring of the discarded fetter will always drown the cry of the starving child'. Minute by Mathieson, 31 December 1954.

18. Minute by Poynton, 21 October 1964, CO 936/925.

19. For the United Nations and the Suez crisis, see especially Michael G. Fry, 'Canada, the North Atlantic Triangle, and the United Nations', in W.R. Louis and Roger Owen, *Suez 1956* (Oxford: 1989).

20. See Piers Dixon, *Double Diploma: The Life of Sir Pierson Dixon – Don and Diplomat* (London: 1968); and Edward Johnson, 'The Diplomats' diplomat', *Contemporary British History*, 13, 2 (Summer 1999).

21. See especially Avi Shlaim, 'The protocol of Sèvres, 1956: anatomy of a war plot', *International Affairs*, 73, 3 (1997); for the crisis itself, Keith Kyle, *Suez* (London: 1991) stands the test of time as the classic work.

22. See Douglas Hurd, *Memoirs* (London: 2003).

23. *New Statesman*, 3 November 1956.

24. See *Foreign Relations, 1955–1957*, XVI, p. 868. Dulles made the remark to the French Ambassador in Washington, Hervé Alphand, who was so incensed that he stood up to leave the meeting. Dulles thereupon retracted or at least, according to the record, 'modified' his complaint.

25. Dixon to FO, Emergency Secret, 5 November 1956, FO 371/121748. Dixon's telegram is printed in full in Richard Lamb, *The Failure of the Eden Government* (London: 1987), pp. 265–6.

26. I.T.M. Pink, 'The United Nations: A stocktaking', Confidential, 7 February 1957, CO 936/540.

27. Dixon diary entry for 7 January 1957, *Double Diploma*, p. 277.

28. Sir Patrick Dean (Permanent Representative at the United Nations 1960–64) to FO, Confidential, 25 January 1963, FO 371/172548.

29. Minute by T.C.D. Jerrom, 19 September 1963, CO 936/921.

30. Minute by Beith, 19 July 1962, FO 371/166803.

31. For the 'Unholy Alliance' see for example FO 371/172548, FO 371/172601, and FO 371/172606, especially the minutes produced by the powerful mind of C.W. Squire, who had served in the Nigerian Administrative Service as well as in the British delegation to the United Nations and later became Ambassador to Israel.

32. See especially Brian Crozier, *Neo-Colonialism* (London: 1964), a book of interest because the Foreign Office commissioned it to disprove the theory of neo-colonialism. (See Edward Youde to Sam Falle, Confidential, 27 May 1966, FO 371/189816.) Crozier, on the staff of *The Economist*, was a journalist of considerable repute, not least because of his highly acclaimed survey of the post-colonial world, *The Morning After* (London: 1963). *Neo-Colonialism* is an inferior work in comparison but is nevertheless useful for its statistical comparisons of the former British and French colonies. For Foreign Office assessments of the theory, see for example FO 371/166835, FO 371/166842, and FO 371/172605. According to *The Times* on 23 August 1963: 'Neocolonialism is the prolongation of colonialism by other means, mainly but not wholly economic.' (Cutting in FO 371/172601.)

33. Sir Colin Crowe to FCO, Confidential, 23 May 1973, FCO 58/773. Crowe, a Supernumerary Fellow of St. Antony's College, Oxford, was Permanent Representative to the United Nations 1970–73. He had begun his career in China before the Second World War and had post-1956 experience in Egypt.

34. Sir Robert Scott to Harold Macmillan, Secret, 13 November 1959, FO 371/143732. Scott was High Commissioner in South East Asia, having served previously in China.

35. Minute by Evelyn Shuckburgh, Confidential, 2 February 1962, FO 371/166819. Shuckburgh was the Under-Secretary supervising Middle Eastern affairs until shortly before the Suez expedition, which he vehemently opposed. See Evelyn Shuckburgh, *Descent to Suez: Diaries 1951–56* (London: 1986).

36. Minute by Martin, 6 October 1964, CO 936/925.

37. The United Nations had established the date of 1960 for the independence of the trust territory of Somalia, which in turn influenced the decision to grant independence to Tanganyika in 1961 with a knock-on effect of helping to determine independence for Uganda in 1962 and Kenya in 1963. For the balance between political forces in East Africa and the causative affect of the trusteeship system, see W.R. Louis, 'The dissolution of the British Empire', in Judith Brown and W.R. Louis (eds), *Oxford History of the British Empire: The Twentieth Century* (Oxford: 1999), pp. 351–2.

38. These are the words of Sir Gladwyn Jebb, himself a grandiloquent and arrogant representative of Britain at the United Nations in the early 1950s (Jebb to FO, Confidential, 13 February 1954, CO 936/319). On the other hand, Krishna Menon held a clear, intellectually vigorous and consistent anti-colonial ideology that attracted a devoted band of followers. On his political thought see Michael Brecher, *India and World Politics: Krishna Menon's View of the World* (London: 1968).

39. Harold Macmillan, *Pointing the Way: 1959–1961* (London: 1972), p. 279. According to the assessment at the time by the British delegation at the United Nations, Macmillan's speech represented far and away 'the most effective expression of a Western political philosophy', which was eye

opening, curiously enough, to 'Mr. Khrushchev himself' – though probably as much because of Macmillan's oratorical skills as because of the content. (Sir Patrick Dean to FO, Confidential and Guard, 14 January 1961, FO 371/160877.)

40. The new African members were: Cameroon, the Central African Republic, Chad, the former Belgian Congo, the former French Congo, Dahomey, Gabon, Ivory Coast, Madagascar, Senegal, Mali, Mauritania, Niger, Nigeria, Somalia, Togo, and Upper Volta. Cyprus also joined the United Nations in 1960.

41. Poynton circular to Colonial Governors, 29 September 1960, *BDEEP: Conservative Government 1957–1964*, II, 405.

42. Minute by D.J. Derx, 31 October 1963, CO 936/922. On the assumption that the members of the United Nations would sympathise with an animal that defended itself rather than submitted passively to slander, the British from time to time replied in kind to the Russians by pointing out the geographical and other circumstances of the Soviet Empire. Much to their surprise, the British discovered that the Russians were taken aback. They were not used to being denounced as colonialists. 'The Russians have shown themselves to be pretty sensitive', Patrick Dean wrote in December 1962 (Dean to FO, Confidential, 1 December 1962, FO 371/166842). On the other hand the British did not carry the assault of 'pinpricks' too far, for reasons concerning China as well as the Soviet Union. According to the Governor of Hong Kong: 'If the Chinese are needled over Colonies, there is a possible danger of provoking them into some kind of action over Hong Kong' (Robin Black to J.D. Higham, Secret and Personal, 14 June 1963, CO 936/921).

43. The 17 original members of the Special Committee on Colonialism created in November 1961 were: Australia, Britain, Cambodia, India, Italy, Madagascar, Mali, Poland, the Soviet Union, Syria, Tanganyika, Tunisia, Syria, the United States, Uruguay, Venezuela and Yugoslavia.

44. The additional members were Bulgaria, Chile, Denmark, Iraq, Iran, Ivory Coast and Sierra Leone.

45. Minute by Eastwood, 20 September 1963, CO 936/921.

46. Eastwood to Sir Andrew Cohen, Confidential, 10 January 1961, FO 371/160902.

47. Minute by Eastwood, 5 September 1961, CO 936/686.

48. Foot to Dean, Confidential, 16 March 1962, FO 371/166822. The sentiment was mutual. 'With Sir Hugh Foot at the helm', Poynton once wrote, there would be all the more need for 'firmness' on the part of the Colonial Office (minute by Poynton, 7 February 1961, CO 936/679).

49. See his autobiography, *A Start in Freedom* (London: 1964). The Foot (Caradon) Papers at Rhodes House, Oxford, contain documents relating only to Cyprus but there are many examples of the principles that sustained him through his official career. For example his friend (Sir) Eugene Melville in the Colonial Office wrote to him of the idealism of Milner: 'It helps to know that the cause is just and the motive unselfish and that, in the end, we shall come through all right' (Melville to Foot, Personal, 10 November 1958, Foot Papers, Box 8 MSS. Medit. S 25).

50. Cohen had been responsible for reshaping and modernising British colonial policy in West Africa after the Second World War and then became Governor of Uganda before his assignment to the United Nations 1957–60. The calibre of such men as Cohen and Foot is an indication of the importance the British

government attached to the colonial problem in New York. On Cohen see especially the entry by R.E. Robinson in the *Dictionary of National Biography 1961–1970*.

51. The Churchillian phrases are a paraphrase of Foot's 'tailpiece' summing up his outlook in his memorandum of 27 December 1961, *BDEEP: Conservative Government 1957–1964*, II, 409. According to Denis Greenhill (Permanent Under-Secretary at the Foreign and Commonwealth Office 1969–73): 'He was a compelling speaker and was a major figure in the United Nations in New York to the benefit of the British reputation particularly in the Third World.' Denis Greenhill, *More by Accident* (Bishop Wilton: 1992), p. 112.

52. For Bunche and Foot, see Brian Urquhart, *Ralph Bunche: An American Life* (New York: 1993), pp. 425 and 429. The FO Personalities Report noted that 'Dr. Bunche now wears a slightly melancholy air, and seems to lack some of the energy which he showed in earlier years.' 'Leading Personalities in the United Nations', Confidential, 10 June 1959, FO 371/145243.

53. The British delegation's assessment of U Thant was mixed: 'U Thant has not Mr. Hammarskjöld's intellect nor is he the dynamo that Mr. Hammarskjöld was. Unfortunately, he is not a very much better organizer. But he is a quiet, sensible, friendly man of great courage' (Dean to FO, Confidential, 25 January 1963, FO 371/172548). Sir Patrick Dean wrote of Stevenson: 'I acknowledge with respect his brilliance, his charm and his political experience and prestige, but even if he were ten years younger I doubt if he would be the right man to lead the United States delegation. As things are, he is not up to it; nor is he really interested. He gives the impression of disillusionment and lack of knowledge, and in negotiations he finds it impossible to get down to details or to stand firm' (Dean to FO, Confidential Guard, 30 July 1963, FO 371/172634).

54. Greenhill to FO, Confidential, 16 August 1963, FO 371/172634.

55. J.D. Hennings to David Jerrom, Secret, 24 April 1962, CO 936/664.

56. Dean to FO, Confidential Guard, 30 July 1963, FO 371/172634.

57. Benjamin Gerig, one of the central figures on the American side of the trusteeship issue, used this phrase several times in conversations with me in the early 1970s. For Gerig see Louis, *Imperialism at Bay*, p. 91.

58. Cecil King of the British delegation in New York to FO, Confidential, 26 September 1963, FO 371/72600. Ironically enough, the phrase 'keep off the grass' was the same one used by Lord Linlithgow, Viceroy of India, during the early part of the Second World War to warn the Americans not to interfere in India. See W.R. Louis, 'British imperialism and the partitions of India and Palestine', in Chris Wrigley (ed.), *Warfare Diplomacy and Politics: Essays in Honour of A. J. P. Taylor* (London: 1986), p. 198.

59. Caradon to Secretary of State for the Colonies, Confidential, 10 March 1965, CO 936/927.

60. Marchant to Falle, Confidential, 10 February 1964, FO 371/178179. Marchant continued to explain the reasons for the Tunisian obsession with decolonisation: 'This is a small country headed up by a number of physically small people – all of them full of bounce. Most have had a French education and on Arab and African standards are more than usually able. Perhaps it is because they are conscious of their superiority in their own continent that they are a little over anxious to cut a figure in the "big league" as well.' Marchant later became the British representative on the UN Committee for the Elimination of Racial Discrimination.

61. See for example FO 371/178179 for very extensive documentation on the work of the committee.
62. Minute by Maudling, 5 July 1962, FO 371/166829.
63. Minute by Jerrom, 3 January 1964, CO 936/922. Emphasis added.
64. Minute by Jerrom, 5 March 1965, CO 936/927. See also especially the minutes by A.N. Galsworthy, who emphasised not only 'a most unwelcome precedent for Rhodesia' but also '*the extreme danger*' of visiting missions in Basutoland and Mauritius as well as in Gibraltar, the Falklands, and British Honduras (minutes by Galsworthy, 29 and 30 June 1966, CO 936/960, emphasis added). (Sir) Arthur Galsworthy had a particular interest in the smaller territories of the colonial empire and later (as High Commissioner to New Zealand) became Governor of Pitcairn.
65. Aden and Rhodesia were the two principal preoccupations of the British delegation in New York: 'Aden, along with Southern Rhodesia, will be one of the main colonial crosses which we shall have to bear in the United Nations over the next few years.' Dean to FO, Confidential, 6 August 1963, FO 371/ 172591.
66. This fundamental point was clearly expressed in a letter from Sir Leslie Monson (who had a long career in the Colonial Office and was High Commissioner in Zambia 1964–66) to Percy Cradock, the head of the Planning Staff in the Foreign and Commonwealth Office (later Ambassador to China). Monson wrote: 'As an administrator I am conditioned to think primarily in terms of accountability to Parliament while you are more concerned naturally enough with accountability in the international sense under the UN Charter' (Monson to Craddock, 26 August 1971, FCO 49/322).
67. See Sam Falle, *My Lucky Life in War, Revolution, Peace and Diplomacy* (Lewes, Sussex: 1996), p. 163: 'The idealistic Hugh Foot, Lord Caradon ... really believed in what he was doing and some of his enthusiasm rubbed off.'
68. Minute by Falle, 5 July 1963, FO 371/172591.
69. Patrick Dean to FO, 6 August 1963, FO 371/172591. In another quirky judgment on the Committee, it was best to follow 'Confucius' advice to the girl about to be raped'. (Minute by C.W. Squire, 29 May 1963, FO 371/172591.)
70. Falle to Jerrom, Confidential, 8 June 1966, CO 936/959. For Brown's ordeal with the Committee see also FO 371/189811. Brown had been educated at Wellington and Trinity College, Cambridge, apparently good training against verbal assault and coarse behaviour.
71. Minute by Le Quesne, 15 February 1966, FO 371/189811.
72. See for example, minute by Falle, 14 February 1966, FO 371/189811.
73. Minute by Gore-Booth, 15 February 1966, FO 371/189811. Gore-Booth's autobiography is *With Great Truth and Respect* (London: 1974), in which he does not dwell especially on the United Nations but see especially 160.
74. Minute by Falle, 13 July 1966, FO 371/189814.
75. Eirene White (later Baroness White) was the daughter of Thomas Jones, the aide to Lloyd George. She knew the history of the Committee of 24 because she had served as Parliamentary Secretary in the Colonial Office (1964–66) before becoming Minister of State at the Foreign Office (1966–67); but, like Caradon, she consistently saw the problem of the Committee as subordinate to the larger issue of Britain's relations with the United Nations.
76. The reasoning is laid out in Greenhill to Sir Roger Jackling, Confidential, 26 August 1966, CO 936/979.

77. The British delegation had considerable respect for Goldberg and thought him a great improvement over Stevenson; Goldberg was tragically portrayed by Sir Leslie Glass during a debate about the 1967 war in the Middle East: 'One picture stands out – the stricken face of Mr. Goldberg, profoundly vulnerable in this dispute, when taunted by the Syrian delegate as being the representative of Israel rather than of the United States' (Glass to FCO, Confidential, 9 August 1967, FCO 58/84; Glass was a former member of the Indian Civil Service, later High Commissioner in Nigeria).

78. Caradon to Goronwy Roberts, Confidential, 11 December 1967, FCO 58/100; *BDEEP: East of Suez and the Commonwealth, 1964–1971*, part II, 148. As events transpired the United States decided to remain, temporarily at least, on the committee. See *Foreign Relations, 1964–1968*, XXXIII, p. 426.

79. Caradon to Goronwy Roberts, Confidential, 11 December 1967, FCO 58/100; *BDEEP: East of Suez and the Commonwealth, 1964–1971*, part II, 148.

80. Minute by Gore-Booth, 27 December 1967, FCO 58/100; see also his minutes in FCO 58/101.

81. George Thomson to George Brown, Confidential, 8 February 1968, FCO 58/101; *BDEEP: East of Suez and the Commonwealth, 1964–1971*, part II, 149.

82. See his minute of c.24 January 1968 and other minutes in FCO 58/101.

83. Brown to Thomson, 9 February 1968, FCO 58/102; *BDEEP: East of Suez and the Commonwealth, 1964–1971*, part II, 150.

84. Roberts to Brown, Confidential, 1 February 1968, FCO 58/101.

85. See Gore-Booth's minute of 2 February 1968, FCO 58/101: 'I do not think Lord Caradon would feel it easy to do this spontaneously unless there was some explicit expression from you ... to take a really (and not nominally) tough line.'

86. See Peter Paterson, *Tired and Emotional: The Life of Lord George-Brown* (London: 1993), especially p. 207 for his troubled relations with Gore-Booth.

87. George Brown to D.E.T. Luard, 5 January 1968, FCO 58/87. This file is useful for letters to and from Luard on the subject of the Committee. See also FCO 58/310.

88. Caradon to FCO, Confidential, 21 April 1970, FCO 58/587.

89. Sir Colin Crowe to FCO, Confidential, 21 January 1971, FCO 58/642.

90. Minute by J.H. Lambert (head of the United Nations Department), 27 July 1970, FCO 58/491.

91. See for example Shirley Hazzard, *Defeat of an Ideal: A Study of the Self-Destruction of the United Nations* (Boston: 1973).

92. F. A. Warner to Sir Denis Greenhill, Personal and Confidential, 15 July 1970, FCO 58/586.

93. Minute by D.J. Derx, 1 July 1964, CO 936/925. The US government had independently arrived at the same conclusion. The two delegations in New York now fixed their timing to leave on the same day, 11 January 1971. On the next day the *New York Times* carried a major story on the first page with these headlines: 'Britain and U.S. Pull Out of U.N. Colonialism Unit: Both Long Critical of Committee, Saying Resolutions Were Forced Through by the African-Asian and Red Blocs.' Cutting in FCO 58/619, in which there is also a cutting from *The Times of Malta* with the headline 'End of an Era'.

94. For the last stage of the Committee and the decision of the Labour government 1974–79 to resume cooperation but not to become a member, see Sankey, 'Decolonisation and the UN'.

10
When (if ever) did Empire End? 'Internal Decolonisation' in British Culture since the 1950s

Stephen Howe

Entitling a chapter for a volume on the 1950s with the phrase '… since the 1950s' is neither (I hope) a simple error, nor is it done out of sheer perverseness. The intention is rather to gesture towards an argument which this chapter seeks to make, which could most succinctly be summarised as ' "the fifties" after the 1950s'.

If the decade was, for the British Empire, one of decolonisation – as clearly it was in many places and on many levels, even if rather few British colonies actually attained juridical sovereignty during the 1950s, as contrasted to both the end of the previous decade and the start of the next – then it is remarkably hard to discern or construct a pattern of internal decolonisation during those years. The 1950s were in this respect, one could almost say, the decade when nothing happened (though I shall, in the second half of the chapter, say a certain amount about what did). Or to make the same suggestion in different and perhaps potentially more illuminating terms: 'the 1950s', as an era of Britain's de-imperialisation, mostly didn't happen in the 1950s at all. Some bits of 'the 1950s' arrived ahead of time and can be seen in the preceding few decades. Most of them, though, came later, even much later – or can be argued still to be happening now. Neither imperial retreat nor revival profoundly shaped British cultural life during the 1950s: at least not in the ways or to the extent that, in light of Britain's declining global strength across the decade, it has often been thought they should, even must, have done.

The notion that emblematic aspects of a decade's developments may actually fall chronologically outside that decade's limits is not unfamiliar – for instance, it is a commonplace that insofar as 'the 1960s' means to some people festivals, long hair, youth and student rebellion, psychedelic drugs, sexual experimentation and very long guitar solos, those 1960s happened mostly in the early-mid 1970s. Something a bit more complex than that, though, will be argued here.

This may possibly be elucidated – some impression given of what an 'internal decolonisation' during the 1950s might have looked like – by a very small exercise in what is sometimes now, rather pompously, called 'virtual history'.

The decade that might have happened ...

The recent death, at age 93, of Lord Williams of Tunapuna provides an apt vantage point for assessing the 'postcolonialisation' of Britain in the 1950s. Eric Williams' contribution to British life needs little rehearsal here. His brilliant Oxford First in History was followed by pathbreaking doctoral research in economic history and well-deserved (if not uncontroversial) election to a Fellowship of All Souls, where he remained for almost two decades. Alongside his distinguished academic career, of course, Williams pursued an even better known path of political activity. Serving as an influential adviser to the post-war Labour governments on colonial and especially Caribbean affairs, he became the first black British MP for two generations in Labour's landslide 1957 victory. His achievements as Minister, then an active Labour life peer and elder statesman, included his role as late-1950s Colonial Secretary in helping create the West Indian, West African and East African Federations, and engineering the Central African Federation's transition to majority rule. The continued existence and success of all four federal structures in the twenty-first century is surely Williams' greatest legacy; though some still think his victorious advocacy of the 1959 Racial Equality Act takes precedence.

This activity left little time for historical research on a par with the early *Capitalism and Slavery* (1944), but Williams continued to write history all his life. His pugnacious historiographical survey, *Caribbean Historians and the British Isles* (1964) traced the impact – already so omnipresent by the mid-1960s – of West Indian intellectuals in Britain. His broad-brush overview of British history, *From Canute to Cripps* (1970) was a hugely influential 'inside-outsider's' perspective on the national story which became a standard text for many years.

Meanwhile Eric's namesake Raymond Williams was perhaps foremost among those transforming the self-understandings of British culture and intellectual history. His *Culture and Society* (1958) and its sequel *The Long Revolution* (1961) placed the experience of empire and decolonisation at the heart of their analysis – as, almost as famously and persuasively, had the other key late-1950s founding text of 'cultural studies', Richard Hoggart's The Uses of Literacy (1957). Partly under the stimuli of these works, an older critical generation underwent a startling renewal and transmutation. F.R. Leavis's Scrutiny passionately championed the cause of the 'new literatures in English', and of immigrant writers and artists in Britain, throughout the following decade. Through Leavis's influence, not only the formal educational system but the cultural coverage of the main print media, the BBC and the new ITV had by the early 1960s become suffused with a trans-cultural and post-colonial ethos. One can only register a few of this new cultural formation's most salient figures and trends: the ferocious anti-colonialism and salutary scorn for Little England nostalgia which suffused the novels of Vidia 'the Red' Naipaul; the eagerness with which the decade's best-loved poets – John Betjeman, Ted Hughes, Philip 'Calypso' Larkin – embraced Indian, African and Caribbean influences; the passionate engagement with non-European intellectual traditions evinced in the 1950s writings of Karl Popper, Isaiah Berlin and Michael Oakeshott; the near-dominance of the pop music charts by African and West Indian performers; or perhaps Princess Margaret's marriage to the brilliant young South African lawyer Nelson Mandela ...

Why didn't it happen – and does it matter?

Most of that did not, of course, take place – though all the names and most of the book titles are real. Eric Williams was turned down by All Souls, went to Howard University instead, and then back home to lead Trinidad's independence movement. Although his Capitalism and Slavery was, in part, a study in British (and Atlantic) economic history, his later works all took a Caribbean or Trinidadian focus, and a strongly nationalist cast. He never again wrote anything substantial about Britain: his later years gave us British Historians and the West Indies, not Caribbean Historians and the British Isles; and From Columbus to Castro rather than From Canute to Cripps. Neither Raymond Williams' hugely important late-1950s work, nor Hoggart's equally momentous investigation of working-class culture, showed any real interest in empire. Colonial themes are only a scattered and very marginal presence in Culture and Society and The Long Revolution, even though Williams's earliest recorded political intervention, as a 14-year-old schoolboy, was to raise at an election meeting the issue of exploitation of black workers in South Africa,[1] and though in his later work they play an increasing if uneven role. In an interview in the late 1970s Williams suggested that a colonial theme, the Governor Eyre controversy, should have been a starting point for Culture and Society.[2] How different might the general picture presented, and a great deal of subsequent cultural and historical writing shaped by Williams' (and Hoggart's) example, have been if it had done so?

Scrutiny folded in 1953, and neither it nor its core contributors' writings then or later showed the slightest interest in colonial or post-colonial literatures.[3] The philosophers mentioned were no more excited by any non-European ideas than the poets (least of all the viciously racist Larkin) were welcoming towards immigration. The pop charts and TV schedules were no more suffused with colonial or Commonwealth culture than Sir Vidia's writing was with leftwing anti-colonialism.

But ... very many of the imaginary 1950s developments sketched above, from the transformation of academic literary studies to that in popular musical tastes or (less fully) that in the ethnic composition of Britain's political class, have happened – not during the 1950s, but anything between one and four decades later. One might, to strike a last semi-frivolous note, may well regret the absence of the rest: all those imaginary (or, in reality, abortive) federations would surely have been rather good things, and a Margaret–Mandela partnership might just have been less unhappy than either of the pair's real, subsequent romantic entanglements.

A little more seriously: one might ask whether there is anything worth investigating in either the timing or the character of the very various post-1950s developments within British politics, society and culture which are sometimes thought to be linked to decolonisation. Is there – deliberately to 'twist' John Darwin's notable question about external decolonisation – either a pattern or a puzzle here at all?[4] Although very few historians have yet engaged at length and in detail with the domestic British consequences of empire's end, the polemical literature making claims or staking positions in the field is enormous, still rapidly growing, and highly polarised. It has also been suffused with doubt and disagreement over what (if anything) is it that requires explanation: a radical transformation of Britain through decolonisation, its post-colonialisation, or the non-occurrence of such a process? The uncertainty derives in large measure from the very divergent answers proposed (or assumed) in relation to a prior set of questions about the significance of empire to 'domestic' British society, culture and politics – and indeed, latterly, the very analytical utility of the category of the 'domestic' in an age of empire. Part of the problem with such exchanges is that, evidently enough, their protagonists are so often arguing past one another, drawing on radically incommensurate kinds of theoretical inspiration and appealing to very different sorts of evidence. Relatively few have sought seriously to bridge these gaps.

The place of empire in British 'domestic' history has recently attained a new and rapidly growing prominence. This partly reverses or corrects – if not overcorrects – a long established pattern by which the empire typically seemed less significant in British politics and culture than it did in the perceptions of most outside observers. The shift in perception, or even in historiographical orthodoxy, has however only just begun to include the history of the post-1945 era. More far-reaching thus far has been the altered tenor of debate on Britain's nineteenth and early twentieth centuries. Cultural historians, the most influential being John MacKenzie, were coming to see Britain, especially between the 1880s and the 1930s, as far more widely and deeply 'permeated', 'saturated', 'steeped' or 'suffused' (all these were key words in major 1980s–1990s texts on the subject) with imperialism than had previously been thought or assumed. There emerged the notion of a 'new imperial history' centred on ideas of culture and, often, of discourse; emphasising the impact of colonialism's cultures on metropole as well as on the colonised, and tending also to urge its continuing effects after the end of formal colonial rule.

Empire, in the shared view of this wave's practitioners, penetrated far more widely and deeply into British society than had previously been thought. Antoinette Burton, perhaps the most insistent evangelist for a 'new imperial history' wrote of its being 'an integral part of "British" social, political, and cultural history'.[5] But she and others went considerably further than this, increasingly arguing that colonial expansion was both ubiquitously constitutive of metropolitan British culture, and equally crucially dependent on it. It then follows naturally that the continuing internal consequences and manifestations of empire's aftermath must be equally ubiquitous. Failure to recognise this, among historians of contemporary Britain, is at best myopic, at worst must be explicable in essentially political terms – as motivated by anxiety or disavowal towards Britan's decline or indeed towards the transformation via mass immigration of British society.

The whole question of the interaction of British and imperial cultures and identities – or, to put it more strongly, the ways in which each constituted the other, so that they are not and never were fully separate entities – was thus placed at the centre of debate. But many of the polemics take as their starting point what they should be trying to find out about: that imperial rule must necessarily have been fundamental to Britishness. Of course, not all contributions to this emerging structure of debate have made such incautiously sweeping claims, let alone attributed scepticism about empire's or decolonisation's domestic impact to such base motives. Yet among the relatively few historians who have thus far sought to go beyond such indiscriminate contentions and look more closely at the domestic impact of decolonisation and its aftermath, one finds considerable interpretive divergence.[6]

The White Man is repatriated: race talk as internal decolonisation?

The most widely advanced, and surely in many ways the strongest, line of argument for a crucial, shaping role of decolonisation in post-1945 British life centres on race. Thus Bill Schwarz, in a series of articles and a major three-volume forthcoming book, takes as his starting point the moment of Enoch Powell in April 1968, in the wake of his notorious 'Rivers of Blood' speech.[7] Why was the popular response to Powell so rapid, so large scale and so passionate? Schwarz suggests that within British civic life there operated self-consciously white identities which echoed or adapted the experience, and imagery, of whites on the frontiers of imperial settler societies – the 'white man's countries'. What 'Powellism' was about was in significant part the retrieval and re-articulation of these experiences within Britain.

Salman Rushdie's claim that much of Britain's history is unknown to the metropolitan British because it took place overseas, in the empire, has been cited approvingly in many recent works: that suggestion provides, indeed, the starting point for much of the critique of historiographical parochialism alluded to earlier.[8] Schwarz proposes instead that a powerful sense of 'overseas', centred on the colonies of white settlement, operated within British culture, but that it was a mythic or fantasised notion – which is not to say that it had no material consequences. They included various attempts to bring the ethos of the frontier – of, as Schwarz puts it, 'the proper white man' – back to the metropolis. In a trope which can be found at least as far back as Rider Haggard or Cecil Rhodes but which was renewed in post-1950s settler populism and then Powellism, Britain itself had become too prosperous, too urbanised, civilised, idle – indeed too feminine, in the terms of such rhetorics – to live up to the ideals of a proper white man's country.[9] Britain itself was no longer fully British, especially in that the best elements in 'the British character' could no longer flourish there.

To all this was added the theme of treachery: a metropolitan, liberal, ruling- and (in a slightly later coinage) chattering-class betrayal of race and nation. In this mental world, decolonisation – at least in those places where British 'kith and kin' had settled – was a cynical act of state, perpetrated by stealth and by a dishonest, complacent political leadership: Macmillan, Macleod, Wilson, Heath. That populism found rallying-points in Roy Welensky, then in Ian Smith – and then, in the late 1960s Powell (a 'postcolonial proconsul', in Schwarz's apt oxymoron) brought it 'home'. It came to centre ever more on non-white migration to Britain, on internal racial frontiers. The true interests and wishes of the people, especially their natural desire to live in a 'properly British', white country, but also, amongst much else, not to 'go into Europe' were being overridden by the amoral technocrats of Westminster and Whitehall, whose 'pragmatism' masked either abject surrender or disloyalty.

This line of argument, like for instance that of John Darwin, sees the importance of empire lasting well into and beyond the 1950s, and attests that the first real moment of 'Britain decolonised' did not occur until the 1970s.[10] But unlike Darwin, it places ideas, discourses, fantasies of race at the heart of the story, sees these as entering into the intimate textures of everyday life in post-war Britain, and finds them persisting and renewing themselves in domestic political developments from the 1970s to the present.

A less historically detailed, more explicitly theoretical, but in many ways convergent critique is mounted in the most recent work of Paul Gilroy. He argues that since 1945:

> The life of the nation has been dominated by an inability even to face, never mind actually mourn, the profound change in circum-stances and moods that followed the end of the Empire and conse-quent loss of imperial prestige ... Rather than work through those feelings, that unsettling history was diminished, denied, and then, if possible, actively forgotten.[11]

In contemporary Britain, arguments over phenomena like institutional racism and historic recompense have therefore become 'tied to an obsessive repetition of key themes – invasion, war, contamination, loss of identity – and the resulting mixture suggests that an anxious, melan-cholic mood has become part of the cultural infrastructure of the place, an immovable ontological counterpart to the nation-defining ramparts of the white cliffs of Dover'.[12]

Actually, Gilroy is more optimistic than this makes him sound: the 'morbid fixation with the fluctuating substance of national culture and identity'[13] that constitutes the long, largely disavowed post-imperial trauma is not 'immovable'. It may be proving so for the political class, but from below flourishes a 'vernacular dissidence' and spontaneous urban 'conviviality' of multiculture. Here, and in multiple, strikingly diverse cultural expressions from Eliza Carthy to Mike Skinner of The Streets, from Maggie Holland to Ali G, may be found the signs of Britain's becoming truly and finally post-imperial, internally decolonised.

Or maybe not? ...

As well as the major, holistic arguments essayed by Gilroy or Schwarz, a series of recent texts in cultural history have attempted somewhat similar though more localised exercises in reinterpreting domestic British developments as distinctively post-colonial.[14] Others, including the present author, have sketched arguments about British political debates and developments since the 1950s – indeed into the 1980s and beyond – as a form of internal decolonisation. But that sketch was not only avowedly tentative, but went on deliberately to cast doubt on the status and explanatory scope of its own claims – naturally, and equally explicitly, suggesting that some other contributions to this emerging structure of debate should also be far less confident than they sounded.[15]

This tentativeness, if not double-mindedness, is surely apt not least because something like a counter-attack against such arguments is already underway. It may be encountered, fairly briefly sketched, in essays by Peter Marshall, and far more fully elaborated in recent work by Bernard Porter.[16] Porter begins by noting (what he considers to be) the near-absence of empire from major nineteenth-century works of British literature, art and music, its neglect in the schools and universities, and so on. Perhaps, he muses, those British historians who used to leave empire entirely out of their accounts of Britain's modern development, or made it utterly marginal, were right all along – distressing though the thought might be to specialists in imperial history.

Porter seeks to investigate what kinds or degrees of support British imperialism received from the domestic culture of its time – urging that he does so in a more open-minded spirit than that shown by much recent writing in the field, which assumes the strength and even ubiquity of such sentiment. He submits moreover that such support as there was may not necessarily have been imperialistic, in the sense of consciously or actively endorsing the 'imperial mission'. Examining imperial themes in a broader British social and cultural context, he believes, better puts imperialism in its (relatively minor) place. He develops an extended metaphor of British society as an archeological site from which thousands of 'imperial' shards can be excavated. Piled up together, they form an impressive-looking mound. Studying them in situ, however, may give a different impression. They are widely scattered, with a few dense concentrations but also huge expanses from which they are, apparently, entirely absent. Those absences may be just as significant as the presence of 'imperial' shards elsewhere.

Porter emphasises (as, albeit perhaps less forcefully, does Andrew Thompson in his relevant recent work[17]) just how divided – above all by class – British society was in its awareness of and attitudes to empire. The major material repercussions of empire for Britain were almost all indirect. And the empire could have existed, and even expanded, with very little commitment towards it or even awareness of it at home. So, indeed, it did. More, that lack of commitment and awareness was preferred by the empire's rulers. Not only did empire not require mass involvement among Britain's own populations, but such involvement might have been downright destabilising and was thus assiduously avoided – except, Porter concedes, for a relatively brief historical moment around a century ago.

Many culturo-political traits which are seen in much recent work as necessarily associated with empire – the other shards, in Porter's metaphor, that have been excavated and pieced together to form an imperial culture, like racism, patriotism, militarism, masculinism, adventure stories, the study of geography and many more – could and in his view did exist quite independently of it. If imperial rule involved, at least in non-settlement colonies, few British personnel, little expenditure, only superficial interference with indigenous life, often more bluff than substance, then it need not have marked British society very deeply either. If many colonies were acquired easily, almost costlessly, by private enterprise, let alone reluctantly or absent-mindedly, then on this count too one should not be surprised to find them remaining marginal to British society in nearly every way. It required little material, cultural or indeed psychological support from the metropolis. Finally, something describable as 'the national culture' could never have become profoundly imperialised, because there was no such thing. So disparate or 'multicultural' a population had almost no shared beliefs or ideals – about imperial matters, or anything much else. The most widely diffused discourses were probably, Porter believes, ones which were indifferent or even inimical to empire, notably the Victorian (or Whig) ideology of progress.

Bernard Porter only briefly discusses the era of decolonisation and its after-effects, but his conclusions there are almost self-evident. There is no particular mystery – no puzzle in the pattern – about either the lack of trauma attendant on decolonisation, or the delayed, indirect or even just insignificant domestic manifestations of 'becoming postimperial'. All this appears, obviously enough, to place his argument at an opposite pole to those of Schwarz or Gilroy, let alone an Antoinette Burton. It is not that there are no points of convergence. Porter, like Schwarz, sees emigrants to the settler colonies and their descendants as having distinctive, and distinctively intense, ideas about the connections among Britishness, empire and race. But whereas it is the interaction – including the post-1950s repatriation or feedback – between these and the metropole which are important to Schwarz, for Porter there is near-total dissociation. He also concedes that his argument might be thought particularly vulnerable in relation to race. But he goes on to elaborate a strong (though in my view greatly overstated) case for a lack of necessary 'fit', or even substantial and demonstrable influence either way, between the facts of empire and domestic British racial attitudes or race relations, whether during the colonial era or in its wake.

A middle way? Signs and portents *c*.1950–60

Can such divergent perspectives be reconciled? Insofar as they cannot be (which is pretty far!) whose version should we prefer, and why? Possible starting-points to answering those questions, as already intimated, come through exploring the idea of a delayed internal decolonisation. The 1950s, it was suggested only half-jokingly at the outset, was the decade when nothing happened in terms of this chapter's concerns. Let us explore, in inevitably somewhat impressionistic style, some implications of and indeed exceptions to that claim.

British forces were involved in at least eight armed conflicts during the decade: Korea, Malaya, Kenya, the Canal Zone in 1951–54, Suez, Cyprus, Aden and the Radfan. Of these, only Suez could be said to have had a sharp, immediate (though some would argue largely ephemeral) impact on domestic politics.[18] Of the remainder, the Mau Mau revolt probably had the widest repercussions for British culture and political life.

As David Anderson says, the very words 'Mau Mau' still conjure up memories of something evil lurking in history's dark shadows. Mau Mau was depicted at the time – and often since – as a struggle between savagery and civilisation, between modernity and a debased tribal past.[19] The revolt seemed not only shocking but puzzling. Why a fullscale armed uprising just as the old European empires were being dismantled? The Kenyan Emergency was also both shocking and surprising on another level – and, one might say, should have been far more so, for British observers and commentators at the time, than it was. White settler and British security force casualties were, of course, very low despite the huge and gruesome publicity given to them in the British newsmedia. Those among the Kikuyu were massive. Official figures gave the total of killed in combat as 12,000, but the real figure was probably over 20,000: and there is little real doubt that a considerable majority of these were neither armed guerrillas, nor killed in actual battle. At least 150,000 Kikuyu were detained (almost all without trial) during the course of the Emergency, often under extremely harsh conditions which not infrequently included ill-treatment amounting to torture. Anti-terrorist laws suspended the rights of suspects, imposed collective punishments, and extended the death penalty to a wide range of offences. Approximately 3000 Gikuyu stood trial on capital charges relating to Mau Mau during the course of the Emergency. 1090 were hanged – at a time when Britain 'at home' was debating the abolition of the death penalty. As Anderson points out, judicial killing had not taken place on such a scale anywhere else or at any other time in the history of British imperialism. The number of executions in Kenya was more than double that carried out by the French in Algeria, and many more than in all the other British colonial emergencies of the post-war period put together. Anderson's description of central Kenya during the 1950s as a 'police state in the very fullest sense of that term', or Caroline Elkins' of the detention camp system as 'Britain's Gulag', seem all too apt.

It seems clear that in the course of suppressing the revolt, Kenya's British rulers were responsible for thousands of unjustifiable killings, for gross abuses of both their own law and the laws of war, and that this was the most brutal episode in Britain's entire twentieth-century imperial history. Just how brutal it was has now been uncovered in unprecedented detail both by Anderson's research on Mau Mau trials and their victims, and by Elkins' on the detention camps. Their books not only transform our understanding of decolonisation in Kenya, but may be expected also to produce political shock-waves both there and in Britain itself.[20] It appears even quite possible (at the time of writing in late 2004) that some former Kenya colonial government officials will face criminal charges arising from the events of five decades ago.

To ask why the shock (if, as predicted, it happens) will be in the early twenty-first century, why not during the 1950s themselves, is on some levels an evidently naïve question – but on others a genuinely intriguing one. It is not, of course, that there was no public controversy in Britain over the conduct of the Emergency, from James Cameron's fierce criticisms of Kenya administration and settlers in the *Daily Mirror*, through Eileen Fletcher's expose of camp conditions, to the famous Hola parliamentary debate of 27 July 1959. Yet these were in many ways surprisingly small storms (as well as highly selective ones: the Hola camp killings, for instance, were clearly just the tip of the iceberg of deaths in custody) not only by comparison with the obvious reference point of near-contemporary French battles over human rights abuses in Algeria,[21] but also as compared to those that occurred in Britain a little later over security force behaviour in Northern Ireland, or much earlier about Governor Eyre in Jamaica.

It ought, one might think, to be possible to trace the effects of Mau Mau and its suppression running, like a barium meal in an X-Ray, throughout 1950s British life, in rather the ways that historians from Bernard Semmel to Thomas C. Holt and Catherine Hall have done for the metropolitan consequences of the 1865 Jamaican Morant Bay revolt. No doubt something of the kind will be attempted – indeed Joanna Lewis is working on it. Yet the archive of metropolitan responses looks, at first glance, surprisingly thin and patchy, whether on political, intellectual or cultural levels. As is well known, very many of the most prominent British thinkers and artists of the day – Mill and Carlyle, Ruskin and Dickens – entered passionately into the fray over Morant Bay. One finds no similar response to Mau Mau, or any other colonial crisis, among their equivalents in the 1950s (whoever we might think were the equivalent British public intellectuals then), nor anything like Sartre's, Camus' and others' engagement with the matter of Algeria.[22]

To leap to another extreme of the cultural spectrum, almost no evident resonances of the Kenya crisis are to be found in British popular culture of the time. Joanna Lewis suggests that 'Mau Mau even had its own pop song'.[23] But actually this song – though no doubt it existed, somewhere, as a street ditty – was certainly not a commercial release. The only clear example of the latter I can find is much later: a performance by veteran US R'n'B singer Screamin' Jay Hawkins, whose 'Feast of the Mau Mau' was first released in 1969 though it had presumably been in his repertoire rather earlier.[24] The song includes allusions which seem to be derived from media reports of Mau Mau oathing ceremonies, but this is no protest song. I can find none of those, even from performers in the highly politicised 1950s British 'folk revival' movement. Rather, like much of Hawkins' work it's a humorous, mock-horrifying, boastful performance in the tradition of Bo Diddley's 'Who Do You Love?'

Mau Mau has, of course, its literary legacy – but remarkably few of the fictions of the Emergency at the time are actually British.[25] The most famous, and probably most important in spreading the image of Mau Mau as purely atavistic, Robert Ruark's *Something of Value* (1955) and *Uhuru* (1962) came from an American author. Liberal – or any serious – metropolitan fiction about Mau Mau, like Michael Cornish's *An Introduction to Violence* (1960) or G.W. Target's *The Missionaries* (1961) mostly comes only in the early 1960s – as does the first major relevant Kenyan or Kikuyu fiction, notably Ngugi's first novel *Weep Not, Child* (1964 – *The River Between*, published in 1965, was actually written first). The contemporary cinematic archive is comparatively larger: three films were released (and at least partly made in Kenya itself) during the Emergency: *Simba* in 1955, *Safari* 1956, and an adaptation of *Something of Value* (very different from, and with a notably more liberal message than, Ruark's book) in 1957.[26] In the theatre, there was of course the 1959 Royal Court workshop production *Eleven Men Dead* (at Hola), largely remembered now because of the young Wole Soyinka's involvement. Yet this appears as an isolated instance of directly agitational, political drama relating to Kenya: though in more oblique and allegorical form, John Arden's powerful *Sergeant Musgrave's Dance*, also in 1959, might be thought to have Kenyan as well as Malayan referents for its unidentified colonial war.[27]

If we now seek to broaden our perspective, from representations of the Kenyan Emergency in 1950s British culture to those of empire more generally, how far or in what ways do we find signs and portents of an internal, imaginative decolonisation? At one extreme it is possible to present all the major currents of modern English literature as being preoccupied by a dialogue with Kipling's ghost and with the loss of empire.[28] The effectiveness of such an exercise, however, will depend heavily on how one chooses to construct the canon of 1950s British literature. For Martin Green, for instance, this centres on Kingsley Amis and Doris Lessing, with sideways glances – or counterpoints – taking in Evelyn Waugh, Graham Greene and V.S. Naipaul. By this kind of selection, plus an over-simple contrast between an imperialist, adventurous patriciate and an anti-imperialist middle class and sweeping assertions about the supposedly all-pervasive psychic influence of empire, one might construct a schematic picture with on the one side empire, glamour, the military, the patrician, the populist and the adventure story, on the other commerce, domesticity, modernism, the middle class and the novel. On this account, the cultural story of the 1950s and after is of the inevitable triumph of the second set of values and forms over the first.[29] Perhaps more convincing, certainly more theoretically complex and supple, is Jed Esty's recent book *A Shrinking Island*. Here a very wide range of twentieth-century British – in the main English – literary and cultural developments (including the invention of cultural studies) are seen as an attempt to invent an English national culture in the face of decline and decolonisation. An ethnographic perspective, 'repatriated' from the empire, is central to this. The 'island story' is (re)made as Englishness is reimagined after empire.[30]

At another extreme of the interpretive spectrum one might naturally do as most British literary and cultural historians did until the 1980s or even later – simply and silently assume the irrelevance of empire or decolonisation to the mainstream of post-war British cultural development.[31] There are good or at least plausible reasons (of a Bernard Porterish sort) for doing so. After all, the major novels, plays or poetry collections of the decade which could effectively be argued to deal centrally and explicitly with a kind of internal decolonisation could almost be counted on one's fingers. Perhaps, even, on three fingers: Colin MacInnes' 'London Trilogy', *City of Spades* (1957), *Absolute Beginners* (1959) and *Mr. Love and Justice* (1960). Or – in a fashion which has become almost an historiographical cliché – one might see 'the works of the break' as being John Osborne's early plays, in which imperial decline, nostalgia and post-colonial resentment play largely oblique but not trivial roles.[32] Finally, one might choose simply to pick on a single text, or a small clutch of them, and treat this as either typical or symptomatic of the phenomena under examination. An obvious candidate in relation to British views of decolonisation would be something like Nicholas Monserrat's hugely popular though distressingly stereotypical *The Tribe that Lost Its Head* (1956) and its post-colonial sequel *Richer Than All His Tribe* (1968).

None of these procedures seems very satisfactory. Yet what are the alternatives to simply oscillating, as so much colonial discourse analysis has done, between sweeping general claims and the close analysis of a tiny handful of texts, the latter selected on no clear grounds except, sometimes, their existing place within the canons of literary scholarship and teaching? Clearly it would be impossible, perhaps even by means of large-scale collaborative work, to survey all cultural production and trace the overt or less direct depiction or allusions to the empire and its legacies across the whole range, and across the decade. Thus far, in the continued focus on 'high' literary texts, whole archives have continued to be overlooked. For instance, as John Newsinger points out, military writings including the vast mass of British imperial military memoirs have been almost entirely neglected, perhaps because of the typical ignorance and dislike of matters military among literary and cultural critics. This is despite the evident importance of the military experience to the British Empire and indeed to British cultures themselves, and the fact that military service in the empire was among the most 'typical', most widely shared colonial experiences for British men and those of other colonial powers. Moreover, as Newsinger suggests, military memoirs were 'a consistently successful publishing venture' through the nineteenth and twentieth centuries. This fact alone offers reasons for taking them seriously as mass-cultural artifacts.[33]

But one would really need to do something far more theoretically ambitious than just survey more widely than cultural historians have usually yet done. One would have to show in some detail, rather than assume, the existence of an elaborate system of 'cultural coding' by which talk about a range of seemingly unconnected phenomena was really talk about empire – the parallel would be, for instance, argument on how in late-nineteenth-century German culture 'Jew' became the cultural code-term for a swathe of incompatible phenomena: international socialism, liberalism and democracy, finance-capitalism, the cultural avant-garde, and more.

Nothing so enterprising will or could be attempted in the remaining sections of this chapter. Instead, far more banally, an impressionistic, even cartoon-like sketch of a few 1950s indices of internal decolonisation will be offered, before we return in conclusion to some ideas about time-lag: 'the fifties after the fifties'. First, we might ask how far, if at all, British popular cultural forms and tastes became 'post-imperial' during the 1950s.

Although performances of Indian music in Britain and elsewhere in the North Atlantic world date at least as far back as Sufi Inayat Khan's international tours before the First World War, this was clearly a tiny minority taste with limited exposure. That did not change substantially during the 1950s. Again the 1960s seems to have been the 'turning point', with the enthusiasms (on their very different planes) of Yehudi Menuhin and Lord Harewood, of George Harrison and other pop stars – though it was actually the Yardbirds, not the Beatles, who first put a sitar on a pop record.[34] Only from the late 1970s did an indigenous British-Indian form, usually labelled Bhangra, take shape.

A Caribbean presence in British music was a little more substantial during the decade. British jazz was dominated in the 1950s by 'trad' with Chris Barber as the leading figure (and with Humphrey Lyttelton in more eclectic, Ken Colyer more 'purist' New Orleans-imitative proximity). Barber's ensembles occasionally included Caribbean players, notably Arthurlin 'Joe' Harriott. Harriott, who moved to London from

Jamaica in 1951, is indeed surely the most important, retrospectively most underrated figure not only among 'colonial' musicians in Britain, but of all British-based jazz musicians of the 1950s. Yet – in what is already becoming a repetitive story of 'it all happened in the 1960s, not before' – Harriott's major works as a leader began only with Free Form in 1960, followed by Abstract and the remarkable Indo-Jazz Fusions with John Mayer.

Harriott was far from alone: other West Indian (mostly Jamaican) jazz performers active in London in the 1950s included Ellsworth 'Shake' Keane and Coleridge Goode – who both played on Harriott's groundbreaking Free Form. Eighteen of the passengers on the *Empire Windrush*, startlingly, listed their occupation as musician. Several of these were calypsonians, of whom the best known, Aldwyn Roberts, used the splendidly and consciously ironic late imperial stage name of Lord Kitchener. His 'London is the Place for Me' has come to be seen – though, yet again, only long after the fact – as perfectly emblematic of the soon to be disappointed aspirations and hopes of these 'first-wave' post-war West Indian migrants.[35]

Many of the early migrant calypsonians seem to have been Jamaicans, even though calypso is of course originally and primarily a Trinidadian form. More distinctively, later globally, Jamaican was the development out of locally recorded R'n'B first of ska, then rock steady, then reggae. All these evolutions, though, date only from the very early 1960s. Elements of Jamaican musical culture did nonetheless take root in Britain before that. The first British JA-style sound system seems to have been founded by Duke Vin in 1955, closely followed by Count Suckle – both were based in Ladbroke Grove, and naturally soon engaged in a small-scale local version of the great Coxsone-Reid sound clashes. By the end of the decade, the key British-based figure was probably George 'Peckings' Price, who acted among other things as British distributor for 'foundation label' Studio One – operating out of his own home until he finally established a shop in Shepherds Bush in 1974. Probably the first actually to produce Jamaican records in Britain was Sonny Roberts in Willesden – but this was only at the very end of the decade, and they were almost entirely acetates for sound system use rather than commercial releases. The first 'Jamaican' record made and commercially distributed in the United Kingdom was, it seems, Laurel Aitken's 'Boogie in My Bones', in 1960.

During the 1950s, however, none of these performers or small-scale entrepreneurs seem to have made any impact whatever on a wider public, on indigenous British consumers or media. The early sound systems were playing for almost entirely West Indian audiences, and the sales patterns of the handful of British-made discs appear to have followed the same pattern. It was first broken only by Millie Small's 'My Boy Lollipop' in 1964.[36] Relative isolation and lack of recognition were the norm. Jamaican-born Andy Hamilton emigrated to the United Kingdom in 1949, settled in Birmingham and played continuously for the following four decades and more – but only released a 'debut' record as leader in 1991! Wilton 'Bogey' Gaynair had his 'Blue Bogey' issued by UK label Tempo in 1959 – but Gaynair then moved to Germany where he enjoyed considerably more success than in Britain. The examples could be multiplied.

For African music in Britain, again the story of the 1950s and before is of a very few isolated pioneers with a marginal and/or ephemeral public impact. Nigerian guitarist Ambrose Campbell played regularly in London during the Second World War years, eventually with a residency at Club Afrique in Wardour Street.[37] There were other, scattered instances: Ghanaian E.T. Mensah played at the Royal Festival Hall in 1955, introduced and sponsored by Chris Barber. Nigerian highlife performer Eddie Edem was in London from the early 1950s, initially as trumpeter with Ambrose Campbell's band. A little later a significant cohort of South African jazz musicians became British residents – Chris McGregor, Dudu Pukwana, Mongezi Feza, Johnny Mbizo Dyani, Louis Moholo and more. But their story, like that of British-based South African exiles also in acting (the 'pioneer' here being Lionel Ngakane), literature and of course politics and scholarship, is once more almost entirely a post-1950s – in effect, post-Sharpeville – one.

Musics from anywhere in the empire were overshadowed by the growing impact of African-American blues and jazz performers – though even here the 1950s presence and influence of touring luminaries was a trickle compared to the 1960s flood.[38] Once more an early 1960s configuration, pioneered by Alexis Korner, Graham Bond, Cyril Davis and John Mayall – and then their protégés including Eric Clapton, Jeff Beck, the Stones and the Who – proved vastly more influential than anything which surfaced in the 1950s. Meanwhile early British rock'n'roll included almost no black or 'colonial' performers. Only Georgie Fame and his Blue Flames seem ever either to have included West Indian and African musicians or played material from those areas – and yet once more this is an early mid-1960s rather than a 1950s development.[39]

Many commentators have argued that the prime 'villain' in the whole story of unheard or marginalised immigrant or colonial artists – beyond the general insularity of British culture in the era – was the startlingly restrictive broadcasting policies of the BBC (though in the musical world, the Musicians' Union also comes in for some deserved retrospective damnation).[40] Almost equally powerful, thus almost equally culpable, however, were the four big record companies: EMI, Decca, Philips and Pye. Only as more independents began to emerge did more non-white performers get their chance, as with the crucial early mid-1960s role in the popularisation of Jamaican music of Chris Blackwell and Island Records.[41]

As a footnote to this rather bleak musical story, it might be asked: where were the protest songs? As noted earlier, I have found none relating to Kenya in the 1950s – but the cupboard is apparently almost bare too in relation to any other colonial issue of the day. The folk revival's prime mover, Ewan MacColl, in his great autobiography *Journeyman*, has lots on anti-nuclear and anti-Vietnam campaigning and songwriting, effectively nothing (and certainly no reference to protest songs performed or written) in relation to the British Empire – unless one counts an allusion to Suez in a song evidently written long afterward, in the 1960s. Almost MacColl's only explicit evocation of empire is via memories of childhood, with a schoolteacher propagandising for empire but young MacColl's reaction being on the familiar lines of 'my family is poor so what's it to do with us?'[42]

Some other cultural spheres must now be addressed only in shorthand. The early black presence on British stage and screen has been traced in great and loving detail by Stephen Bourne.[43] There was a little more of it than one might expect, including figures like Guiana-born Robert Adams with his rather erratic career beginning in the mid-1930s (the BBC froze him out for most of the 1950s) including foundation of the London Negro Arts Theatre in 1944. There was Edric Connor from Trinidad – an enthusiast for, promoter of and broadcaster on Caribbean musics as well as actor – and his wife, Pearl (nee Nunez), also from Trinidad. There was music the remarkable Sylvia Wynter from Jamaica: actress, playwright, novelist, social and cultural theorist. But it is only a little. Indeed among both musicians and actors, there were repeated suspicions or complaints that British- or empire-born blacks were discriminated against not only in favour of whites, but also vis-à-vis African Americans. ITV, which began broadcasting in 1955, may have seemed more receptive to black entertainers than the Beeb: its 'Sunday Night at the London Palladium' was important to the early careers of British-born performers like Shirley Bassey and Cleo Laine, though here too the number of black American stars was far greater.

Professional sport remained almost entirely white during the 1950s – indeed it was only in the 1980s that a dramatic transformation in the ethnic composition of major professional soccer clubs, and of county cricket, took place. The first traceable black British professional foot-ballers, Arthur Wharton and Walter Tull, date to the very first years of the century, but not only were they (the phrase becomes tiresome) iso-lated pioneers but their successors remained so for over six decades. More important probably was international sport, and although no African or Asian soccer team made a serious impact in the 1950s (indeed very few even played in or against England during the decade), in cricket it was a somewhat different story. The 1950s rise of Caribbean cricket has subsequently been viewed, surely with some justice, as a cultural and even political phenomenon of some significance.[44] The West Indies' first major Test success against England came in 1950 – but apparently there were only 30–40 West Indian spectators present at Lords' for the triumph.[45]

In imaginative literature the decade witnessed, naturally, some notably early landmarks in what was soon to be called 'Commonwealth', much later 'post-colonial', literature: Doris Lessing's *The Grass is Singing* nd Edgar Mittelholzer's *A Morning at the Office* in 1950; Nirad Chaudhuri's *Autobiography of an Unknown Indian* (1951), Amos Tutuola's *The Palm-Wine Drinkard* (1952, and the first black African novel to achieve any attention in Britain, albeit only as a curiosity), George Lamming's *In the Castle of My Skin* in 1953, Samuel Selvon's *The Lonely Londoners* (perhaps the first notable 'novel of colonial immigration') in 1956, Chinua Achebe's *Things Fall Apart* in 1958. Yet only in retrospect could such works be seen as presaging a major and lasting transformation of the metropole's literary culture. Those of the authors who resided in Britain were in the main as marginal to London literary culture as the characters in Selvon's aptly titled book. Mittelholzer's ever deepening sense of fail-ure and frustration, culminating in his hideous suicide by burning, was an extreme but in some eyes symptomatic outcome. Far more attention, and far greater sales, continued to be commanded by the colonial fictions of white, often still explicitly pro-imperial writers like John Masters (notably *Bhowani Junction* in 1954 and its cinematic adaptation), Monserrat or Ruark.

In relation to scholarly – or indeed polemical – writing about empire during the 1950s, one finds again a dual but still markedly asymmetrical picture. On the one hand is an emerging chorus of anti- (or indeed in some cases already distinctively post-) colonial voices, but on the other a considerably greater weight of material which, for all its internal variety and for that matter often its increasing scepticism about the continued viability of the imperial mission, still espoused distinctively

British-imperial viewpoints or assumptions. In the first camp might be placed pioneering studies of African agency like George Shepperson and Thomas Price's 1958 *Independent African*, the first modern fruits of indigenous African historical scholarship like Kenneth Dike's *Trade and Politics in the Niger Delta* (1956), works on African nationalism which powerfully mingled analysis and advocacy such as Thomas Hodgkin's *Nationalism in Colonial Africa* and George Padmore's *Pan-Africanism or Communism?* (both 1956), or indeed early imperial obituaries from the British left like John Strachey's *The End of Empire* (1959). On the other, more 'traditionalist' side might be placed – to select again just a handful of the most important books – Nicholas Mansergh's *Survey of British Commonwealth Affairs* which began appearing in 1952, Roland Oliver's *The Missionary Factor in East Africa*, also in 1952, Philip Woodruff (Mason) *The Men Who Ruled India* (1954), Elie Kedourie *Britain and the Middle East* (1956), and the first volume of Perham's *Lugard*, also in 1956.

Outside such relatively specialist circles, in the most influential general British history writing of the day, it is the sheer absence of empire or decolonisation which is most striking. Among the towering figures of the profession during the 1950s, neither Butterfield nor Namier ever engaged substantially with imperial themes, (except insofar as 'empire', for Namier, meant almost exclusively North America), while – an odder case – A.J.P. Taylor penned a number of essays and reviews on colonial themes across the decade, but entirely excluded these from his conception of 'British', by which indeed he meant near-exclusively English, history.[46]

One could, naturally, continue much further in tracing 'postcolonialising' signs in the British metropolitan culture of the 1950s: but one would, I think, repeatedly find these to be minority enclaves, embryonic though perhaps prefiguratory. Maybe one should not expect much more. Apart from all else, insofar as (following Schwarz and Gilroy) one expects to find such signs above all in the effects of migration and multiculture, the numbers were still small. According to the 1951 census 138,072 people in Britain had been born in the Caribbean or Indian subcontinent – the vast majority (110,767) of these Indian-born, a substantial proportion of whom will have been white. By comparison there were 716,028 Irish-born, 162,339 Polish-born, 38,427 Italian.[47] Few commentators seem surprised at or retrospectively upset about the lack of a profound or pervasive Polish or Italian impact on British life in the 1950s.

Maybe, then, on this particular cultural front 'the fifties' only happened in the 1970s – rather like Teddy-Boys, of whom there were undoubtedly more in their 1970s 'revival' than in the original incarnation. Maybe, even, the 1950s are happening now. It is in the last years of the twentieth century, if not beyond, rather than at any earlier time, that one finds with real force and prominence both the pattern and the puzzle of internal decolonisation, the deeply scored marks both of imperial retreat and revival. Britain in the 1950s was 'post-' many things, perhaps above all post-war and post-austerity. It was certainly very far still from being post-imperial.

Acknowledgements

I am profoundly indebted to David Anderson, Paul Gilroy, Bernard Porter, and Bill Schwarz for the opportunity to read their forthcoming works, as well as to all participants in the 2004 Wiles Symposium.

Notes

1. Fred Inglis, *Raymond Williams* (London: 1995), p. 58.
2. *Politics and Letters: Interviews with New Left Review* (London: 1979), p. 109.
3. See Francis Mulhern, *The Moment of 'Scrutiny'* (London: 1979). C.L.R. James took close note of the evolution of *Scrutiny* and its newer rivals – see for instance 'Britain's New Monthlies' *Saturday Review* 22 May 1954 – but the interest was not reciprocated in relation to James or any other 'colonial' writer.
4. Darwin, 'British decolonization since 1945: a pattern or a puzzle', in R.F. Holland and Gowher Rizvi (eds), *Perspectives on Imperialism and Decolonization* (London: 1984).
5. Antoinette Burton, 'Rules of thumb: British history and "imperial culture" in nineteenth- and twentieth-century Britain', *Women's History Review*, 3, 4 (1994), 486.
6. Compare, for instance, John Mackenzie 'The persistence of empire in Metropolitan culture', in Stuart Ward (ed.), *British Culture and the End of Empire* (Manchester: 2001) with Ward's 'Introduction' in ibid. or Wendy Webster, 'There'll always be an England: representations of colonial wars and immigration, 1948–1968', *Journal of British Studies*, 40, 3 (2001).
7. Relevant published work includes ' "The Only White Man in There": the re-racialization of Britain, 1956–68', '*Race and Class* 38 (1996); 'Reveries of race: the close of the imperial moment', in Becky Conekin, Frank Mort and Chris Waters (eds), *Moments of Modernity? Reconstructiung Britain, 1945–1964* (London: 1999); 'Actually existing postcolonialism', *Radical Philosophy* 104, (2000); 'Claudia Jones and the *West Indian Gazette*: Reflections on the emergence of post-colonial Britain', *20th century British History* 14, 3 (2003); 'Crossing the seas', in Schwarz (ed.), *West Indian Intellectuals in Britain* (Manchester: 2003). I am drawing especially, however, on the unpublished *Memories of Empire*: vol. I *White Tribunes;* vol. II *'We Have Met Before';* vol. III *Post-Imperial England?* (forthcoming, Oxford, 2006).

8. Salman Rushdie, 'The new empire within Britain', *New Society*, 9 December 1982, reprinted in his *Imaginary Homelands* (London: 1992).

9. See also, on this syndrome, Peter Godwin and Ian Hancock, *'Rhodesians Never Die': The Impact of War and Political Change on White Rhodesia c.1970–1980* (Oxford: 1993).

10. Darwin, *Britain and Decolonisation: The Retreat from Empire in the Post-War World* (Basingstoke: 1988), p. 324 which refers to 'the 1970s, the first real post-imperial decade' and *The End of the British Empire: The Historical Debate* (Oxford: 1991).

11. Gilroy, *After Empire: Melancholia or Convivial Culture?* (London: 2004). p. 98.

12. Ibid., p. 15.

13. Ibid., p. 13.

14. See for instance (from authors based respectively in Illinois, Japan and Singapore!) Jed Esty, *A Shrinking Island: Modernism and National Culture in England* (Princeton, NJ: 2004). Michael Gardiner, *The Cultural Roots of British Devolution* (Edinburgh: 2004), C.J.W-L. Wee, *Culture, Empire, and the Question of Being Modern* (Lanham, MD: 2003).

15. Howe, 'Internal decolonization? British politics since Thatcher as post-colonial trauma', *20th Century British History* 14, 3 (2003).

16. Peter Marshall, 'No fatal impact? The elusive history of imperial Britain', in *Times Literary Supplement*, 12 March 1993. Porter, ' "Empire, what empire?" or, Why 80% of early- and mid-Victorians were deliberately kept in ignorance of it?' *Victorian Studies* 46, 2 (2004); and above all idem. *The Absent-minded Imperialists: The Empire in English Society and Culture, c. 1800–1940* (Oxford: 2004).

17. See especially Thompson, 'The language of imperialism and the meanings of empire', *Journal of British Studies* 36, 2 (1997) – and his forthcoming, wider-ranging work on the domestic consequences of empire.

18. On which see now Jonathan Pearson, *Sir Anthony Eden and the Suez Crisis* (Basingstoke: 2003) and for longer term, 1960s consequences Saki Dockrill, *Britain's Retreat from East of Suez: The Choice Between Europe and theWorld?* (Basingstoke: 2002) and Frank Heinlein, *British Government Policy and Decolonisation 1945–1963: Scrutinising the Official Mind* (London: 2002).

19. Anderson, *Histories of the Hanged: Britain's Dirty War in Kenya and the End of Empire* (London: 2005). I am indebted also for advance sight of Caroline Elkins' equally important, in many ways complementary *Britain's Gulag: The Brutal End of Empire in Kenya* (London and New York: 2005).

20. In the meantime parts of Anderson's and Elkins's work are in E.S. Atieno Odhiambo and John Lonsdale (eds), *Mau Mau and Nationhood* (Oxford: 2002). A.W.B. Simpson, *Human Rights and the End of Empire: Britain and the Genesis of the European Convention* (Oxford: 2001) also includes substantial discussion of abuses in late colonial wars.

21. See for instance Martin S. Alexander, Martin Evans and J.F.V. Keiger (eds), *The Algerian War and the French Army, 1954–62: Experiences, Images, Testimonies* (Basingstoke: 2002), and Paul Aussaresses, *Services speciaux: Algerie, 1955–57* (Paris: 2001) which provoked an intensely heated debate in the pages of *Le Monde* during May 2001.

22. It is not just that Sartre was intensely politically engaged with the Algerian crisis, but that the problematic of colonialism became and in many ways

remained a central concern of his philosophy: see not only the writings translated and collected in *Colonialism and Neocolonialism* (London: 2001) but the crucial role of colonial violence in the whole architecture of the *Critique de la raison dialectique* – or indeed the continuing importance of Algerian experience in French thought from Althusser to Derrida or Cixous. Nothing even distantly similar may be encountered in British philosophy of the 1950s or since.

23. Lewis, 'Daddy wouldn't buy me a Mau Mau: the British popular press and the demoralization of empire', in Odhiambo and Lonsdale (eds), *Mau Mau and Nationhood*, 227. She credits Richard Rathbone for the reference.

24. It can be found on the live recording *What That Is!* (Philips 1969) and *Feast of the Mau Mau* (Edsel, 1988).

25. For a survey – albeit one marred by a very rigid political framework – see David Maughan-Brown, *Land, Freedom and Fiction: History and Ideology in Kenya* (London: 1985).

26. David M. Anderson, 'Mau Mau at the movies: contemporary representations of an anti-colonial war', *South African Historical Journal*, 48 (May 2003), 1–17, as well as Jeffrey Richards 'Imperial heroes for a post-imperial age: films and the end of empire', in Ward (ed.), *British Culture*.

27. Awam Amkpa, *Theatre and Postcolonial Desires* (London: 2004) relates Nigerian post-colonial theatre very effectively to the 'theatre of decolonisation' he discerns among British radical playwrights, centring on close readings of Arden's *Sergeant Musgrave's Dance*, David Edgar's *Destiny* and Caryl Churchill's *Cloud Nine*.

28. As is done in Martin Green's *The English Novel in the Twentieth Century: The Doom of Empire* (London: 1984).

29. A very similar narrative is constructed in Daniel Bivona, *Desire and Contradiction* (Manchester: 1990). For less schematic accounts see Michael Gorra, *After Empire: Scott, Naipaul, Rushdie* (Chicago, IL: 1997), Thomas Richards, *The Imperial Archive: Knowledge and the Fantasy of Empire* (London: 1993).

30. Esty, *Shrinking Island*. The ethnographic impulse and its 'domestication' deserve much further exploration in this sphere.

31. As is done in perhaps the best-known overview of 1950s British culture, Robert Hewison, *In Anger: Culture in the Cold War, 1945–60* (London: 1981). Maybe the most effective survey of the popular media and arts at the start of the 1950s is in Ross McKibbin, *Classes and Cultures: England 1918–1951* (Oxford: 1998) – though it too includes almost no explicit discussion of the role of empire, and almost nothing on racial attitudes or images.

32. The cliché is effectively challenged by Dan Rebellato 'Look back at empire: British theatre and imperial decline' in Ward, *British Culture*. See also David Cairns and Shaun Richards, 'No good brave causes: the alienated intellectual and the end of empire', *Literature and History* 14, 2 (1988).

33. Newsinger, 'The military memoir in British imperial culture: the case of Malaya', *Race and Class* 35, 3 (1994) quotation from p. 47.

34. Reginald and Jamila Massey, *The Music of India* (London: 1976).

35. Stuart Hall, 'Calypso Kings' *Guardian* 28 June 2002; and the CD collecting early British-recorded calypso performances *London Is the Place for Me* Honest Joe Records 2002.

36. See Lloyd Bradley, *Bass Culture* (London: 2000) esp. 111–29, and Michael de Koningh and Marc Griffiths, *Tighten Up! The History of Reggae in Britain* (London: 2004).
37. Chris Stapleton and Chris May, *African All-Stars* (London: 1987), p. 297.
38. Bob Groom, *The Blues Revival* (London: 1971).
39. On rock'n'roll's early British impact and exponents, perhaps the best overview is still Charlie Gillett, *The Sound of the City* (London: 1970, rev. edn 1983) esp. ch. 11.
40. The great, but yet once more very isolated, exception to the BBC's cultural myopia was Henry Swanzy's influential 'Caribbean Voices': see Glynne Griffith, 'Deconstructing nationalisms: Henry Swanzy, Caribbean voices, and the development of West Indian literature', *Small Axe* 10 (September 2001).
41. I have not here discussed classical music. Jeffrey Richards, *Imperialism and Music: Britain 1876–1953* (Manchester: 2001) sees the imperial era in British music as running out in the early 1950s (actually he says very little about anything after the 1930s), but doesn't offer any real explanation for this.
42. Ewan MacColl: *Journeyman* (London: 1990), pp. 373–85.
43. Stephen Bourne, *Black in the British Frame* (London: 1998) and his numerous entries on relevant individuals in the new *Oxford Dictionary of National Biography* (Oxford: 2004).
44. For instance in Mike Cronin and Richard Holt, 'The imperial game in crisis: English cricket and decolonisation', in Ward *British Culture*, and of course C.L.R. James, *Beyond a Boundary* (London: 1963).
45. Hall, 'Calypso Kings'.
46. Taylor's volume in the Oxford History of England, *English History 1914–1945* (London: 1965) has in its index only two, rather delightfully revealing, sub-heads under 'colonies': 'in war because of British declaration' and 'a burden'. 'Commonwealth' fares still worse, with just one brief mention. Perhaps more surprising still is the paucity of allusion to empire in *The Troublemakers: Dissent Over Foreign Policy, 1792–1939* (London: 1957).
47. Colin Holmes *John Bull's Island* (Basingstoke: 1988), pp. 212, 214, 216, 226.

Index